Marvelous Recipes
from the
French Heartland

Régis Marcon

Text by Jean-François Abert
Photographs by Patrick André

ici
la
PRESS

English translation rights © 2002 by Ici La Press

Copyright © 2000 by éditions du miroir

Text by Jean-François Abert
Photographs by Patrick André
All rights reserved. No part of this book may be reproduced
or transmitted in any form or by any means, electronic or
mechanical, including photocopying, recording, or by
any information storage and retrieval system, without
permission in writing from the publisher.

Published by Ici La Press
694 Main St. South
Woodbury, CT 06798
www.icilapress.com

Printed in Singapore by Imago

ISBN 1-931605-08-4

10 9 8 7 6 5 4 3 2 1

Table of Contents

Spring

Appetizers

Fish

Meat

Desserts

Summer

Appetizers

Fish

Vegetables and Side Dishes

Meat

Desserts

Autumn

Appetizers

Fish

Vegetables and Side Dishes

Meat

Desserts

Winter

Grains

Appetizers

Fish

Vegetables and Side Dishes

Meat

Desserts

Editor's Notes

A few notes about the ingredients: The salt used should always be sea salt, and the pepper should always be freshly ground. Use unsalted butter, unless specified otherwise. In some recipes we have offered substitutions for ingredients that may be unavailable.

Each recipe is coded for its relative ease of preparation:

Easy

Moderate

Advanced

Marvelous Recipes
from the
French Heartland

My parents

Our hotel-restaurant has undergone a progression of changes to become the Auberge des Cimes, but this has not disrupted the history of the family establishment. It is just as impossible to force a place one loves into becoming something else as it is to, when cooking, force ingredients to be other than what they are. In this sense, any evolution we have undergone has been the result of only gentle subversion.

Saint-Bonnet-le-Froid

My journey to become a chef was more eventful than one would imagine. The chef's hat did not simply slip onto my head overnight. As a child, I was not overly excited watching food being prepared. My mother did instill a culinary interest in me, but I did not realize it at the time. The flavors infused very slowly. I was not one of those little boys eager to seize saucepans or to even taste their contents. At the time, painting and drawing seemed to be much more worthwhile pursuits. If I had a fondness for food in any way, I was content just to eat, without afterward yearning to become a chef. The charm of childhood, after all, is about savoring the present moment.

Artisan Cook in Saint-Bonnet

As summers went by, however, the natural warmth and hospitality of our family restaurant made an impression on my youthful sensibilities. The ambiance there was simple, as informal and welcoming as could be. If necessary, the guests did not hesitate to join in and prepare vegetables themselves—and even I was required to pitch in from time to time. I believe that this same friendly and comfortable spirit, entirely without airs, still permeates the Auberge des Cimes at the start of the third millennium. I consider sincerity and warmth to be essential values, particularly here in the demanding climate of our mountains. They testify to our desire to keep Auberge at the heart of our humble village, supporting its inhabitants in their everyday concerns. Unfortunately for the gossip columnists, I have always considered recognition from those nearest and dearest to me to be more meaningful than media fame.

Of course, this search for simplicity is not always appreciated by those guests who believe that restaurants should impose formalities, create theatrical illusions, and titillate with luxurious fare. One day, at Alain Chapel's restaurant, a diner was furious to find only a bouquet of lupins on his table. He crumpled the flowers and cast them to the floor like a sullied napkin. The field flowers were an offense, an aggression, a provocation. To what, one might ask? At Saint-Bonnet-le-Froid one day, a guest complained about the presence of my three-and-a-half-

Amandine, returning from picking flowers

Thomas, with helping hands cutting dough

year-old son in the restaurant. I found myself wondering: Does a chef's honor require him to conceal his life and hide his children as if they were less legitimate progeny than his mushroom gratin or lentil *tuiles*? The child, however, was not more offensive than the lupins of Chapel. My son had merely wished the angry guest a "Bon appétit!" One can only hope that the man's digestion was not as easily upset.

A book like this would have no meaning if it did not pay homage to those who made it possible by providing the author with both culinary knowledge and, more importantly, human understanding. I will begin with Guy Blin, a pastry chef who taught at the hotel college of Grenoble. He helped me realize that cookery could be a passion. He worked and expressed his ideas with great regard for others—a quality without which even the most excellent cooking is pig's swill. I was fortunate enough to go on and study with other great chefs—Claude Patry (today, the chef at the Relais Saint-Jean-de-Levroux near Châteauroux in the Indre region), Charles Janon (former chef at the Paris intercontinental where such chefs as Pierre Gagnaire, Roland Durand, and Christian Etienne have also served), and the talented and sadly missed Jean Peyronnet (of the Michelin-recognized Chapeau Rouge in Feurs in the neighboring Loire region). Their cuisine, along with Escoffier's unquestionable influence, enabled me to make headway. I have always enjoyed a close relationship with these masters. Charles Janon visited Saint-Bonnet regularly right up until his death.

I was later influenced by other chefs. Pierre Gagnaire is an incredible improviser and a constant fount of inspiration. Joël Robuchon taught me precision in technique, and Bernaud Pacaud instilled in me the demand for perfect products. I also feel a certain complicity with Michel Bras. His restaurant in Laguiole, in the Aveyron, is also situated about a mile in the sky, as we are here at Saint-Bonnet-le-Froid. His village's rustic traditions are similar to ours, and resources are just as scarce. His knowledge and fame gave me confidence in my environment, freed me from my early inhibitions, and released a raging desire for freedom like his. My response was to work locally, with local products and producers, to create synergies among them, and develop traditional recipes without distorting them. To achieve this, it was essential—and still is today—to remain faithful to local inhabitants and their environment.

My profession offers me the chance to discover a little more about nature each day. I like to explore herbs and imagine the subtle nuances that, say, a sprig of lovage may lend to pike perch and tomato. There is a rich variety of mushrooms in the region, and I have discovered many dif-

My Saint-Bonnet restaurateur friends

ferent species and developed closer ties with mycologists. Fortunately, humankind is never far removed from those products we choose.

The faith I have placed in my village has been returned a hundred-fold by the village itself. I give great thanks to Saint-Bonnet-le-Froid, which has so greatly inspired both the life and cuisine I have created here.

Marie's passion is reading and history

Taking in nature with Jacques

*U*nscrupulous manufacturers and certain remiss restaurateurs toss about the notion of "region" purely for selling purposes. Major supermarkets distort the meaning to create a mystique. I have seen lentils imported from Canada that bear the label "authentic green du Puy lentils" or "genuine green lentils from the Auvergne." This sort of false advertising doen't benefit anyone.

To me, the word "region" is meaningless if it ignores the region's character and people. The virtues of the soil—essential to breeding milk-fed veal or to producing fine Hermitage wine (each estate has its own climate)—are belittled by vague and indiscriminate clichés. A "region" is not an abstract, philosophical world, nor is it a world measured in market value, without moral standards or substance.

Instead, our preoccupation with region involves reawakening a forgotten heritage, rediscovering a species of game bird, or a type of lost cereal grain. This desire is not born simply of nostalgia—each revived

The Region

flavor contributes to a richer present. Furthermore, our regional heritage affects how we present our restaurant, bar, rooms, and a whole host of other activities, too. At Saint-Bonnet-le-Froid, all decoration, interior and exterior, draws upon the rural influences of the surrounding Velay and Vivarais regions. One day, a guest was upset to see "some kind of farm machine" from the window of his room in the Auberge—a slice of life in Saint-Bonnet that one does not find on the Place de la Concorde in Paris.

It is worthwhile to seek out the profound tenderness of such seemingly rugged lands. The solitude of the place always threatens to dominate and, as the will to resist it grows, so does one's love of the land. At one time, the inhabitants of Saint-Bonnet started to move away, and the school was in danger of closing. In winter, people abandoned their empty houses to the numbing, desolate snows. Those people who chose to stick out the rigors of the season developed a passionate sense of solidarity. With shared determination, they set up an artisans' workshop, a cross-country ski center, a winter sports club, and a tourist office. Their collective efforts seemed like Hansel and Gretel's bread crumbs, strewn on the forest path. But each of these "bread crumbs" was as flavorful as the meals that Yvonne Bernard now serves up for her guests.

Today, the village offers visitors a bounty of choices, which will ensure the village's longevity and character. The cuisine offered in the village, for example, is firmly rooted in the landscape of the Haute-Loire. It shares those same long-lasting qualities as the granite and volcanic rock used in the walls of the region's houses—although, these days, some people strip the characteristic facade from their houses. I don't believe that my cuisine will ever evolve to the point that it is unrecognizable, absorbing so many other influences that it becomes what London and New York refer to as "fusion-cuisine." If people want to eat Tex-Mex Italian ravioli with Thai green curry sauce, then they will have to dine elsewhere. The lessons I learn from nature, when I am out collecting mushrooms, for example, drive me to create recipes strongly based on the ingredients and their authentic context. My culinary style pays homage to all those who live and work on this land, which defines their destinies. I use the word "region" not as a label or a marketing ploy, but to describe a heart that beats in rhythm with a great being, a landscape, a culture, a history.

The mountains of Ardèche

A recipe does not just fall from the sky or from the rafters onto the stage. It requires hours of work and days of reflection, particularly in winter when Saint-Bonnet-le-Froid is held in snowbound silence, which enhances the feelings of belonging to a land. The idea that leads to a recipe sometimes emanates from the ingredients themselves. I like to imagine, for example, what trout tartare might yield when combined with green du Puy lentils. The impulse arises almost as an image—a fresh water lake, for example, on stark and rugged land.

When adapting a recipe, you never know quite where it may lead. Sometimes the final appearance of the dish becomes more important than first imagined. For example, glazing seemed obvious for the roast pork, as I imagined its caramelized rind vibrant with spices and rich fragrances. A recipe may change direction even before the flavors are considered.

The spirit of the recipes

At Saint-Bonnet-le-Froid, recipes are often written in the "stone" of the land's traditions and integral to the history of the community. I discovered the famous Margaridou brochette in the local library. I followed the recipe to the letter, then I tried to adapt it—but the recipe resisted my meddling. Everything I added or took away upset it, disturbed its balance, ruined it. I came to realize that the recipe had to be respected in its entirety, as an essential and familiar part of the region's landscape, belonging to a local "nature reserve" of traditions and customs.

A recipe can build a bridge, almost physically, with the past, by tying a present-day feeling with a childhood memory, as in the Two-Mushroom Ragout that I borrowed from my mother. Similarly, a conversation with a friend can lead to a recipe as easily as to a book reference or recommended wine. "Lactaire" Mushroom Salad in this book is the result of a conversation I had with Jean Delaveyne, another chef with a passion for mushrooms, whose renown has unfortunately never matched his talent. The recipe itself is perhaps less significant than the homage it pays to him.

I also like to compliment two different recipes, align them together, and direct their union. When I place two fine dishes on the same plate, the result is a mini-celebration. When I serve blood pudding fricassée together with stewed eels in a red wine sauce, I feel a great pleasure—as though monotony has been averted and life has been restored.

Naturally, the creation of a recipe should not be a frivolous act. Work is the key ingredient here. It no doubt makes the chef what he is. The best place to create is right in front of the stove. When I started creating dishes at Saint-Bonnet-le-Froid, the restaurant was modest and functional, situated next to a gas pump. There was a lack of *savoir-faire*. I progressed slowly, discovering techniques as I went along and dining in other restaurants, my nose in the troughs of others. I read extensively. Christian Millau helped me realize my strengths, as I myself was not aware of them. He had a strong intuition about the restaurant and what it could become. He helped me understand the necessary balance between cuisine and its context. He helped me to grasp the principles underlying my cookery and to regard it as a cuisine with a story to tell, as history, as a description of a landscape. It is not a abstract cuisine, born of brilliant intuition, like a flash of poetry. It has form, like prose, and is faithful to the principles governing matter, like an account of natural history. When I serve my Mushroom and Tansy Consommé to guests at the Auberge, I like to explain why we use a teapot. When I mix lentils with grains, I take great satisfaction as they discover the virtues of spelt and quinoa. Cuisine has much to gain when the pleasure comes not just from simple gratification but also from knowledge, which provides the meal with as many hidden surprises as pieces of china and enhances all the flavors.

By "knowledge," however, I do not mean erudition or sophistication. At Saint-Bonnet-le-Froid, we favor simplicity, which can be as flavorful as puréed porcini potatoes.

Most important of all, each recipe has to be accepted by the guests. It is physically painful for me when a guest does not like one of our dishes. In this respect I am very different from some colleagues who can pursue their craft while remaining indifferent to reaction. That said, for the first time since the Auberge opened—thanks to the excellent team I now work with—I can leave the stoves to meet our guests and welcome them to Saint-Bonnet-le-Froid. After all, considering all the time I have spent in the kitchen, I no longer need to keep blinders on under my toque.

The Auberge garden at sunrise

Along with
the meal

The dining room

I have always believed that a meal at the Auberge des Cimes starts long before the appetizer, on the roads approaching Saint-Bonnet-le-Froid. The miles of countryside that our guests travel to the village provide the perfect transition from city to country, allowing them to leave their worries far behind. Arriving at the Auberge des Cimes is nothing like arriving at the Crillon Hotel on the Place de la Concorde in Paris. The tight, winding roads, with their hairpin turns, are not made for limousines. The solitary landscape does not require much attention, which stimulates the appetite and heightens the anticipation of the meal. The feeling of isolation that pervades the land around Saint-Bonnet emphasizes the congenial feeling of the dining room when one finally arrives. It is a study in contrasts, just as the wind and snow outside make the warmth of the room even more pleasurable. The great advantage of these effects is that they catch the attention of even the most distracted guests.

The village never seems to change, and it barely has enough bricks to fill a whole paragraph in a guidebook. There is a small main street with several shops — but it is a street without inhibitions. Everybody greets and talks to each other. People are genuinely at home — they joke and occasionally even have a rowdy time. A sentence left unfinished, a nod of the head — the people in the village understand one another. The local patois no doubt seems somewhat obtuse to the outsider.

Once they have passed through the entrance, what first strikes our guests is the unorthodox reception. All the usual hotel trappings are absent, or, more precisely, hidden. There seems to be, at first, something illogical about it. All those brochures, keys, computers, telephones, and newspapers that usually clutter up hotel entrances are missing. There is only the hint of a reception area, tucked away in one corner.

The guest passes through glass doors with engraved mushroom motifs, our house symbol. First, one arrives in the welcoming room, with its low tables and sofas, where guests may have a pre-dinner drink, prepare for their meal, read the menus, assess their appetites, and consider their choices. It is an interim stop, where one can sit at the bar and settle down after the long journey. François is the hotel's "man of many masks." He greets new arrivals, makes them feel welcome, brings menus, and takes orders. He knows the Auberge's score, like a composer. His experience is essential to ensuring that all runs smoothly.

This before-dinner period is also a preview, of sorts, providing a chance to awaken the senses for what is to come. It allows us to provide a sampling of what we have to offer — vegetable fritters, for example, to be eaten with the fingers. At each meal, it is important to serve one food, whether slices of sausage or some other dainty delight, that can be eaten with the hands. A true celebration brings all the senses into play.

A pre-dinner aperitif at the Auberge des Cimes often means a Rhône valley white wine, recommended by my wife Michèle. She creates our wine list, with the knowledgeable and reliable assistance of Georges-Albert Aoust, a man whose eyes are always open to new discoveries. The wine cellar reflects our proximity to the Côtes-du-Rhône and the region's improvement in quality and diversity over the last fifteen years. Michèle and François are on hand to advise guests, when required, as to possible combinations of food and wine. They never offer any hard and fast rules, however.

The view from the Auberge des Cimes

In the dining room, guests discover a new landscape—not the brick-red carpeting and fir-tree paneling that evokes the view on the long approach to Saint-Bonnet, but rather the Doux River Valley and the Ardèche, which can now be seen through the windows.

The tables are set simply, adorned with wild flowers from the surrounding countryside. At the beginning of the meal, I often leave the kitchen to wish the guests "bon appétit." I believe that meeting the chef and talking with him for a while increases the guest's confidence. It at least proves that Régis Marcon is not off in Tokyo or Singapore preparing gala dinners. So the meal will gain from this familiarity. There is nothing esoteric about the recipes I produce at Saint-Bonnet. The reader will have understood by now that I believe in the instructive virtues of cooking. Michèle and François, among others, will happily tell the biography of porcini, chanterelles, or cauliflower mushrooms. It would be a terrible icing on the cake if cookery's own fantastic insight was not shared. Vive la culture!

When the meal is over, the diners return to the lounge—to carry on their conversations and sustain the friendly spirit in a tranquil environment. Some gather the strength to leave, despite the invigorating aroma of coffee wafting across the room. Others stay for a while, like children who do not want to leave the playground, prolonging their visit to Saint-Bonnet-le-Froid with an after-dinner drink or a cigar. After all, as the Irish proverb says, "God made time and plenty of it!" If only we had the room, we would invite (almost) everyone to stay.

Respect for
the products

Chestnut burs

My parents were farmers in Saint-André-en-Vivarais, without personal fortune, who lived frugally. Once, while working a gala presentation in Los Angeles, I was outraged to see mountains of food destined for the garbage bin. I was disgusted by the frantic accumulation of food for the purpose of surreal and almost morbid bingeing. The amount of waste was terrifying. Back in Saint-André, my mother would work magic with leftovers. She lived courageously, from hand to mouth.

The journey from my parent's house to Los Angeles seems long. In our home, waste was forbidden. My mother had to feed seven children, who responded well enough under the circumstances, and learned to finish their bread and mop up their ragout. The imprints of my upbringing still mark my everyday existence, several decades later. I constantly monitor the store room and manage the foodstuffs as strictly as any bank account. This is as fundamental to me at the Auberge des Cimes as it would be to the owner of a modest country bistro. It's especially important because most foods should not be stored in the cold room for more than 24 hours.

Of course, today, many chefs feature the most choice cuts of certain products—the back of the turbot or the belly of the tuna, for example. Preferential selection only has meaning, for me, if it includes a broad range of choices. At Saint-Bonnet-le-Froid, we prepare the whole pigeon, rabbit, and lamb, for example. After all, a book cannot be truly appreciated on the basis of a few brief extracts. This desire for "integrality" is perhaps also an instinct to maintain "integrity." Pulling out the stops in our kitchen means the team has to rely on their imaginations and their entire range of skills. It is not difficult, even for the lay person, to subtly modify combinations and form new relationships with straightforward, honest intelligence. For example, one might incorporate the rich flavors of pike perch trimmings into a mushroom lasagna (gratin, pâté, or other) that would then accompany the finest cut of the fish.

The diner should also retain a somewhat naive appetite, whetted by curiosity. Without an inquisitive spirit, visiting restaurants becomes a mere show of social decorum, a laborious comparison of the merits of one and the other—the club champions, the new recruits, and the hanger-on recipes.

Excuse me, but I don't believe that the pleasure of dining consists in tasting halfheartedly, leaving half a plateful, brandishing a fork to make a point, stirring up debate while stirring your coffee, leaving a tip instead of tipping, or behaving in any other way befitting a caricature of a restaurant critic. That said, the Auberge des Cimes owes much to certain specialist journalists, in particular Christian Millau.

A guest should also avoid focusing primarily on luxury—in this way, the very sheen of luxury itself may be preserved. It was not long ago that salmon was still a highly valued ingredient. Today, it is bred in such quantity that it has all the flavor of wet bandages. The Brittany or Irish lobster is a much sought-after commodity. In the nineteenth century, however, noses would turn up at it. Today, it is under threat from its cheaper and less flavorful cousin in Maine. A scrupulous chef, on the other hand, benefits greatly by taking an interest in the humble and familiar foodstuffs, ennobling them through this rare, deferential treatment.

Just such an ingredient for us is the green du Puy lentil, which thrives in a very specific microclimate. Thanks to the efforts of Pierre Ambert and the CilverPuy producers cooperative, lentil production in the region has increased tenfold. The du Puy lentil, which dislikes being overcooked as much as being undercooked, is better today than ever before. Lentils are versatile and lend themselves to a wide range of preparation methods—including baking. One of our favorite dishes is delicately caramelized lentils, with sliced truffle to bring out the flavor, mellowed by the yolks of poached eggs. There are, of course, as many different ways to bring out the flavor of lentils as there are lentils on a plate. They may be combined with luxury foods, such as foie gras or lobster, prepared alone (we use two different cooking methods), in elaborate stocks, or in playful variations, with different spices or sauces.

Green du Puy lentils on the bush

One can find a little humor in recent culinary history. These days, luxury products are losing their appeal while other, more modest, less expensive ingredients are proving their worth. When we were children, lentils were of little interest—they were badly prepared and seemed out of place anywhere but in the school cafeteria. The gravel we picked out of them required better eyesight than taste buds.

Recently, the INAO (National Institute for Certificates of Origin) attempted a blindfolded taste-testing of the local lentil and decided that it was worthy of the quality-control award. We are now awaiting the creation of our own lentil museum, which, rather than wallowing in the lentil's past, will recount the story of the du Puy legume's culinary evolution.

Another subject, made fashionable by today's chefs, is the timeless art of bread making. Here, at Saint-Bonnet-le-Froid, our specialty is chestnut bread, inspired by our endless obsession with the region. Bread can hide its own magic chemistry beneath the cloak of night. Like ragout, it has to be abandoned for hours on end and left to its own devices. Having become accustomed to the vigors of kneading, a chef can easily doze off during this waiting period. The bread, then, seems to just make itself, without the chef's intervention. Any anxiety the chef may have felt while waiting will be further heightened by a feeling of powerlessness.

Bread plays to the concerns of many new chefs, eager to delve deep into the heart of their ingredients to discover all there is to know about flour and the nutritional content of cereal grains. When I was a child, simply beholding the miracle of baking bread, a miracle repeated each day, made me want to become a baker. You will never know, dear readers, the number of baguettes I have denied you when I turned my back on the bread oven.

Editor's Note: The producers that are featured in this book have been selected by Régis Marcon, but their portraits have been written by Jean-François Abert. Unlike Louis XIV, the chef of Auberge des Cimes, whom one would not mistake for the Sun King (difficult to do at Saint-Bonnet-le-Froid, during the long winter months), is not in the habit of speaking about himself in the third person.

The Auberge seems to be more accessible than its isolated location would suggest. Why? Because its employees choose to stay there rather than work somewhere more conveniently located. When I interviewed the staff, I frequently heard the phrase, "I never expected to stay this long." You might think that Saint-Bonnet-le-Froid has only limited opportunities for restless young people. The Auberge also stops serving during the winter, an additional inconvenience for the committed employee, who is forced to find other work in the off-season. Again, I often heard, "I'd continue working for Régis Marcon for much longer if it wasn't a seasonal job." One chef, who has worked for other big names in French cuisine, such as Pierre Gagnaire and Antoine Westermann, said, "It's a pity, because he creates a really good atmosphere in this place."

Editor's Note: For obvious ethical reasons, this text was not written by Régis Marcon, but by Jean-François Abert, who was in a better position to interview the Auberge team and express their feelings.

Nobody demonstrates this desire to linger better than Renée Dumas, the family's "right-hand woman." Renée has a real talent for courtesy and kindness. She has been a part of Auberge life continuously since 1989. She first met Michèle Marcon in a wine-tasting course and has since become part of the family. When Régis

Behind the scenes at Auberge des Cimes

and Michèle's youngest son, Paul, was born, Renée brought him home from the maternity ward for his father to see—because, that day, our prize-winning chef was in the thick of a competition and had mushroom terrines on his mind. With an open mind, Renée has assumed a wide range of roles at the Auberge—she handles reception, supervises rooms, embroiders table linens, and more. Previously, she worked in Puy, and she lives in Langeac, so she is the exemplary Haute-Loire citizen. In her opinion, the Auberge des Cimes has not changed much through the years. It is still "somewhere you can feel at home." Her mere presence in Saint-Bonnet makes one feel very much at home, even if she is threatening to retire soon.

The staff of the Auberge are an equal match to the eager and enthusiastic summer clientele. Michèle, Renée, or whoever is working reception, takes a deep breath and steadily works through the long list of reservations. Fortunately, the Haute-Loire is conducive to the development of ample lung capacity. Often, whole weeks will be solidly booked at a time. Ten years ago, this phenomenon would occur only on weekends. Those who wish to dine at the Auberge often have to alter their plans.

Restaurants like this, where personnel and clientele genuinely speak the same language, are rare. In the general hubbub of warmth and hospitality, it is easy to overlook the unified efforts of kitchen and dining room. To notice, it takes a particularly clairvoyant visitor—or a chef used to working in the anonymous surroundings of a chain hotel, who is overjoyed to see what is going on in the kitchen.

Situated one mile above sea level, Saint-Bonnet-le-Froid has never

been rich in natural resources The village was once surrounded by forest. Historically and geographically, it has always been rather isolated. People living on a "island" of this sort form strong bonds, and in the small world of the Auberge, everyone grows to know each other well. Employees happily spend their days off together. They keep in close contact during the off-season. Sometimes, a romance may blossom between a young chef and waitress or chambermaid.

Régis and Michèle Marcon—who favor every kind of authenticity and reject all pretense—encourage this kinship among their personnel. François Lofficial has been their long-time accomplice in creating this spirit as manager of the restaurant. François is the model of fidelity to the Auberge, in a profession where such a quality is rare. After finishing his studies, he did an internship at Saint-Bonnet. His career then led him to England, then to Bordeaux, and then to a ski resort. He returned to the Auberge des Cimes in 1994, where he has supervised the service and personnel ever since. François gives his all to finding a position for a new chef or bolstering a chef's professional pride (by assigning him the task of carving in the dining room). He has high praise for Régis Marcon's patience, attentiveness, generosity, teaching abilities (also frequently mentioned by the Auberge team), and friendly, open manner with staff. François admits to having an aversion for the kind of hysterics that other establishments indulge in. "I hate working for people who shout all the time," he says. He greatly appreciates the serenity of the Auberge des Cimes, which allows him freedom of movement—even financial movement, as he had no reservations about investing in the Marcons' business.

François feels at home at the Auberge because, there, luxury service is not incompatible with true simplicity. He mentions other establishments that maintain a natural and spontaneous atmosphere, such as Michel Bras's restaurant in Laguiole and Patrick Henriroux's *Pyramide* in Vienna. These restaurants are not straitlaced or stuck in their ways, he says. They satisfy their clients without surrendering their own rhythms and identity.

In Saint-Bonnet-le-Froid, as elsewhere, it takes a psychologist to run the dining room. François has to respond to clients with unreasonable expectations. He has to know how to sidestep comments comparing the merits of France's major restaurants. Some guests have their own restaurant championship league and forget that a tablecloth is not the same as a soccer ball. Needless to say, they are not always infallible referees. To such guests, one might quote Montaigne, whose words seem as relevant today as they were yesterday: "My opinion is my opinion and not necessarily right."

There are also the more affable diners, who extend their after-dinner euphoria with a drink or two until 3 o'clock in the morning. For François and the others, the ideal guest is open to suggestions and enjoys being initiated in the pleasures the Auberge has to offer. One of the team's chefs notes that local guests are always "bowled over by what we have in store." With excited curiosity, they ask for explanations about everything. So, it is important to have service personnel that are not as "wet behind the ears" as the Saint-Bonnet snow. The entire staff agrees, "Seniority at the Auberge des Cimes is a definite plus." The long-time employees also understand the familial nature of the business. "The atmosphere created by Régis Marcon and Michèle makes the restaurant much friendlier. You can't help but feel more comfortable here than in a more-structured hierarchy, where everything is so much fussier."

As in all restaurants, service at the Auberge des Cimes must be precisely timed. The rates at which guests dine are as dissimilar as the relative cruising speeds

The staff behind the scenes at the Auberge des Cimes

of the Concorde and the bus to Saint-André-le-Gaz. The forks of some diners move in a blur, while others move as slowly as customs officials during a slowdown. Service personnel should always inform their colleagues in the kitchen as to the rhythm of the table—hence, the need for perfect harmony between the dining room and kitchen. Although this system is rarely in place in larger restaurants, it is the law in Saint-Bonnet-le-Froid. Clear communication is easier in an establishment like the Auberge, which has preserved its rural spirit and refused to renounce its origins. Those palatial eateries and the Auberge are as different as hot and cold, as unlike each other as two snowflakes in a storm. The Auberge des Cimes, tucked away in the hills yet exposed to the elements, has benefited from its adversity. The warmth and friendliness of the kitchen staff, dining room staff, and guests keep out the cold and greatly contribute to the pleasure of spending a day—or longer—there.

Mushrooms seem closely tied to our rural history, hinting at a deep but diffused relationship to ancient times. When I was a child, mushrooms marked the seasons of the year, as did daffodils, narcissus, or the white nettles we sold at the drug store. Like blueberry picking in the summer, collecting mushrooms was a way to earn some pocket money from our neighbors.

Mushrooms were not just child's play, however. They also had great culinary value. My father, at that time a vintner, would gladly interrupt his rounds to go mushroom picking. Aromas linger in the memory, and for me, mushrooms were the breeding ground of my love of food. How could I forget the simple fairy ring mushroom omelet that Marie Dentressangle—the "grandmother" of all Saint-Bonnet's children—used to prepare? How could I forget the scent of the crate loads of russulas and man-on-horseback mushrooms that permeated my mother's kitchen? Today, the Auberge pays homage to these aromatic memories.

Mushroom country

I had my first culinary impulses during this stage of my life. I would spend hours sorting through the mushrooms. I would love finding the *Gyromitra*. (It is still illegal to sell them in France because they are considered poisonous—but it is not the mushroom that is responsible for the deaths of the young hero's parents in Sacha Guitry's famous film, *Roman d'un tricheur* . . .).

Through the years, I have been able to improve my knowledge of mushrooms by walking with friends, in particular, with mycologist Gilles Liège (see page 183). I learned, for example, that fairly mediocre-looking mushrooms—such as the strange cauliflower mushroom, which looks like an old kitchen sponge—actually have a fine flavor that make them much more presentable. I now know that one should be wary of such epithets as "common" chanterelle or "trumpet of death," as, actually, the opposite is true in both cases. I also became aware of how tree species contribute to the flavor and how the weather—wind, rain, and snow—affects harvests. In this sense, there is a close relationship between the practical knowledge of a mycologist and a ski instructor. Waxing skis also requires training in meteorology.

The Massardier family returns from mushroom picking.

To me, mushroom preparation seems the most natural thing in the world. It is also a way to work the local geography and history onto the menu. In a way, mushrooms are inextricably linked to the Marcon family, too. An invisible thread connects them to our shared existence, just like the garlands of mushrooms that the people of Haute-Loire hang over the mantels to dry (the mushrooms are gathered, strung one after another, and evenly spaced to preserve them).

Each mushroom variety must be prepared according to its distinct identity. To me, the fairy ring mushroom requires a recipe to suit its name, something light and airy, such as a creamy velouté, well whisked, which could be topped with parasol mushrooms and porcini. On the contrary, the horn-of-plenty mushroom loves to lap up sauce, so basks contentedly in a lentil and quail's egg ragout. Many more associations are possible, too — of forest and freshwater lake, for example, as with char and chanterelles. In every way, the mushroom is a tremendous muse for a chef's imagination.

The dried mushroom fair in November

The recipe seems to have found its home in glossy magazines. Photographs of finished dishes frolic among details of the latest fairy-tale marriage, the wonders of a beach holiday, and interviews with celebrities, conducted with such seriousness it seems as if germ warfare were imminent. In this inaccessible world, the recipe is the icing on the cake, suspended between desire and fantasy. Not altogether surprising. These days, cooking has very different meanings for the swelling battalions of professional chefs and the working people who do not eat at home. The latter may find it difficult to tell shallots from onions, but they understand that a knowledge of exotic dishes and local wines is part of good taste and culture. Cooking leads a double life: one for those who do it and another for those who eat it. Fortunately, between the two, there is the true enthusiast who will spend a day off from work concocting a salmi of guinea fowl rather than painting the bathroom or sprawling in front of the television.

In the beginning, the cooking lessons at Saint-Bonnet-le-Froid were linked to cross-country ski lessons. The instructor's name for both courses was Régis Marcon. The chef would swap his ski gloves for oven mitts. The atmosphere was fun, and the concept was unusual and difficult to replicate on the Champs-Elysées or the Promenade des Anglais in Nice. The only problem was that the snowfall in Haute-Loire is as temperamental as the inhabitants. Cooking lessons and skiing lessons eventually became separate concerns. Today, Régis's brother, André, takes care of the mountainsides.

Cooking lessons at Saint-Bonnet-le-Froid

Cooking and skiing require similar methods of instruction. Both, in their own way, require a journey "cross-country." Both need a patient approach and careful planning to glide smoothly toward the goal. Once over the peaks, the rest is downhill. I never tire of my students' lively curiosity or their cheerful, sometimes flabbergasted, willingness. Nor do I tire of the never-ending flood of questions. I don't give lectures. Anyone can interject at any point during the making of a recipe. Unlike many culinary demonstrations, these open sessions enable students to overcome their apprehension, awkwardness, and imagined ignorance, which is, most often, just modesty in disguise. Everybody lives under one roof at the Auberge, sharing mealtime (in the company of an egalitarian chef, I like to think) and together ruminating over scallop and mushroom dishes and lobster hotpot. These conditions create great warmth and intimacy. The recipe for success is simple: the friendly atmosphere makes many people want to return, two or three times, or more. Each year, we have to turn some people away. The cooking lessons are so popular that, between foie gras terrines and Yule logs, I wonder whether I will ever see the cross-country slopes again. This may seem nostalgic on my part, but the way that the snow falls on Saint-Bonnet is truly the sugar icing on the cake.

The cooking lessons are open and friendly.

Magazines ramble on and on about the supposed success of their "slimming" diets. Each one claims to have found the secret for shedding pounds—and all are as certain to be ineffective as the air is fresh in Saint-Bonnet. In many foreign cultures, such as Japan or China, the cuisine is linked to health constraints. In the chaos of diets and counter-diets, the French—whose knowledge of medicine is equal to their knowledge of geography—soon lose their bearings. It is easy to forget the basics of nutrition when so-called balanced diets lead, inevitably, in the wrong direction and away from satisfying the appetite. To me, "substitutes" provide no solution to the problem of excess eating. The word itself has as much to do with food as, say, "parking ticket" or "indictment." The magical weight loss that these diets promise conjure the image of an animal flattened on the road, like a pastry dough rolled out by a truck.

Healthy cooking

If the idea of a balanced diet has been lost somewhere along the way, it is clearly because we have generally lost the habit of cooking. People are eager to satisfy hunger as quickly as possible, with as much as possible, in one, huge, high-calorie, junk-food frenzy. Some follow a fast-food diet (bun plus burger plus cola), which, to me, seems to require a heroic performance by the stomach lining, somewhat akin to John Wayne's in *The Alamo*. Other diets focus on snacks and pastries, bars of industrially made candy, additive-crammed ham sandwiches, or the hot dog—the sports fanatic's meal. Worst of all is that such so-called "treats" are oozing with fat and are far more fattening than any lobster ragout or mushroom fricassee.

Nutritional balance is, for me, quite opposite to the process of constraint and coercion imposed on the guilty eater. People should make their own choices and not be forced to transform mealtime into a stressful chore. These same sentiments have been expressed by many people better qualified to judge nutritional matters than I am—for example, Scott Serrato, head chef of the Hélianthal Hotel at the seawater therapy institute of Saint-Jean-de-Luz. Some people have phobias to certain foods and experience complex fascination and repulsion syndromes, which are difficult for trained psychoanalysts to unravel. Because food is such a sensitive issue for the human body, it cannot be subjected to military discipline. Breakfast and dinner should not be obstacle courses, after all.

Germinated wheat

In Saint-Bonnet-le-Froid, we try to promote a diet based on well-being. This approach requires a precise knowledge of food products and their merits and potential dangers. Today's chef must establish trusting relationships with producers, selected for their respect of nature. The chef should watch them work, see whether they avoid the systematic, excessive use of chemicals, and—if need be—act as the "voice of reason" and encourage organic methods. At the same time, the chef should try to inform clients of the quality of the produce and the need for both healthfulness and flavor. These days, why should we tolerate a whole-meal bran bread that is full of pesticides?

We should vary the foods we eat and rediscover forgotten grains and "obsolete" vegetables, as the Celle brothers encourage us to do. We should revive what I call "open air" cuisine—allowing herbs, plants, and mushrooms free expression, as my friend, Michel Bras, does so well at Laguiole. Such a cuisine would not, however, preclude the enjoyment of a freshly caught river bass, a milk-fed veal roast, or a mushroom fricassee. I have no bones to pick with vegetarians or vegans. I respect their convictions and would never encourage them to renounce their lifestyles—but I cannot help but think that they are missing out on something.

Cereal grains and legumes

To the motorist in a hurry, the town of Saint-Bonnet-le-Froid looks like one long road with three or four stores. There is little to make one want to stop there. The town's 195 full-time inhabitants are certainly not going to stand in the way of a speeding car. Yet, there is more to Saint-Bonnet than meets the eye. It occupies a strategic position on several invisible lines of demarcation. It shares water with both the Mediterranean Sea and the Atlantic Ocean. Linguistically, it is divided between the *langue d'oïl* of the north and the *langue d'oc* of the south. In culinary terms, it is between the two Ardèches: the "Ardèche à l'huile" ("made with oil") on the low plateaus to the south and the "Ardèche au beurre" ("made with butter") on the high pastures to the north. In the kitchen, one can play on both, without denying the regional character of either.

In 1985, the Auberge des Cimes crossed its own line of demarcation. We were faced with a choice. We could continue the tradition of catering for the village's businesses—the café, gas station, etc. Or, we could open ourselves up to the outside world by promoting a distinctly regional cuisine, to demonstrate that the region was not stuck in the past but did indeed have a future. Opening up to the outside world may seem a tall order for a village that, in winter, only opens up to the wind, the *burle*, which howls around the houses like bagpipes, rattling the windows, tearing branches from trees, and toppling signposts. The stakes were high—but at least we would be attempting to escape what one writer has called the "knack for oblivion." Yet those who do not dare remain above criticism, safe and sound, as untainted as a newborn lamb. Sounds easy, doesn't it?

The risks were not mine alone. Sharing is an integral part of restaurant life, and I took those risks with my wife, Michèle. When there are two of you, it seems that it is easier to confront obstacles, overcome difficulties, and compensate for shortcomings. The individual ego has to sit back as the two of you learn to understand, support, and listen to each other. An effective couple also learns to talk to one another.

The challenges we faced included questioning our own abilities, assessing our strengths and weaknesses, and evaluating our relationships to others. In this regard, competitions have always seemed to me perfect opportunities to learn more about oneself. They are less about collecting scalps and raising trophies as a measure of one's individual progress. My own experience demonstrates my steep learning curve. First, there was a competition in Vichy, then the Taittinger prize (in 1989), then the *Bocuse d'Or*, in which I represented France in 1995—the year Saint-Bonnet-le-Froid took on Tokyo, Amsterdam, Toronto, and New York. If my head ever grows too big beneath my chef's hat, I will

Of men and medals

The *Bocuse d'Or* trophy, a compressed sculpture by the artist César

count on the chill *burle* to ruffle my hair, as it does on family walks, when it invariably sends my son Paul's hat flying.

For me, winning the *Bocuse d'Or* brought honor to the village in which I chose to make my life. To keep my ego in check, I dedicated my first dish to Brother Joseph, the director of the Saint-Chély Hotel College, who has devoted his life to helping young people. I dedicated the second dish to Margaridou, an unassuming chef from the Auvergne, who was more attached to the region than to glory. Her recipes were published posthumously by Troisgros two or three decades ago. With these people in mind, any temptation to indulge in vanity was quickly quashed. This suited me just fine. After all, modesty has always been a trait of the chef, tucked away in the kitchen. These days, television threatens to transform our great chefs into circus clowns. But before the media took over, many chefs, despite their important roles in shaping

culinary sensibilities, spent their professional lives behind the scenes. Nobody today talks about Denis, or Jacques Manière, or Georges Garin, whom the writer Malraux called the finest chef in Paris. Since he retired, no one mentions the name of Claude Peyrot, who put native Ardèche into his cookery. It warms my heart when I see him cycle through Saint-Bonnet-le-Froid from time to time. I will never forget those who helped me win my first competition: Jean-Marc Allix, Gilles Eteocle, André Barcet, Guy Legar, and my friends Michel Roth and Christophe Quantin, among others.

Modesty aside, I was filled with emotion when I won the *Bocuse d'Or*. The national anthem was playing, and it unleashed a torrent of feelings in me. Everything happened so quickly, and my memory of it is a blur. I hugged my wife, children, and friends. I was inundated with congratulations, and radio and television interviews. I thought about my father who

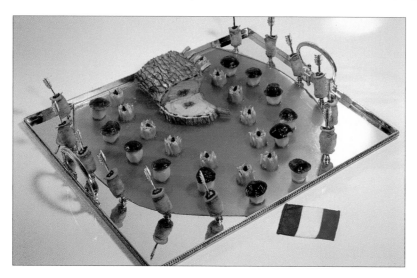

died too young; about my mother and the sacrifices she made; and about Michèle, who has courageously faced the Saint-Bonnet adventure with me. Their names should be on the trophy, too. The award that I won on January 25, 1995—a compressed sculpture designed by the artist César— sits in a place of honor at the Auberge des Cimes. So, although one is never sure where they will lead, the long hours of effort and practice have not been in vain. Culinary training is a lot like sports training: hours of preparation that takes time away from family and friends, and only occasional breaks for physical exercise, for which my former profession prepared me. My years as a ski instructor also taught me a bit about composure, which was put to good use in front of audiences and before cameras that circled so close they tickled the veal loin and garnish. I am a firm believer that a chef also benefits from what is learned outside the kitchen.

I will certainly never be able to thank **Paul Bocuse** enough, or all the people of Lyons who supported me at that moment.

To my wife, Michéle, my children, and all my family, with whom I share the same attachment to this land and to the village of Saint-Bonnet le froid.

To my parents, who taught me the true values.

To everybody who accompanies us on our adventure, our staff and clients of today, yesterday, and tomorrow...

Régis Marcon

Spring

René Chatelard

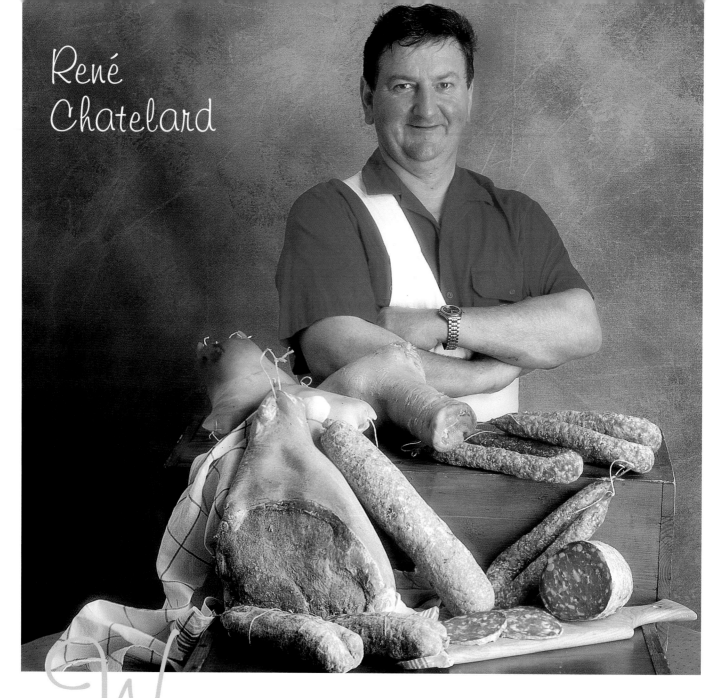

ithin "Néné" Chatelard's store, the history of the village and the vibrant high plateaus comes to life. Visitors come from afar—and there must indeed be many, for this butcher employs 3 people, although the town has only 195 residents. Instead of being made to feel like outsiders, these customers receive a warm welcome. The quality of their reception is in keeping with the quality of the shop's wares. From time immemorial, the tradition here has been to serve the very best—delicious marbled beef from local Mézenc cattle, milk-fed veal, prize-winning produce from the annual Estables fair, and salted meats, dried to perfection in the country air.

The shop is also filled with memories of warmth and friendship. René's father was known in the region as a very genuine and generous man. His mother had the same qualities. When Régis was a child, sulking at the bus stop, dreading his return to boarding school, the thoughtful Madame Chatelard would appear to cheer him and surreptitiously slip a dry sausage into his pocket as a treat. Since then, René says, "we've always had some sort of game going." In Saint-Bonnet, to say that the Chatelard and Marcon families are close friends is to state the obvious. So it would not be possible for Régis Marcon to write a book without including "Néné" Chatelard and his family.

Monkfish Studded with Dried Sausage

The sauce

In a heavy sauté pan, heat 3 tbsp. oil with the onion. Add the pepper, crushed garlic cloves, and chorizo. Brown slowly for 20 minutes to caramelize.

Crush the fresh tomatoes and add to the pan with the bouquet garni and parsley. Add the fish stock. Boil, skim the surface, and simmer for 30 minutes.

Remove from the heat, and let the flavors infuse for 10 minutes. Pass through a fine china cap strainer, pressing the ingredients. Reduce the liquid to a syrupy consistency.

The monkfish and sausage

Preheat the oven to 300°F (150°C). Slice the pieces of dry sausage into sticks ⅛ in. (3 mm) wide. Freeze for about 10 minutes.

Pierce the surface of the fish, about ½ in. (1,5 cm) deep, with a trussing needle to hold the sausage, and insert the sausage. Brush with a little olive oil and place in a shallow baking dish.

Brown the fish over a high flame and season with salt and pepper. Bake for 20 minutes, basting with the cooking juices from time to time.

Presentation

Warm the sauce. Arrange the monkfish in the center of the dish and pour the sauce around it. Serve with fresh fava and white beans.

Fish 🌲🌲
Serves 4

Ingredients
1 whole monkfish, 1¾ lb. (800 g)
8 strips dry sausage
½ cup (10 cl) olive oil
4 tbsp. (50 g) butter

Sauce
1 medium onion, minced
1 thinly sliced red pepper
2 cloves of garlic, sprout removed
3 oz. (80 g) sliced chorizo
2 fresh tomatoes
1 small bouquet garni
Several sprigs of parsley
2 cups (40 cl) fish stock (pg. 291)

Salt, pepper, and Espelette pepper (a type of chili pepper from Espelette in the Basque region of France)

The flesh of fish is sometimes bland, which is why I like to enhance its flavor by studding it with smoked salmon, haddock, or herring. Here, I thought it would be interesting to combine monkfish with dry sausage, a specialty of the mountainous Haute-Loire region. Everyone in the region has a favorite—some prefer sausage that is rich in fat; others prefer it lean. It is an essential food there because the region's dry air facilitates the drying process.

Terrine of Escargot and Herb Veal Mousseline with Pistachio Vinaigrette

Appetizer 🌲 🌲
You may replace the pistachio oil with olive oil.
Serves 10

Ingredients
Forcemeat
10 oz. (300 g) lean veal
Salt, pepper, cumin
1¼ cups (30 cl) crème fraîche
2 egg whites
7 oz. (200 g) mushroom duxelle
(pg. 294)
1½ oz. (50 g) coarsely chopped herbs: parsley, tarragon, sorrel (or other early spring garden herb)
20 large spinach leaves
40 escargots
2 cloves of garlic
¼ cup pastis
1½ tbsp. blackberry or black currant liqueur

Pistachio herb vinaigrette (pg. 295)

I use the young shoots of fresh herbs found throughout the garden in spring, when they are their most fragrant.

The terrine

Prepare and trim the meat. Season with salt, pepper, and cumin. Set aside overnight. The next day, grind the meat in a food processor until smooth. Whip half the crème fraîche and gently beat the eggs. Gradually add the remaining crème fraîche, the cold mushroom duxelle, herbs, whipped crème fraîche, and beaten egg whites.

Blanch the spinach leaves in boiling water. Refresh in cold water and drain on paper towels.

Sauté the escargots with the garlic. Flambé with the pastis, then deglaze the pan with the blackberry liqueur. Remove the garlic and set aside.

Line the bottom and sides of a terrine mold with spinach leaves. Fill the mold with alternate layers of mousseline and escargots. Cover with spinach leaves.

Cook in a *bain-marie* (water bath) at 275°F (140°C) about 30 minutes. Insert a knife to check for doneness. If the blade comes out clean, remove the terrine from the oven.

Presentation

Slice the terrine while it is still warm. Drizzle each serving with pistachio herb vinaigrette. This dish may be accompanied by escargot fritters (by dipping them in batter).

Scallop Carpaccio with Acorn Squash Remoulade

Appetizer
Serves 4

Ingredients
14 to 16 scallops (without the coral)

Remoulade sauce
1 acorn squash or
celeriac, 10 oz. (300 g)
½ cup (10 cl) crème fraîche
1 tsp. prepared dijon mustard
Juice of ½ lemon
Salt, Szechwan pepper,
coriander seeds

Marinade
1 celery stalk
¾ cup (20 cl) extra virgin olive oil
Juice of 1 lemon
1 large shallot, 2 oz. (50 g),
finely chopped
1 tomato, peeled and finely diced
½ bunch chives, snipped

¼ bunch of chervil

This carpaccio is dedicated
to my friends, the Prades,
for whom the squash holds
no secrets. Acorn squash
is very nice with the vinaigrette.
The squash in the rémoulade
sauce may be replaced with
celeriac.

The remoulade sauce

Peel the squash and remove the seeds. Grate into fine strips.

Whisk together the cream, mustard, and lemon. Pour the sauce over the squash and season with a little salt, Szechwan pepper, and crushed coriander seeds.

The scallops

Brush each plate with olive oil. Slice each scallop across into thirds and arrange the slices around the circumference of each plate. Refrigerate.

Peel and finely dice the celery.

To make the marinade, mix the celery, olive oil, lemon juice, shallot, tomato, and chives. Season to taste. Preheat the oven to 350°F (180°C). Warm each plate in the oven for 1 to 2 minutes and remove.

Presentation

Arrange the grated squash remoulade in the center of each warm plate. Sprinkle with salt and Szechwan pepper. Drizzle with marinade and decorate with sprigs of chervil.

Chicken Liver
and Juniper Mousse

Appetizer 🌲
Serves 12

Ingredients
*1 lb. 2 oz. (500 g) very fresh chicken
livers (light colored, if possible)
3 oz. (80 g) lightly salted
bacon, diced
1 tbsp. butter
1 cup (25 cl) white wine
½ cup (12 cl) white port
8 juniper berries plus 12 to garnish
Pinch of allspice
2 medium shallots, minced
2 small cloves of garlic*

*½ cup (12 cl) crème fraîche
½ lb. (225 g) butter
Salt, pepper, cognac (1 shot)*

*If I were to ask each of my
children, I believe they would say
that this chicken liver mousse,
served in little pots, is their
fondest culinary memory. This
cold starter is easy to make and,
above all, very practical to
serve to guests.*

The mousse

One day ahead, lightly brown the chicken livers and bacon in the teaspoon of butter. Flambé with the cognac, then add the white wine and port. Season with salt and pepper. Add the crushed juniper berries, allspice, shallots and garlic. Cover and gently simmer for 20 minutes.

Drain the chicken livers, reserving the cooking juice, and transfer them to the bowl of a food processor. Let them cool.

During this time, reduce the cooking juice to a syrupy consistency and pour over the chicken livers. Add the crème fraiche and the butter, cut into small cubes. Blend in the processor to obtain a smooth and light mousse.

Spoon the mousse into small individual terrines and refrigerate overnight.

Presentation

Before serving, decorate the center of each mousse with juniper berries. (You may also pour a little melted gelatin or butter on top.)

Serve with slices of grilled chestnut bread. The mousse should be served within 2 days.

Sole Meunière with Jerusalem Artichokes and Bacon

The Jerusalem artichokes
Peel and dice the artichokes. Plunge them into a bowl of water to keep them from turning brown.

Drain and dry the artichokes. Over high heat, sauté the artichokes in the butter to brown them lightly. Add the chopped onion and sprinkle with salt, lower the heat, cover and cook till tender.

Dice the bacon and brown in a frying pan. Add to the artichoke mixture and keep warm.

The sole
Remove the dark skin from all the sole and then scale the white skin. Gut, wash, and dry the fish. (Or ask your fish seller to prepare the fish for you.)

Flour the four sole, tapping off the excess. Heat the peanut oil and a little clarified butter in a nonstick pan. When the oil is hot, add the fish, laying it on the skinless side. Brown slightly and carefully turn with a long metal spatula. Season with salt and pepper.

Baste the fish with the cooking oil. Place a small piece of potato under the tail to prevent it from overcooking.

Transfer the fish to a warm serving dish. Cut the two outer fillets from each fish and remove the backbone. Cover each fillet with an equal part of artichokes and bacon, place the remaining fillets on top.

Presentation
Melt 7 tbsp. (100 g) of fresh butter in a pan. When the butter foams, add the lemon juice and chopped parsley. When sizzling, pour over the sole and serve immediately.

Fish 🌲 🌲
If you wish, ask the fish seller to prepare the whole fish for you.
Serves 4

Ingredients
4 whole sole, 8 oz. (225 g)
Handful of flour
4 tbsp. peanut oil
6 tbsp. (80 g) clarified butter
Salt and pepper

Garnish
1¼ lb. (600 g) Jerusalem artichokes
3 tbsp. (40 g) butter
1 onion, finely chopped
5 oz. (150 g) lightly salted slab bacon

Meunière sauce
7 tbsp. (100 g) butter
Juice of 1 lemon
1 tbsp. chopped parsley

The Jerusalem artichoke is a tuber originally cultivated by North American Indians. The explorer Samuel de Champlain introduced the vegetable into France. Its French name, "topinambour," derives from "Topinambous," the name of a Brazilian Indian tribe. Unfortunately, the Jerusalem artichoke has lost its popularity to the potato. In France, it is considered the poor man's vegetable because it was one of the only root vegetables grown during World War II.

Photograph of the recipe shown on the next two pages.

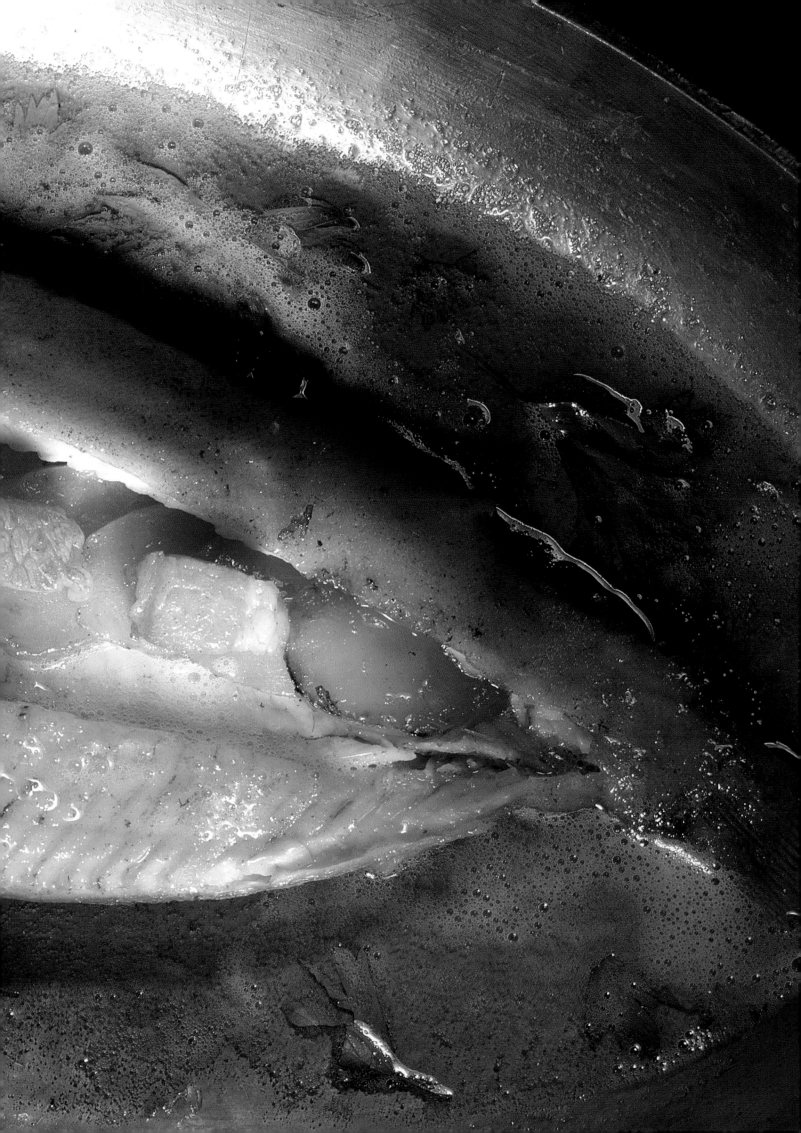

Trout with Auvergne Blue Cheese Sauce

Fish
Serves four

Ingredients
Trout
4 trout, 8 oz. (225 g)
Handful of flour
4 tbsp. (6 cl) peanut oil
6 tbsp. (80 g) butter

Cabbage and celery
¼ green cabbage
2 celery stalks
3 oz. (80 g) smoked bacon
2 tbsp. (30 g) butter

Sauce
1 cup (25 cl) chicken jus (pg. 290)
1 oz. (30 g) Auvergne blue cheese
1½ tbsp. (20 g) butter
1 tbsp. chopped parsley
2 to 3 celery leaves, chopped

Scrambled eggs
4 eggs
1 tbsp. butter
2 tbsp. (3 cl) cream

Salt, pepper, and celery salt

In Auvergne, there are many different types of blue cheese, and there are still a few small producers who cultivate varieties from unpasteurized milk. Blue cheese is the perfect cheese for this type of recipe as it has a slightly acid flavor that goes nicely with trout.

The cabbage and celery

Boil a pan of salted water. Remove the cabbage leaves and discard the thicker parts of the stalks. Boil the leaves for 2 to 3 minutes until tender. Refresh in cold water, drain, and set aside.

Peel the celery and cut into sticks about 2 in. (5 cm) long. Cook in boiling salted water, retaining their crispness. Refresh in cold water, drain, and set aside.

The sauce

Pour the chicken jus into a sauté pan and boil to reduce by half. In a bowl, combine the softened butter, blue cheese, half the chopped parsley, and the celery leaves. Whisk the mixture to make a sauce and keep warm.

The scrambled eggs

Break the eggs into a bowl and gently beat them.

Heat the butter in a small skillet. Add the beaten eggs and cook until scrambled. Stop the cooking by adding several spoonfuls of crème fraîche. Keep warm.

The trout

Flour the trout and season with salt and pepper. Heat the peanut oil in a nonstick pan. Lay the trout belly up, with their heads in the same direction. Brown on one side, turn carefully with a long metal spatula. Add the butter and baste the fish frequently. Check for doneness by inserting the tip of a knife. Allow about 8 to 10 minutes of cooking time.

Presentation

Dice the bacon and brown in a hot pan. Mix the bacon and butter into the cabbage leaves and celery. Season with a little celery salt. Place the trout on a serving dish. Arrange spoonfuls of scrambled eggs around the plate and lay the celery and cabbage leaves on top. Serve the sauce on the side.

Beef with Parsley in a Hermitage Wine Sauce

Meat
Serves 10

Ingredients
4¼ lbs. (2 kg) beef tenderloin
3½ oz. (100 g) marrow
2 tbsp. (30 g) butter

Hermitage wine sauce
2¼ lb. (1 kg) oxtails
2 tbsp. (30 g) butter
2 tbsp. (3 cl) peanut oil
3½ oz. (100 g) carrots, finely diced
3½ oz. (100 g) onion
2 cloves of garlic
2 tbsp. flour
1 bottle (750 ml) Hermitage wine
1½ cups (30 cl) veal jus (pg. 292)
Several sprigs of parsley
Sprig of thyme

Vegetables
1 green cabbage
10 carrots with tops
10 turnips with tops
10 small white pearl onions
2 tbsp. (30 g) butter
5 oz. (150 g) morel mushrooms
salt, pepper and sugar

Potato purée
1 lb. 2 oz. (500 g) potatoes
3 tbsp. (40 g) cream
6 tbsp. (80 g) butter
2 egg yolks
2 tbsp. (20 g) fresh bread crumbs

Sea salt and pepper

The Hermitage wine sauce
In a large sauté pan, lightly brown the oxtails in the butter and oil. Add the carrots, onion, garlic, parsley, and thyme, and continue cooking until browned. Sprinkle with the flour and mix, deglaze with the wine. Add enough veal jus to cover the oxtails and vegetables. Bring to a boil and season with salt and pepper. Cover and bake in the oven at 300°F (140°C) for 6 hours.

Carefully remove the pan from the oven. Transfer the oxtails onto a plate and cover with a damp cloth. Strain the cooking juices into a saucepan through a china cap strainer.

Let the sauce rest, then skim off the fat. Reduce to 1½ cups (30 cl). Keep warm.

The beef
Cut the beef into 10 thick equal pieces. (If you have a smoker, cold-smoke the meat for 15 minutes.) Set aside.

Heat a small pan of salted water. Poach the marrow for 1 minute, then refresh in iced water.

The vegetables
Peel and wash each vegetable. Blanch the cabbage leaves, refresh and set aside. Braise the carrots, turnips, and onions in separate pans. Glaze the vegetables in the butter with salt and a pinch of sugar.

Wash and rinse the morels. Sear them over high heat. Season with salt and pepper and keep warm.

The potato purée
Cook the potatoes in their skins. Remove the skin and press the potato pulp through a sieve. Add a little cream, the butter, and the egg yolks. Adjust the seasoning. Coarsely chop the oxtails.

Fill half of a buttered bottomless mold with the puréed potatoes. Add the oxtails and a little cooking juice. Spoon the remaining purée on top. Sprinkle with bread crumbs and place in a 350°F (180°C) oven.

In the photograph, the potato purée is wrapped in a large slice of carrot that has been cooked in salt water. This presentation is optional.

Presentation

Heat all the vegetables in a sauté pan. Season with salt and pepper.

Heat a little oil and 1 tbsp. of butter in a pan. Sear the beef slices, browning all surfaces. Season with salt and pepper. Serve rare or medium, according to taste.

Whisk the sauce with the butter and correct the seasoning. Place a slice of beef in each plate. Top each serving with 2 slices of warm marrow. Season with a pinch of sea salt and ground pepper. Arrange the vegetables at top right and the potato purée to the side of the beef. Serve with a generous portion of sauce.

Each year on Palm Sunday, tradition requires our local butcher to decorate his beef cows and parade them through the village. The beef from these cows is, in my opinion (influenced by local pride, no doubt), the finest I have ever tasted—well aged and from animals of the highest quality. The cattle are fattened with Mézenc hay, which is ideal for the purpose. The animals then spend six months in the cow shed. The process requires patience, and the beef is only available between March and June. The stock is a local breed from an area between the Ardèche and the Haute-Loire.

Chicken Breasts Gratinée with Asparagus Fritters and Truffle Sauce

Meat 🌲
Serves 4

Ingredients
Chicken
4 tbsp. melted butter
4 free-range chicken breasts
with skin, 5 oz. (150 g) each
4 thin slices fourme d'Ambert
blue cheese

Fritters and vegetables
12 asparagus stalks
2 egg whites
4 tbsp. (60 g) bread crumbs
7 oz. (200 g) leaf spinach
4 chicken livers
3½ tbsp. (5 cl) olive oil
1 clove of garlic
1 cup (25 cl) peanut oil

Truffle sauce
½ cup (12 cl) port
1 medium shallot, finely minced
1 cup (20 cl) of chicken jus
(pg. 290)
1 tbsp. of truffle slices
crushed with a fork
1 oz. (30 g) butter

Salt, pepper, and nutmeg

The chicken breasts

Preheat the oven to 250°F (120°C).

Heat the melted butter in a pan. Cook the chicken breasts to brown the skin. Then roast in the oven for about 20 minutes. Remove from oven and cover each breast with a slice of cheese. Keep warm.

The asparagus and spinach with chicken livers

Peel the asparagus and cut in half along its length. Put the tips in boiling salted water and cook for about 3 minutes, depending on their thickness. Refresh in cold water, drain, and lay on a cloth to dry.

Dip the asparagus tips in the egg whites and then in the bread crumbs. Remove the stalks of the spinach. Wash and drain the leaves.

Prepare the chicken livers, removing the nerves. Warm a pan over high heat and add the olive oil. Sear the chicken livers and brown on both sides. Remove and keep warm. Add the spinach and half the garlic clove to the same pan and stir gently with a fork. Season with salt and pepper, and keep warm.

Heat the peanut oil in a small pan. As soon as it starts to smoke, fry the asparagus tips. Remove and drain on paper towels. Season with salt and pepper, and keep warm.

The truffle sauce

Pour the port into a small saucepan. Add the shallot and reduce by half. Then add the chicken jus and reduce by half again to obtain about ½ cup (12 cl) of sauce.

At the last moment, add the truffle crumbs. Whisk the butter into the sauce. Adjust the seasoning.

Presentation

Brown the chicken breasts under the broiler. Remove and slice at an angle.

Place each sliced breast in a serving plate. Arrange the spinach on top of the chicken livers and lay the asparagus tips across the spinach. Coat the plate with truffle sauce.

Fourme d'Ambert cheeses have the French government's guarantee of origin and quality. Its cylindrical form has a dry crust speckled with white, yellow, and red mold; and the traces of the needle pricks that encourage the development of the fungi penicillium. This cheese is delicious when hot.
For this recipe, the cheese should be very thinly sliced.

Chestnut Soufflé Tart with Vanilla Ginger Ice Cream

Dessert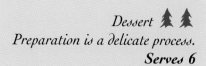
Preparation is a delicate process.
Serves 6

Ingredients
Sweet pastry dough
9 tbsp. (130 g) butter
½ cup + 1 tbsp. (75 g)
confectioner's sugar
1 egg
1¾ cup (250 g) flour
½ cup (60 g) ground almonds
Pinch of salt

Chestnut mixture
6 tbsp. (80 g) butter
10 tbsp. (150 g) chestnut purée
¼ cup (50 g) sugar
2 egg yolks
1 egg

Vanilla ginger ice cream
2 vanilla bean pods
2 cups (½ l) milk
6 egg yolks
½ cup (100 g) sugar
½ cup (10 cl) heavy cream
¾ oz. (20 g) crystallized ginger

Chestnut tart is a specialty of the Ardèche region. I wanted to make the dish lighter so decided to mix the chestnut purée with a cold zabaglione-style sauce. This tart may be made with candied lentil purée or butternut squash instead of chestnuts.

The pastry
To make the pastry, soften the butter. Add the sifted confectioner's sugar, then the egg, sifted flour, and ground almonds.

Knead the dough, then cover with plastic wrap and refrigerate for 20 to 30 minutes. Roll out the pastry and press into a buttered pastry mold. Refrigerate the formed pastry dough for another 20 minutes. Pre-heat the oven to 350°F (180°C). Bake 10 to 15 minutes, until the tart shell just begins to color.

The chestnut mixture
Melt the butter and chestnut purée over double boiler.

Whip the sugar, cold egg yolks, and whole egg until light and creamy. The chestnut-butter mixture should be slightly warm. Blend the two mixtures with a spatula and pour into the tart shell. Bake 7 to 8 minutes at 350°F (180°C), until the center of the tart is lightly cooked.

The vanilla ginger ice cream
Split and scrape the vanilla bean pods into the milk and bring to a boil in a saucepan.

In a mixing bowl, whisk the egg yolks and sugar until light and creamy. Add the hot milk while stirring with a spatula. Return the mixture to the heat and continue to stir gently until the custard thickens. Be careful it does not boil. Pass through china cap strainer and set aside in a cool place.

Presentation
When the custard has cooled, add the cream. Process the mixture in an ice-cream maker. Finely dice the crystallized ginger and add just at the end of making the ice cream.

Morel Mushroom Crème Caramel

Dessert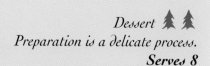
Preparation is a delicate process.
Serves 8

Ingredients
Morel caramel
2 oz. (60 g) quality morel
mushrooms, dried
1¼ cups (250 g) sugar
½ cup (12 cl) dry Vermouth
½ lemon, juice only

Crème caramel mixture
1¼ cups (250 g) sugar
1 cup (25 cl) cream
3 cups (75 cl) milk
¾ oz. (20 g) dried morel mushrooms
4 eggs
8 egg yolks

*This crème caramel may be served
with a pear cake.*

Prepare the morels one day in advance by soaking in warm water.

The morel caramel

The following day, drain the mushrooms, reserving the water. Sort the mushrooms and wash thoroughly to remove excess sand. Filter the soaking water and reduce to ¼ cup of liquid.

Heat the sugar with a little water until golden brown. Deglaze with the vermouth, being careful of hot splashes. Add the lemon juice and reduced mushroom juice and reduce again, until it begins to turn golden caramel color. Pour the caramel into the individual ramekins.

Cook the mushrooms in a little water. Chop them and portion into each ramekin. Set aside in a cool place until the caramel hardens.

The crème caramel

Heat 1 cup (200 g) of the sugar with a little water until it turns a rich brown. Deglaze with the cream and boil. Add the milk and mushrooms. Return to a boil while mixing with a whisk.

Beat the eggs, egg yolks, and the remaining sugar until light and creamy. Add the boiling milk and pass the mixture through a fine china cap strainer.

Line the bottom of a baking dish with parchment paper. Arrange the ramekins on the paper, then fill each ramekin with the crème caramel. Pour water into the baking dish to mid-height of the ramekin to make a water bath.

Bake about 45 minutes in a preheated 275°F (135°C) oven. Insert a knife to check for doneness—the blade should come away clean. Remove the ramekins from the oven and refrigerate.

Presentation

Unmold each crème caramel onto a plate. To make this step easier, first slip a thin knife around the edges of the ramekin, allowing some air into the bottom of he mold. Serve with pear cake.

Daniel turned up at the Auberge one day to invite Régis to sample his goat cheeses. He timed his visit well as the chef had been looking for just this ingredient. By happy coincidence, Daniel's cheese resembled those that had been cultivated at a farm in Saint-Bonnet several years earlier. In no time at all, Daniel Mounier and the Marcon family formed a successful alliance, capped by the marriage of Daniel and Marie-Christine, Régis's sister. In his laboratory in the neighboring village of Dunières, Daniel excels in varying flavors and forms. He produces everything from the more traditional rectangular block to the small round *blanchardon*, which is masterfully matured to bring just the right amount of fruitiness to the flavor. (The *blanchardon* takes its name from the village where it is produced, not far from the home of the small round cheeses called *picodon*.) He also produces a surprising *fourme de chèvre* (mild blue goat cheese), which resembles a *tomme de Savoie* but has a very different flavor and is matured longer to be sold in summer.

Daniel Mounier is not content simply to produce goat cheese from his alpine herds. He also cultivates cheese from his herds of Montbéliard cows and, occasionally, blends goat's and cow's milk together. Daniel only turned to cheesemaking in 1992, to improve his farm's chances of economic survival. The Auberge des Cimes provides a good "showcase" for his wares, and Régis's customers often visit his farm.

With his brothers and sisters, Daniel Mounier has created a local farming cooperative to market quality farm produce. Clearly, Daniel is a dear friend of the Auberge chef for reasons beyond the fine quality of his cheeses.

Brochette Margaridou

Appetizer
Serves 4

Ingredients
Veal sweetbreads
14 oz. (400 g) plump veal sweetbreads
8 medium-sized morel mushrooms

Roux
4 tbsp. (50 g) butter
⅓ cup (50 g) flour
¾ cup (15 cl) light cream
½ cup (12 cl) milk
1 tbsp. powdered mushrooms (pg. 29)

Brochettes
2 slices of cured ham
4 tbsp. (50 g) butter
6 egg whites
1 cup (150 g) white bread crumbs
1 medium shallot, finely sliced
½ cup (12 cl) port
1 cup (25 cl) veal jus (pg. 29)
1 tbsp. butter
1 tbsp. chopped truffle
Peanut oil

Salt, pepper, and nutmeg

See pages 94 and 95 for step-by-step photos.

The veal sweetbreads

One day in advance, wash the sweetbreads in cold water. Remove the nerves and as much of the skin as possible. Cut strips of sweetbreads about 1 in. (3 cm) wide. Arrange the strips on a sheet of plastic wrap, about 5 in. (12 cm) long. Enclose the sweetbreads by rolling them in the wrap several times, tie both ends to form "sausages." Plunge in boiling water, reduce heat and gently poach for about 15 minutes. Remove the sweetbreads to cold water. Drain and refrigerate.

The morel mushrooms

Sort and carefully clean the mushrooms, washing thoroughly to remove any sand. Dry on a clean cloth or paper towels.

The brochettes

Remove the sweetbreads from the plastic wrap and cut into 1 in. (2 cm) long pieces. Slice the ham into squares of about the same size. Thread the sweetbreads, ham, and mushrooms onto wooden skewers.

Heat the butter in a pan and brown each brochette. Season with salt and pepper. Refrigerate.

To make the roux, melt the butter in a small pot, whisk in the flour and cook over medium heat stirring constantly about 3 to 4 minutes. Add the cream, milk, and powdered mushrooms. Cook another 4 to 5 minutes stirring to make a bechamel sauce. The sauce should be fairly thick. Season with salt, pepper and nutmeg.

Holding the skewers, dip each brochette into the hot sauce. Place two rulers across a platter and lay the brochettes between them so that the sauce does not come into contact with the dish.

Freeze the brochettes about 1 hour.

Gently beat the egg whites. Dip each frozen brochette into the egg whites and then into the bread crumbs to coat well. Dip into the bread crumbs a second time if necessary. Roll each brochette in plastic wrap to hold their shape. Refrigerate.

The sauce

Boil the port and shallot to reduce the liquid by half. Add the veal jus. At the last moment, add the butter and truffle.

Cooking

Heat oil to 325°F (160°C) and deep-fry the brochettes until crisp and golden. After frying, finish cooking in a 350°F (175°C) oven for 5 or 6 minutes, depending on the size of the brochettes.

Presentation

Serve the brochettes with the truffle sauce. Accompany with a small mache lettuce salad or a ragout of asparagus tips and black morel mushrooms, as shown in the photograph on the following pages.

I first came across this recipe in the archives of the library of the Haute-Loire.

I came across it a second time in book by Margaridou, a legendary chef from the Auvergne region, with whom I feel a great affinity. We share the same desire—to give pleasure while cooking in a close relationship with nature.

Photograph of the recipe shown on the next two pages.

Young Turnips Stuffed with Escargots and Thyme Butter

Appetizer
Serves 4

Ingredients
24 young turnips, with tops
2 tbsp. (30 g) (butter)
1 tbsp. granulated sugar
Salt
Several grains of coriander, crushed
1 tbsp. butter
48 large escargots
4 tsp. pastis liqueur

Herb butter
11 tbsp. (150 g) butter
1 tbsp. chopped parsley
1 large shallot, minced
1 clove of garlic, finely chopped
Several sprigs of fresh thyme,
leaves picked
3 tsp. ground almonds
4 tsp. pastis liquer
Salt and pepper

Garnish
2 tbsp. (30 g) butter
1 clove of garlic
½ lb. (225 g) fresh spinach
salt

The turnips
Remove the tops of the turnips and set aside. Peel the vegetables and core them with a melon baller.

Place the turnips in a large sauté pan. Add the butter, sugar, salt and ground coriander. Add enough water to cover the vegetables. Cover the pan with parchment paper or lid.

Cook gently until a knife can be easily inserted into the vegetables. Remove the turnips, and reduce the cooking liquid to a syrup. Caramelize the insides of the vegetables.

The herb butter
First whip the butter and add the parsley, shallot, garlic, thyme, almonds, and pastis. Season with salt and pepper.

Heat the tablespoon of butter and sauté the escargots. Season with salt and pepper and flambé with the pastis.

Preheat the oven to 400°F (200°C).

Stuff each turnip with the herb butter and snails. Arrange in a baking dish and bake about 10 minutes.

The garnish
Meanwhile, heat the butter in a pan with the clove of garlic, cut in half. Add the spinach and salt lightly.

Stir to wilt, then drain on paper towels. Keep warm.

Presentation

Remove the dish from the oven. Serve the escargots while very hot.

The turnips may be served without the spinach garnish as an hors d'oeuvres with cocktails.

For this recipe, you may replace the turnips with mushroom caps.

For several years now, Alain Charras has been cultivating escargots in Grazac in the Haute-Loire region. He restricts their diet to thyme. The petit gris escargot (Helix aspersa), once enjoyed by the ancient Romans, has no problem getting nourishment. It feeds on the abundant wild plants in the region.

Foie Gras Terrine
with Cured Ham

Appetizer 🌲 🌲

*This terrine can be made
without the cured ham.*
Serves 15

Ingredients
*3 duck foie gras, A quality, each
about 1¼ lb. (550 g)
6 slices of good quality ham*

Seasoning for foie gras
*1 tbsp. (15 g) salt
1 tsp. (5 g) pepper
Pinch of sugar
4 tbsp. (6 cl) white port*

Fig marmalade
*10 oz. (300 g) fresh figs
2 tbsp. (30 g) butter
1 clove
3 pieces star anise
¼ stick of cinnamon
Pepper
½ cup (12 cl) muscatel
10 dry figs, diced*

*The duck liver should be very
fresh with bright color. As a guide,
duck foie gras weighs from 1 to
1¼ lb. (500 to 600 g). Goose foie
gras is larger and has a milder
flavor. The cooking method I
recommend allows the duck liver
to cook evenly.
The plastic wrap is necessary
as it protects the iron-rich foie
gras from oxidizing when in
contact with the air. Be careful
not to add too much salt, as the
ham also seasons the dish.*

The foie gras

One day in advance, buy fresh foie gras with good color. Cut each lobe widthwise to form scallops about 1 in. (2,5 cm) thick. Remove the nerves and blood vessels.

Line a rectangular porcelain or glass baking dish with plastic wrap and sprinkle with half the seasoning. Arrange the foie gras in the dish and sprinkle with the remaining seasoning. Lay plastic wrap over the foie gras and press down to form an even layer, about 1½ in. (4 cm) thick. Cover the dish with plastic wrap and aluminum foil to protect it from light. Marinate in the refrigerator for about 12 hours.

The next day, preheat the oven to 170°F (75°C). Unwrap the foie gras an hour before cooking. Place in the oven until the center is slightly warm, about 15 minutes. Do not let the foie gras become too soft.

To finish

Line the bottom of a terrine mold with plastic wrap. With a large spatula, place a layer of foie gras into the terrine. Cover with a slice of ham and another layer of foie gras. Repeat these steps 3 times. When the terrine is full, cover with a plastic wrapped cardboard and about 2 lbs. (1 kg) weight.

The fig marmalade

Chop the fresh figs. In a heavy saucepan, brown them in the butter. Wrap the spices in a cheesecloth pouch. Add the spices, dry figs, and muscatel to the pan. Cook about 1 hour, stirring frequently so that the mixture does not stick. Remove to a bowl and refrigerate. Serve with the foie gras.

Duet of Morel Mushrooms Stuffed with Langoustines

The morel mushrooms

Sort and wash the morels. Sauté the morels and shallots in the butter, then deglaze the pan with vermouth. Sort and wash the asparagus, blanch, drain, and set aside.

The langoustines

Peel the langoustine tails, retaining the last ring and tail fin. Season with salt and pepper. Cook in clarified butter in a very hot nonstick pan. Drain immediately on paper towels and keep warm.

The sauce

Reduce the seafood stock until it coats the back of a spoon. Whisk in the butter and add several leaves of parsley. Whip the sauce well to incorporate the butter.

Presentation

Stuff all the morels with the langoustine tails. Place 2 stuffed mushrooms on each plate. Cover with the sauce and arrange the asparagus tips. Garnish the plates with the langoustine claws and small drops of parsley oil.

Fish
Serves 4

Ingredients
Morel mushrooms
4 large fresh white morel mushrooms
4 large black morels
2 shallots, finely minced
4 tbsp. (55 g) butter
5 tbsp. white Vermouth
20 stalks of white or small green asparagus

The langoustines
8 large langoustines
2 tbsp. (30 g) clarified butter
Salt and pepper

The sauce
2 cups (½ l) seafood stock (pg. 294)
2 tbsp. (30 g) butter, cut into small pieces
Several leaves of parsley

Garnish
Langoustine claws
Parsley oil

This recipe further reveals the mushroom. Here, I combine the black morel (Morchella deliciosa) and its round, white counterpart with large langoustines from the fishing town of Guilvenec in Brittany.

Pike Perch Fillet in a Cheese Crust

with Stuffed Baby Onions and Asparagus Purée

Fish
Comté may be substituted for the Lavort cheese. You may change the vegetables if they are not in season. Spinach sautéed in butter will complement this dish.
Serves 4

Ingredients
1¼ lb. (600 g) skinless fillet of pike perch
6 tbsp. (80 g) clarified butter

Cheese crust
7 tbsp. (100 g) butter
3½ oz. (100 g) grated Lavort or Comté cheese
3½ oz. (100 g) soft white bread, without crusts

Garnish
8 new spring onions, about 1½ in. (3,5 cm) round, with shoots
⅔ cup (150 g) mushroom duxelle (pg. 294)
Pinch of salt
24 green asparagus
4 tbsp. (50 g) butter

Red wine sauce
¾ cup (18 cl) red wine (Crozes Hermitage, for example)
1 tbsp. sugar
½ tsp. potato starch
3 tbsp. (40 g) butter

Salt and pepper

The cheese crust
Cream the butter and mix with the grated cheese and white bread in a food processor. Spread the mixture on a sheet of plastic wrap and cover with another sheet. Roll out the paste to a thin layer, about ⅛ in. (3 mm) thick. Refrigerate or freeze.

The stuffed onions
Cut the caps from the onions and remove the inner pulp with a melon baller. Secure each cap to the onion with toothpicks on each side to hold in place while cooking.

First blanch the onions and caps. Refresh in cold water and dry. Stuff each onion with mushroom duxelle.

The asparagus purée
Drop the asparagus into a pot of boiling salted water. After cooking, refresh in iced water. Set aside 8 asparagus tips to use as a garnish. Dry the remaining asparagus, removing as much water as possible. Process with the butter to create a purée. Keep warm.

The red wine sauce
Boil the wine in a sauté pan to reduce to ½ cup (12 cl). Add the sugar and return to boil. Mix the potato starch with a little cold water and whisk into the sauce to thicken it slightly. Whisk in the butter, season with salt and pepper to taste. Keep warm.

The pike perch fillet
Preheat the oven to 300°F (150°C)

Cut the fish into four 5 oz. (150 g) portions. Heat the clarified butter in a frying pan. When the butter is very hot, sear the four portions of fish on each side. Season with salt and pepper. Remove to a buttered baking dish.

Cut 4 rectangles of cheese crust to the same size as the fish. Cover each piece of fillet.

Bake about 15 minutes. Then, place the dish under the broiler until the cheese crust turns golden brown.

Presentation
Remove each portion of fish from the baking dish, dab with paper towels, and position on the plate. Place some asparagus purée on the plate, top with three of the asparagus tips. Place a stuffed onion and sauce on each plate.

Lavort is a cheese from the Auvergne, the product of one man's toil and passion. Patrick Beaumont's cheese farm, Terre-Dieu, is in Puy-Guillaume. The ewe's milk cheese he produces there has a very distinctive, slightly smoked flavor. It is called Lavort, from the French words "lave" (lava) and "or" (gold). This charming name well suits this delicious cheese, which seems to have emerged from the depths of time, just like the volcanoes of the Auvergne region.

Young Pigeon with Fresh Peas and Walnut Wine

Meat
Serves 10

Ingredients
Pigeons
5 pigeons, 1 lb. 2 oz. (500 g) each
2 tbsp. (30 g) butter
10 sage leaves
10 sheets of phyllo pastry

Pigeon sauce
4 tbsp. (60 cl) olive oil
1 tbsp. butter
2 shallots, minced
5 tbsp. (80 g) diced carrots
1 clove of garlic
1¼ cups (30 cl) chicken jus (pg. 290)
1 fresh tomato, chopped coarsely
1 sprig of thyme
A pinch each of ground cinnamon,
ginger, star anise, and allspice
1 tbsp. honey
4 tbsp. (6 cl) vinegar
½ cup (12 cl) walnut wine

Pea ragout and purée
4¼ lbs. (2 kg) fresh green peas
2 tbsp. (30 g) butter
2 oz. (60 g) slab bacon, diced
1 head of lettuce, shredded
(Boston or bibb)
1 cup (25 cl) heavy cream

Celery root and truffle napoleon
3 oz. (80 g) fresh truffles
2 oz. (60 g) fresh white bread, without
crusts
3 oz. (80 g) beef marrow
1 white celery root
½ lemon, juice only

Salt and pepper

The pigeons
Preheat the oven to 350°F (180°C).
Singe the pigeon skin (if necessary). Remove the thighs and refrigerate. Keep the breast meat attached to the birds. Reserve the carcasses.
Heat the butter in a pan and brown the breasts. Season with salt and pepper. Make a series of incisions lengthwise in the skin along each side of the breast bone. Place in the oven about 10 minutes, basting occasionally.

The pigeon sauce
De-bone the pigeons by removing the two breasts. Chop the carcasses. Heat the oil and butter in a sauté pan. Brown the carcasses and the wings. Add the shallots, carrots, and garlic, cook slowly to color.
Deglaze with a little water. Add chicken jus and water to cover. Add the tomato, thyme, and spices. Salt lightly and simmer for 30 minutes.
Remove from the heat and let the flavors infuse for 10 minutes. Pass the sauce through a fine china cap strainer, remove the fat that rises to the surface. Reduce to 1¼ cups (30 cl).
Caramelize the honey in a pan, then deglaze with the vinegar and walnut wine. Reduce the mixture to a syrup. Add the pigeon sauce and boil until the liquid is thick enough to coat the back of a spoon. Adjust the seasoning and keep warm.

The peas and pigeon thighs
Remove the bones from the pigeon thighs. Stuff each thigh wih a sage leaf and wrap in two buttered and layered phyllo sheets. Bake in a 350°F (180°C) oven, then set aside.
Blanch the peas, refresh in cold water, and drain.
Brown the bacon and lettuce in butter. Add the cream and peas. Season with salt and pepper. Cook gently, uncovered, to keep the peas' green color vibrant.
Purée half of the peas in a food processor, then pass through a sieve. Adjust the seasoning. Keep the purée and the pea and bacon ragout warm.

The celery and truffle napoleons

Chop the truffles and mix in a food processor with the bread and beef marrow. Spread the mixture onto a sheet of plastic wrap to form a layer ⅛ in. (3 mm) thick. Freeze.

Slice the celery root into ⅛ in. (3 mm) slices, and cut 1½ in. (4 cm) rounds from each slice. Cook in boiling salted water with a squeeze of lemon juice. Refresh and set aside on a cloth to drain.

Form the napoleons in a buttered baking dish by alternating celery root rounds with layers of the truffle mixture. Bake until hot, about 10 minutes.

Presentation

With a pastry bag and fine tip, pipe the pea purée into a circle on each plate. Place some ragout and a pigeon thigh in the center. Position a napoleon at the top of the plate and a pigeon breast below. Pour sauce over the breast.

The walnut comes from northern India and the coastline of the Caspian Sea. It was introduced into Europe by the Romans. The walnut tree was considered sacred, and at that time, as today, every part was used. The leaves have medicinal properties. The edible part of the nut has many uses, in particular to make walnut oil. The shell is used as a veneer dye, and the husk, which covers the fresh nut, is used to make liqueurs, ratafias, and the famous walnut wine.

Lamb and Quince Spice Bread Charlottes with Mint Sauce Drizzle

Meat 🌲 🌲
*Meticulous attention is required
to assemble the charlottes.*
Serves 8

Ingredients
Lamb
2 to 3½ lb. (1 to 1,5 kg) lamb saddle
or loin, with its belly flaps
3 tbsp. olive oil
1 onion, minced
2 medium carrots, diced
2 garlic cloves, minced
1 tomato, crushed
1 tbsp. soy sauce
1 bouquet garni
½ stick of cinnamon
5 green cardamom pods, crushed
½ garlic bulb, cut across

Vegetables
10 oz. (300 g) snow peas
12 small white sping onions
10 baby carrots
2 tbsp. (30 g) butter
Pinch of sugar

Charlottes
4 quinces or pears in syrup
3 tbsp. (80 g) butter
1 onion, minced
Pinch of ground cumin
10 slices of white bread, ⅛ in.
(5 mm) thick
10 slices of spice bread, ⅛ in.
(5 mm) thick

Mint sauce
1 tbsp. honey
4 tbsp. honey vinegar
10 mint leaves
2 tbsp. (30 g) butter

Salt and pepper

The lamb

Prepare the saddle of lamb. Remove the belly flaps. Cut away the fat and cut the flaps into large pieces.

Heat 2 tbsp. of oil in a sauté pan. Brown the flap pieces, stirring with a wooden spatula. Add the onion, carrots, and garlic. While browning the vegetables, add the crushed tomato, soy sauce, and bouquet garni. Caramelize the cooking juices and deglaze with a little water. Be sure to scrape the bottom of the pan well. Add enough water to cover. Add the cinnamon and crushed cardamom pods and bring to a boil. Reduce the heat, cover, and simmer gently for about 1 hour. Check that the contents remain immersed in liquid, adding water as needed.

After cooking, remove the meat and set aside on a plate. Pass the cooking juices through a fine china cap.

Boil the cooking juices in a sauté pan, reduce to 1¼ cups (30 cl) of jus. Keep warm.

The vegetables

Wash and trim the vegetables. Blanch the snow peas in salted water. Halve the onions lengthwise, brown them in a pan, and cook in 2 tbsp. of the lamb jus.

Cook the carrots, covered, in a liquid that is 2 tbsp. each of lamb jus and water. Whisk in the butter. Glaze the cooked vegetables with the sugar and keep warm.

The saddle of lamb

Preheat the oven to 350°F (180°C).

Heat a tbsp. of oil in a pan over high heat. Rub the saddle of lamb with salt, pepper, and half a head of garlic. Brown the meat on all sides. Place in the oven for 15 minutes. Transfer the cooked saddle to a plate; blood should still run from the meat. Set aside to rest.

The charlottes

Dice the quinces. Brown the onion in a tbsp. of butter. Add the diced quince and sauté. Season with salt, pepper, and ground cumin. Dice the lamb flap and mix into the quince mixture with a little juice.

Generously butter 8 small charlotte molds. Cut the bread slices into ⅛ in. (5 mm) sticks. Position the white-bread sticks and spice-bread sticks, alternately, around the insides of the molds. Cover the bottom of each mold with a round of white bread, then fill the mold with the quince and lamb mixture. Press down well. Place the charlottes on a baking tray and bake for 15 minutes. Be sure that the ends of the bread do not burn.

The mint sauce

Caramelize the honey in a sauté pan over medium heat. Deglaze with the vinegar and reduce until syrupy. Add a cup of lamb jus, bring to a boil, adding chopped mint leaves. Remove from the heat and let the flavors infuse, then pass through a fine china cap. Whip the remaining butter into the sauce before serving.

Presentation

Heat the vegetables in a little lamb jus. Remove the charlottes from their molds and arrange on the plate with the lamb saddle slices, glazed vegetables, and mint sauce.

The "Nior du Velay" black lamb is a variety of sheep that originates on the Velay peaks. Its lambing season is earlier than other varieties and sometimes occurs twice a year. This lamb is easy to breed and butcher, and its meat is of excellent quality.

Goat with Capers in Two Styles

Be sure that the goat you buy is top quality.
Serves 10

Ingredients
1 young goat, 26 lb. (12 kg), with liver and kidneys
3½ tbsp. (5 cl) oil
4 tbsp. (55 g) butter

Aromatic garnish
1 green onion, finely sliced
1 carrot, finely diced
2 cloves of garlic
1 small bouquet garni

Parsley seasoning
2 tbsp. dijon mustard
1½ oz. (50 g) fresh white bread crumbs
Pinch of fresh thyme leaves
1 clove of garlic, minced
4 tbsp. chopped parsley

Sauté preparation for the shoulder cuts
4 tbsp. (55 g) butter
4 tbsp. (6 cl) oil
1 onion, minced
1 clove of garlic, chopped
6 tbsp. (8 cl) pear eau-de-vie
Handful of flour
½ cup (12 cl) white wine
1½ cup (30 cl) chicken jus (pg. 290)
1 small bouquet garni
4 tbsp. (60 g) small capers
1 to 2 egg yolks
¾ cup (18 cl) cream

Salt and pepper

The goat

Ask your butcher to prepare the goat: leg, shoulder, loin, liver, and kidneys.

The legs and loins

Preheat the oven to 325°F (165°C). Heat the butter and oil in a pan. Brown the leg and loin, season with salt and pepper. In a roasting pan, brown the bones and meat trimmings with the aromatic garnish. Deglaze the pan with a cup of water. Place the leg and loin in the pan with the jus. Roast, allowing 20 minutes for the loin and 35 to 40 minutes for the legs. Just before the end of cooking, spread the mustard on the meat, coat with the breadcrumbs mixed with thyme, garlic and parsley. Cook the meat 2 more minutes then remove the meat from the roasting pan and continue to brown the vegetables. Add water and cook another ½ hour. Pass through a medium china cap strainer, check the seasoning, and keep warm.

The shoulder sauté

Cut the shoulder into pieces. Heat the oil and butter in a casserole. Brown the goat, add the onion and crushed garlic and cook until golden. Flambé the meat with the eau-de-vie. Sprinkle with flour and cook for several minutes until the mixture browns. Deglaze with the wine and reduce by half. Add the chicken jus and the bouquet garni. Bring to a boil and reduce heat to simmer gently about 15 minutes—goat meat is delicate. Season with salt and pepper and add the capers. Thicken the sauce with egg yolk beaten with cream. Do not boil. Keep warm.

Presentation

Slice the liver. Flour the slices and sauté with 1 tbsp. butter, a clove of garlic, and a sprig of thyme. Season with salt and pepper. Carve slices from the legs and loin. Arrange on a plate with the livers and kidneys and pour the sauce on top. Serve the sautéed shoulder along with it.

The goat should not be too young, or its meat will be too soft. It shouldn't be too old either because the flavor will be too strong. The best are those weaned on goat's milk, although it is important that they also feed on early spring grasses. Daniel and Marie-Christine and Yvette and Didier breed their goats this way in Dunières. My mother likes to accompany this recipe with early spring snow peas.

Fresh Goat Cheese Blancmange with Warm Apricot Compote

The apricot compote

Select attractive, ripe apricots. Wash and halve them. Boil the sugar in 1 cup of water and add the verbena leaves. Add the apricots and return to a boil. Remove the pan from the heat and cover. Refrigerate.

The blancmange

Soak the gelatin in a small amount of cold water. In a bowl, fold ¼ cup (60 g) of sugar into the goat cheese. Whip the cream until it forms stiff peaks. Melt the gelatin leaves in a little boiling water.

Stir the gelatin into the goat-cheese mixture. Gently fold in the whipped cream. Gradually add 2 to 3 drops of almond extract, checking the flavor, as there should only be a hint of almond flavor.

Pour the mixture into 8 small molds or ramekins. Press down well and refrigerate. Set aside the most attractive apricot halves. Blend the remaining apricots and syrup in a food processor, then pass through a fine china cap strainer, to make a "coulis" fruit sauce.

Presentation

Dip the molds in hot water to loosen the blancmange. Slip the fine blade of a knife around the edges and unmold each blancmange into the center of a plate. Pour the apricot-verbena coulis around the blancmange and garnish with apricot compote.

Dessert 🌲
Serves 6

Ingredients
Apricot compote
2⅛ lbs. (1 kg) apricots
1¼ cups (250 g) sugar
10 verbena leaves

Blancmange
1 pkg. or 4 sheets of gelatin
⅓ cup (70 g) sugar
10 oz. (300 g) very fresh goat's cheese or fromage blanc
1¼ cups (30 cl) whipping cream
2 to 3 drops almond extract

On Daniel and Yvette's farm, the best goat cheeses are enjoyed in the spring. For this recipe, select a fresh, smooth cheese that is well suited to appetizers and desserts.

Frozen Verbena Parfait with Candied Fennel

Dessert 🌲
It's best to prepare this dessert in large quantities.
Serves 4 or more

Ingredients
Verbena parfait
2 cups (½ l) milk
12 egg yolks
1½ cups (300 g) sugar
2 cups (½ liter) whipped cream
⅓ cup. (8 cl) verbena liqueur

Candied fennel
½ bulb of fennel
⅓ cup (70 g) sugar

Chocolate-hazelnut leaves
1 cup (25 cl) milk
6 egg yolks
⅔ cup (140 g) sugar
¼ cup (40 g) flour
7 oz. (200 g) bittersweet chocolate, finely chopped
4 tbsp. hazelnut oil

Verbena coulis
½ cup (12 cl) orange juice
5 verbena leaves
1 tsp. or 1 sheet of gelatin
2 tsp. (10 g) sugar

Chocolate sauce
2 tbsp. cream
½ cup (100 g) sugar
3 tbsp. (30 g) cocoa powder
½ oz. (15 g) bittersweet chocolate, chopped

Shortbread cookies
¼ lb. (100 g) sugar pastry dough (pg. 297)
Cocoa powder
Several verbena leaves

The verbena parfait
Boil the milk. Whip the yolks and sugar for several minutes, add the boiling milk. Pour mix back into a pot and over a low heat continue to stir with a spatula until the mixture has the consistency of custard. Immediately pour into a mixer and whip until cool. The custard should thicken enough to leave a ribbon trail. Gently fold in the whipped cream and verbena liqueur.

Fill small cone-shaped molds or ramekins with the mixture. Freeze at least 1 hour.

The candied fennel
Wash the half-bulb of fennel and remove the stringy fibers. Cut into fine pieces. Boil the sugar in ½ cup (12 cl) of water for 5 minutes. Add the fennel and slowly cook to candy for 30 minutes.

The chocolate-hazelnut leaves
Preheat the oven to 400°F (200°C).

Boil the milk. Whip the yolks and sugar. Add the flour and then the boiling milk. Mix and bring to a boil, whisking continuously like making a pastry cream. Remove from heat and fold in the chocolate and the hazelnut oil. Pour the mixture onto a nonstick baking sheet, spreading it as thinly as possible. Bake for about 5 minutes, watching the color to be sure it does not burn. Allow to cool for a very short time, then break into 4 chocolate-hazelnut leaves.

The verbena coulis
Boil all the ingredients together in a pan. Allow to cool until slightly warm, then pass through a fine china cap strainer.

The chocolate sauce
Mix the cream, sugar, and ½ cup (12 cl) of water. Whisk in the cocoa powder and boil. Remove from heat and fold in the chocolate. Cool.

The shortbread cookies
Heat the oven to 350°F (180°C). Roll out the pastry to ⅛ in. (3 mm) thickness. Cut four rounds about 1 in. (3 cm) in diameter. Bake about 10 minutes, checking their color, do not brown to much.

Presentation

Before serving, place a cookie in the center of each plate and unmold a verbena parfait on top. Sprinkle with cocoa powder. Press a chocolate-hazelnut leaf into the peak of the parfait. Make a trail of chocolate sauce around the plate and pour verbena coulis around the base of the frozen parfait. Arrange a small amount of candied fennel on each plate. Decorate with verbena leaves.

For many years, the Pagès establishment, in the village of Puy-en-Velay, has been producing a liqueur infused with verbena and other aromatics. The product owes its reputation to Raymond Pagès, a marvelous ambassador for the region, who is also responsible for establishing the Logis de France chain of hotel-restaurants around the country.

R ed berries and pink meats. The Haute-Loire's granite terrain is favorable for wild
fruits, and its breeding traditions produce quality stock. Michel Peyrard has made a
career from both. He founded the first Monts du Velay red fruit producers cooperative and also
dedicates part of his time to his mountain veal cows.

Thanks to farmers like Peyrard, agricultural revenues have increased more in the Haute-Loire
than in any other region of France. And thanks to farmers like him, the local economy is going
somewhere.

Naturally, Régis Marcon could not just stand by and watch this revival. To win the international Bocuse d'Or prize, all he had to do was simply select a veal calf from the Haute Loire. Once
again—this time, through our chef—Michel Peyrard had rubbed elbows with success.

Tomato Fritters with Fairy Ring Mushrooms

Appetizer
Serves 4

Ingredients
8 medium-sized, firm tomatoes
1 tsp. confectioners' sugar
1½ cloves of garlic
½ cup (12 cl) olive oil
¼ bulb of fennel, diced
3 shallots, chopped
1 sprig of thyme, leaves picked
9 oz. (250 g) fresh fairy ring
mushrooms

Fritter batter
⅔ cup (100 g) flour
½ cup (50 g) cornstarch
2 tbsp. (15 g) baking powder
⅓ cup (75 g) fromage blanc
1 egg
½ cup (12 cl) water
8 cups (2 l) peanut oil
Salt and pepper

This technical recipe requires a little time. Prepare it at the beginning of the tomato season. The combination of the bitter almond taste of the fairy ring mushrooms and the fruity tang of the tomatoes is remarkable. This recipe is from the "Finest Artisan of France" competition of 1996, which was won by my former chef, Jacques Decoret.

The tomatoes
Preheat the oven to 200°F (100°C).

Cut the tops and peel the tomatoes, quarter 4 of them lengthwise, and remove the seeds. Arrange on a baking sheet lined with parchment paper. Season the tomatoes with salt, pepper and a pinch of sugar. Place a slice of the halved garlic clove on each and drizzle with olive oil. Bake for 45 minutes to 1 hour to dry.

In a small sauté pan add a little olive oil and brown the fennel and shallots.

After removing the seeds, chop the remaining tomatoes. Place the tomatoes, the cooked fennel and shallots, with the whole garlic clove and thyme in a pan. Season with salt, pepper and a little sugar if needed. Dry the mixture over low heat, stirring occasionally.

Sauté the fairy ring mushrooms in olive oil and season with salt and pepper. Drain and add to the cooked tomatoes.

Line 4 round molds with plastic wrap. Arrange slices of oven-dried tomato around the sides of each mold. Fill with the tomato-mushroom mixture. Use the plastic wrap to shape the mixture into balls. Freeze at least 2 hours.

The fritter batter
Mix the flour, cornstarch, baking powder, *fromage blanc*, and egg. Add the water, little by little, to make a batter. Cover and set aside.

Preheat the oven to 350°F (170°C).
Heat the peanut oil to 325°F (160°C).

Presentation
Remove the tomatoes from the freezer and carefully roll them in a little cornstarch. Then, with a wooden skewer, dip them into the fritter batter. Deep-fry to a beautiful golden color.

Put the fritters in the oven to warm the interiors.

Serve as an accompaniment to fish or meat dishes or as a starter with a mixed green salad.

Fairy Ring Mushrooms Marinated in Hazelnut Oil with Burnet and Chives

Appetizer 🌲
Serves 4

Ingredients
6 hazelnuts, shelled and crushed
30 to 40 fresh fairy ring mushrooms,
with stems

Marinade
1 tsp. salt
1 tsp. pepper
Juice of 1 lemon
1 tsp. soy sauce
6 tbsp. (8 cl) hazelnut oil
2 shallots, very finely minced
Several stalks of chives, finely
chopped, with flowers if possible

Handful of burnet and other
small salad greens

The fairy ring mushroom, sometimes mistaken for the Saint George's mushroom, is a field mushroom. Its Latin name, Marasmius oreades, signifies that its foot twists but doesn't break. The fairy ring mushroom is so-named because it grows from the center outward in "fairy rings" on damp unfertilized grass. It is my favorite spring mushroom, with the fragrant, tart aroma of bitter almonds.

The mushrooms
Chop the hazelnuts and toast in the oven for 5 to 10 minutes.

Select healthy fairy ring mushrooms that have been harvested in dry weather. Cut the stems to about 1 in. (2 cm) in length. Place the mushrooms, cap down, in a soup plate.

The marinade
Prepare the marinade by mixing the ingredients in this order: salt, pepper, lemon juice, soy sauce, hazelnut oil, and shallots. Pour the marinade over the mushrooms, making sure that it coats the gills.

Sprinkle with chives and cover with plastic wrap. Refrigerate for about 1 hour.

Presentation
Arrange the burnet and salad greens in the center of each plate. Scatter mushrooms around the greens and pour marinade over the salad. Sprinkle with chive flowers and toasted hazelnuts.

Enjoy this as an appetizer, eaten with the fingers.

Creamy Mushroom Soup

The cream soup
One day in advance, soak the dried porcini mushrooms in 3 cups (750 cl) of warm water.

The next day, wash and thinly slice the vegetables. Wash and quarter the white mushrooms.

Heat the butter and 1 tbsp. of olive oil in a deep saucepan. Add the leek, fennel, garlic, and potato. Sweat over low heat for about 5 minutes. Add the white mushrooms and sweat a little longer.

Add the chicken stock, thyme, the soaked porcini, and the strained soaking water. Cover and cook over medium heat for 45 minutes.

Blend the soup in a food processor or with an immersion blender, and pass through a fine china cap strainer.

Add the crème fraîche and boil. Adjust the seasoning and consistency. If the soup is too thick, add a little water.

Wash and thinly slice the fresh porcini. Brown gently in 1 tbsp. of olive oil. Drain on paper towels and keep warm.

Heat the milk in a small saucepan.

Presentation
Portion the sautéed porcini into mugs and cover with the soup.

With an immersion blender, whip the hot milk into a foam. Place a tbsp. of foam on each serving. Sprinkle with powdered mushrooms and serve immediately.

Appetizer
Serves 8

Ingredients
4 oz. (120 g) dried porcini
1 leek, white part only
½ fresh fennel bulb
2 cloves of garlic
1 large potato, 3 oz. (80 g), peeled and cut into large cubes
2 tbsp. (30 g) butter
2 tbsp. (3 cl) olive oil
10 oz. (300 g) white mushrooms
4 cups (1 l) chicken stock (pg. 290)
1 sprig of fresh thyme
⅔ cup (15 cl) crème fraîche
5 oz. (150 g) fresh porcini mushrooms
¾ cup (18 cl) milk

Pinch of powdered mushrooms (pg. 293)

Served on special occasions, this mushroom soup has become one of our restaurant's classic appetizers. My colleagues at Saint-Bonnet and I prepare more than 80 gallons (300 l) of this soup for the mushroom festival in November.

Dried porcini mushrooms

Fricassée of Frogs' Legs with Bear's Garlic and Hazelnut Crusts

Appetizer 🌲 🌲 🌲
Serve this dish very hot.
Serves 4

Ingredients
Hazelnut crusts
⅓ cup (50 g) flour
2 egg whites
Pinch of salt and sugar
2 tbsp. (30 g) butter, melted
5 tbsp. (30 g) crushed hazelnuts

*Frog's legs and
mushroom fricassée*
2 dozen frogs
4 tbsp. (55 g) butter
4 shallots chopped
4 tbsp. (6 cl) white wine
7 oz. (200 g) fairy ring mushrooms
2 handfuls of fresh spinach
1 clove of garlic

Bear's garlic butter
1 bunch of bear's garlic
(bulbs and leaves)
8 tbsp. (100 g) creamed butter

Jerusalem artichoke coulis
10 oz. (300 g) Jerusalem artichokes
2 tbsp. (30 g) butter
Chicken stock (pg. 290)

Salt and pepper

The hazelnut crusts
Preheat the oven to 400°F (200°C).

Mix the flour, egg whites, salt, and sugar with a spatula. Add the melted butter and set aside. Butter a nonstick baking sheet and roll the pastry into very thin rounds. Sprinkle with crushed hazelnuts.

Bake for 5 to 8 minutes. Keep warm.

The frogs' legs
Cut to separate the frogs' legs. Dress 12 to cook later and set aside.

In a sauté pan, brown the shallots with the remaining frogs' legs in 2 tbsp. of butter. Season with salt and pepper and then deglaze with the wine. Heat covered until the legs are cooked, about 5 to 6 minutes.

Sort and wash the mushrooms. Wash and stem the spinach.

The bear's garlic butter
Set aside 4 bear's garlic leaves.

Finely chop the remaining bear's garlic leaves and 2 or 3 cloves (or use cloves of regular garlic instead). Mix into the creamed butter and refrigerate.

The Jerusalem artichoke coulis
Peel and dice the Jerusalem artichokes. Brown half in a tbsp. of butter in a frying pan and keep warm to use as garnish. Brown the other half in another tbsp. of butter in a sauté pan, moisten with chicken stock, cover, and simmer. Season with salt and pepper. Blend in a food processor to obtain a coulis and pass through a fine china cap strainer. Set aside.

Place the 4 reserved bear's garlic leaves on a baking sheet. Dry in the oven at 175°F (80°C) for 15 to 20 minutes.

Presentation
Heat a tbsp. of butter and add the garlic clove and a pinch of salt. Wilt the spinach and set aside on paper towels. Keep warm.

Sauté the 12 reserved frogs' legs in a tbsp. of butter with the cloves of bear's garlic (or 1 clove of regular garlic).

Remove the bones from the frogs' legs cooked in white wine. Add the mushrooms and keep warm.

Heat the Jerusalem artichoke coulis. Whisk in the garlic butter and adjust the seasoning.

Pour a small amount of coulis into the bottom of each plate and let it spread to form a circle.

Arrange spinach in the center of the circle and place a hazelnut crust on top. Spoon on the frogs' legs fricassée and diced Jerusalem artichokes.

Top with another hazelnut crust. To the side, position a dried garlic leaf and three sautéed frogs' legs. Serve very hot.

This is a recipe to make just as winter turns into spring — when the last Jerusalem artichokes of the season can still be found, the pre-Easter frogs appear, the bear's garlic is in flower and deliciously crunchy, and the first fairy ring mushrooms appear in the fields.

Grandpa Romezin's Char with Spring Herbs and Sautéed Potatoes

Fish 🌲

You might have difficulties finding all the herbs, so I have indicated possible substitutes.
Serves 4

Ingredients

Creamed butter with herbs

6 small leaves of sheep
or garden sorrel
1 tsp. wild thyme or
fresh garden thyme
1 tsp. spring mint or peppermint
2 tsp. spignel or dill
6 juniper berries, ground
4 tbsp. flat-leaf parsley
10 tarragon leaves
1 clove of garlic, crushed

1⅓ cup (300 g) butter
½ cup (12 cl) olive oil
1⅔ cups (40 cl) vegetable stock
(pg. 293)
½ lemon, juice only

Sautéed potatoes

14 oz. (400 g) new potatoes
(ratte variety)
4 tbsp. peanut oil
4 tbsp. (55 g) butter

Char

4 char, 9 oz. (250 g) each
8 tbsp. (110 g) butter
2 cloves of garlic, unpeeled
1 sprig fresh thyme

Salt and pepper

The creamed butter with herbs

Finely chop all the herbs and mix with the butter and olive oil in a food processor.

Transfer the mixture onto a sheet of plastic wrap and roll into a sausage shape. Freeze.

I have deliberately made a large amount of herb butter to make the preparation easier. For this recipe, you will use about 4 to 6 tbsp. (60 to 80 g) of herb butter. You can freeze the rest to use in another recipe—a vegetable dish, for example.

The sautéed potatoes

Scrape the skin of the potatoes with a knife. If they are very new potatoes, you can remove the skin simply by rubbing them with your hands.

Pour the peanut oil into a hot pan. Sauté the potatoes, season with salt and pepper.

Cover, lower the heat and cook, turning them from time to time. Three quarters of the way through the cooking add the butter. Keep warm.

The char

Gut the char and wipe the insides thoroughly with paper towels. Do not wash. Season with salt and pepper.

Heat the butter in a large pan. Dust the char with flour and brush off any excess. Gently lay them in the pan, in the same direction. Add a little butter.

Brown the skin. Slip a long spatula under the length of the fish, hold the fish in place with your finger, and gently turn it, being careful not to drop it and burn yourself. Brown the other side. Baste frequently.

To cook a fish this size takes about 15 minutes. Check inside the flesh for doneness.

The creamed butter sauce

While the char is cooking, reduce the vegetable stock by half in a small, deep saucepan. Add about 4 to 6 tbsp. (60 to 80 g) of herb butter, according to taste. Finish with the lemon juice. Mix together and whisk the sauce with an immersion blender.

Presentation
Lay the fish in a hot platter and generously pour the creamed butter sauce around it. Arrange the potatoes around the fish and serve immediately.

The plateaus of Velay and Vivarais, with their volcanic granite terrain and unfertilized pasture, are a veritable paradise for aromatic herbs. To really know the herbs of this region, you need to spend a great amount of time traveling through the countryside. Here's to Michel Bras and Marc Veyrat, who make their region known through their recipes.

Chicken Fricassée with Crayfish

Meat 🌲🌲

Meat 🌲🌲
Preparing crayfish requires a little practice.
Serves 6

Ingredients
Crayfish and chicken
48 crayfish
4 tbsp. (6 cl) vinegar
1 free-range chicken, 3 lbs. (1,2 kg), cut into 8 pieces (reserve the carcass and neck for stock)

Pea garnish
2 lbs. 2 oz. (1 kg) garden peas
1 tbsp. butter

Sauce
2 cups (50 cl) chicken stock (pg. 290)
6 tbsp. (8 cl) olive oil
1 onion, chopped
2 cloves of garlic, crushed
1 medium-sized carrot, diced
1 fresh tomato, quartered
4 tbsp. (6 cl) cognac
1 cup (25 cl) white wine
½ cup (12 cl) port
1 bouquet garni
1 cup (25 cl) crème fraîche
Several tarragon leaves, chopped

Salt and pepper

The crayfish

Prepare the crayfish by peeling away the black gut from the tail. To do this, hold the central part of the tail tip between thumb and index finger, then gently twist back and forth and pull off the gut.

Heat the vinegar and 4 cups (1 l) of water in a deep pan. Add the crayfish and boil for 1 minute before draining. Reserve 12 unpeeled crayfish. Peel the remaining crayfish tails and crush the empty shells.

The garden peas

Shell the peas. Plunge into a pot of boiling salted water. Cook for 2 to 3 minutes, depending on their size. Refresh in iced water.

Drain the peas. Remove the skins if they are very large.

The chicken and sauce

Make chicken stock with the chicken carcass and neck. In a large sauté pan, heat 4 tbsp. of the olive oil. Brown the chicken pieces with the crushed crayfish shell.

Add the onion, garlic, carrot, and tomato. Brown the mixture, then flambé with cognac. Cover and simmer.

After 12 minutes, remove the breast pieces. After 3 more minutes, remove the wings. Cook the legs for an additional 10 minutes. Transfer all the chicken pieces onto a large plate and cover with foil. Keep warm.

The chicken carcass, crushed crayfish shells, and vegetables remain in the sauté pan. Skim off the excess fat, then deglaze with the white wine and port. Scrape all the caramelized juices at the bottom of the pan. Reduce the liquid by half and then add enough chicken stock to cover. Boil, skim, and gently simmer for about 30 minutes.

Let the flavors infuse for 10 minutes. Pass through a fine china cap strainer into another pan. Reduce to 1¼ cups (30 cl) of sauce, then add the crème fraîche. Boil until the sauce coats the back of a spoon. Season with salt and pepper to taste. Add the tarragon, chicken pieces, shelled crayfish tails, and the reserved whole crayfish. Keep warm.

Presentation

Diagonally slice the chicken breast. Place some breast meat and a thigh or wing on each plate. Reheat the peas with a tbsp. of butter and sprinkle over the chicken. Decorate the plates with the crayfish tails and whole crayfish. Pour on the sauce.

This is a traditional recipe from the Allier region, when there were still crayfish in the Doux and Lignon Rivers. The dish is usually served with rice, but you can also serve it with other grains, such as wheat, spelt, or millet (see the discussion of grains on pages 224–227).

Veal with Chanterelle Mushrooms and Purée in Three Styles

Meat 🌲

This recipe requires several different cuts of veal. If it seems too complex, you could use just the tenderloin. This is a fine, festive dish.

Serves 8

Ingredients
Veal
3 lb. (1,2 kg) veal rump
from a milk-fed calf
4 (6 cl) tbsp. olive oil
1 onion
1 carrot, finely sliced
½ cup (12 cl) white wine
1 fresh tomato, halved
1 clove of garlic
1 sprig of thyme
Veal jus (pg. 292)

Veal sweetbreads and chanterelle mushrooms
9 oz. (250 g) veal sweetbreads
10 oz. (300 g) chanterelle mushrooms
4 tbsp. (60 g) butter
1 tbsp. flour
2 shallots, finely chopped
½ cup (12 cl) white vermouth

Veal kidneys and chanterelle mushroom purée
4 tbsp. (60 g) butter
1 large onion, finely chopped
2 medium-sized carrots, thinly sliced
14 oz. (400 g) large chanterelle mushrooms
1 cup (25 cl) chicken stock (pg. 290)
10 oz. (300 g) veal kidneys, without fat
1 sprig thyme, leaves picked

The veal rump

Preheat the oven to 250°F (120°C).

Heat a little of the oil in a large frying pan. Brown the meat on all sides, season with salt and pepper. Remove from the heat.

In the same pan, brown the onion and carrot. Deglaze with white wine and reduce by half. Add the tomato, a glass of water, garlic and thyme. Pour the liquid and vegetables into a casserole dish. Add the meat. Cook 1½ hours, basting frequently.

At the end of cooking, the veal should be 136°F (58°C) at the center. Cover the meat with a plate and keep warm. Pass the cooking juices through a fine china cap strainer. Reduce to obtain ¾ cup (18 cl) of veal jus.

The veal sweetbreads

One day in advance, wash the sweetbreads in cold water. Drain, place in a pan, and cover with water. Bring to a boil, then simmer about 5 to 8 minutes, depending on its size. Drain, refresh with cold water, and drain again. Press between two plates with a weight on top.

Clean the mushrooms and sauté in a pan with 1 tbsp. of butter. Reserve the cooking juices.

Cut the sweetbreads into ¼ in. (½ cm) slices. Flour and brush off any excess. Heat 1 tbsp. butter and a little oil in a pan. Brown the slices, season with salt and pepper, and keep warm on a plate. Repeat this process twice to cook all the sweetbreads.

Wipe the pan clean and reduce the heat. Add 1 tbsp. of butter and sweat the shallots. Deglaze with the vermouth and reduce. Add the mushroom cooking juices and some veal jus. Cook, stirring with a spatula, until the sauce coats the back of a spoon. Add the mushrooms and keep warm.

The veal kidneys and chanterelle purée

Brown the onion in 2 tbsp. of butter in a heavy pan. Add the carrots, mushrooms, and chicken stock. Cover and cook over medium heat, until there is no liquid left in the pan. Season with salt and pepper.

Purée the mixture in a food processor and pass through a sieve. Add 1 tbsp. of butter, check the seasoning, and keep warm.

Cut the veal kidneys into thick slices.

Heat 1 tbsp. of butter until it foams. Brown the kidney slices for 2 minutes on each side. Add the thyme leaves, season with salt and pepper, keep warm.

Presentation

Carve the loin into slices about ⅓ in. (8 mm) thick and place in a serving platter. Arrange the sweetbreads and mushrooms, the chanterelle purée, and the kidney slices around the meat. Pour veal jus over the loin and kidneys. Season the slices with salt and pepper before serving your guests.

This dish may be accompanied by green vegetables and new potatoes.

Raising veal calves "under the mother" is a tradition in the Monts du Velay region. And when it comes to breeding veal calves, Michel Peyrard is an expert— with a lot of patience! Each calf is raised in an individual stall, sheltered from light, and is weaned exclusively on its mother's milk. Cleanliness—of the bedding and the mother's udders—is essential. The low iron content of the milk produces a pale pink or white flesh. Every day, the calf is also fed eggs, and sometimes biscuits soaked in milk. Some say, jokingly, that the calves do not inhabit stalls but their own "royal palaces." We are far removed from intensive farming here.

Candy Sugared Leaf and Flower Surprise

Dessert

Ingredients
Leaves
Black currant, mint, peppermint, lemon balm, verbena, sage, and basil

Flowers
Violets and fragrant roses

1 egg white
Handful of superfine sugar

The leaves and flowers

Preheat the oven to 150°F (60°C).

Wash the leaves and flowers in cold water and drain on paper towels. With a soft brush, gently coat each with egg white. Immediately dip each leaf into the sugar.

Lay the leaves and flowers on a baking sheet and dry in the oven for 1 to 2 hours, until crisp.

Presentation

Present these sugary treats any way you wish—perhaps as decoration, as shown in the photograph, or as a garnish for desserts or ice cream. Use your imagination.

This recipe is surprisingly easy to make. The drying process concentrates the flavor of each leaf variety. Delight your friends!

Baked Strawberry Tart

On a lightly floured surface, roll the pastry dough into a circle, about 12 in. (28 cm) diameter and ⅛ in. (2 mm) thick. Line a buttered, 8 in. (20 cm) tart pan with the dough, draping it over the edges. Trim the excess by rolling a rolling pin across the rim of the pan. Prick the bottom of the shell, pinch the edges between thumb and forefinger, and refrigerate. Preheat the oven to 350°F (180°C).

Line the pastry shell with a layer of aluminum foil, being careful not to tear the dough. Place weights or beans on top of the foil and bake for 15 minutes. Remove from the oven, and remove the aluminum foil. (Save the foil and beans to bake another tart.)

The almond cream
Mix the creamed butter, egg, almonds, sugar, and cream in a bowl with a wooden spoon.

The tart filling
Hollow out each strawberry with a small melon baller. Turn the strawberries upside down on a wire rack to drain.

Spread a ¼ in. (5 mm) layer of almond cream in the bottom of the pastry shell. Break the ladyfingers and sprinkle them over the cream. Place the strawberries on top, setting them close together, hollowed ends up.

Using a pastry bag and a fine tip, about ¼ in. (½ cm), pipe cream into the hollowed centers of each strawberry and between them. Sprinkle with confectioner's sugar then bake about 20 minutes.

Presentation
Remove the tart from the oven and carefully slide onto a wire rack to cool. Serve at room temperature.

Dessert
Serves 8

Ingredients
10 oz. (300 g) sugar pastry dough (pg. 297)
8 ladyfingers

Almond cream
6 tbsp. (80 g) creamed butter
1 egg
1 cup (100 g) ground white almonds
¾ cup (100 g) confectioners' sugar
1 tbsp heavy cream

Baked strawberries
20 firm wild strawberries
3 tbsp. (50 g) confectioner's sugar

I wanted to make a strawberry tart with cooked rather than raw strawberries, anticipating the pleasant aroma of strawberry jam that would fill the house when the tart came out of the oven.

Photograph of the recipe shown on the next two pages.

French Toast Brioche with Strawberries, Blueberries, and Peach Wild Thyme Sorbet

Dessert
Serves 4

Ingredients
French toast brioche
3 eggs
⅓ cup (75 g) sugar
1 cup (¼ l) milk
7 tbsp. (100 g) butter
4 slices of brioche

Pistachio pastry cream
2 cups (½ l) milk
5 egg yolks
1 tbsp. (25 g) sugar
6 tbsp. (50 g) cornstarch
4 tbsp. (60 g) butter, cubed
1 tbsp. of pistachio paste

Garnish
9 oz. (250 g) wild strawberries
9 oz. (250 g) wild blueberries
1½ tbsp. (20 g) butter

Peach wild thyme sorbet
*1 lb. 10 oz. (850 g) peach pulp,
from ripe peaches*
1¼ cups (30 cl) water
4 oz. (120 g) superfine sugar
1 tbsp. of wild thyme flowers
Juice of ½ lemon

*It's difficult to make a small
quantity of pastry cream, so
I recommend that you simply
use the remaining custard
to make a tart or other dessert.*

The French toast brioche

Whisk together the eggs, sugar, and milk. Heat half of the butter in a large, nonstick pan over high heat. When the butter foams, quickly dip a slice of brioche into the batter. Drain and place in the pan. Brown each side and place the brioche in a buttered oven dish. Brown the remaining slices in the same way.

The pistachio pastry cream

Boil the milk in a stainless saucepan reserving 2 tbsp.

In the meantime, whisk the yolks and sugar until light and creamy. Add the cornstarch and 2 tbsp. cold milk. Pour the boiling milk into this batter, whisking constantly. Transfer the mixture back to the saucepan and cook on high heat, whisking vigorously. The custard will soon thicken. Leave the custard on the heat for 30 seconds to 1 minute after it boils. Transfer to a bowl and stir in the butter, then the pistachio paste. Mix well and refrigerate. With a metal spatula, spread the pistachio custard on the brioche slices. Arrange alternate rows of strawberries and blueberries on top.

The peach wild thyme sorbet

Boil 1¼ cups (30cl) of water. Add the thyme flowers and infuse for about 1 hour.

Purée the peaches in a food processor. Pass through a medium china cap strainer if the peaches are stringy. Remove the thyme flowers, and add the infusion with the lemon juice to the purée. Process in an ice-cream maker.

Presentation

Preheat the oven to 400°F (200°C).

Lightly sprinkle the strawberries and blueberries with sugar and add 1 or 2 tbsp. of butter. Bake the brioches for about 4 minutes. Arrange the slices on the plates. Serve with the peach wild thyme sorbet, as shown in the photograph, or with ice cream.

Brochette Margaridou

1. One day in advance

Rinse the sweetbreads in cold water and remove the nerves. Dry with paper towels and roll in plastic wrap to form "sausages." Poach in simmering water in a large pan for 15 minutes. Refrigerate.

2. The brochettes

Thread the skewers, alternating the slices of sweetbread, pieces of ham, and uncooked morel mushrooms.

3. Cooking the brochettes

Heat the butter in the pan, brown the brochettes, and season with salt and pepper.

4. The sauce
Make the sauce with the roux, mushroom powder, and cream. Season the sauce with salt and pepper. Coat each brochette and freeze for at lest 1 hour.

5. Coat each frozen brochette with beaten egg whites and then with white-bread crumbs.

6. Presentation
Heat the peanut oil in a deep pan to 325°F (160°C), until the oil is steaming slightly. Lay the brochettes in the oil with a skimming ladle. Remove when crisp and golden. Finish cooking in the oven. Sprinkle with salt and drain on paper towels.

Serve with a truffle or morel mushroom sauce or alone as an appetizer.

Complete recipe is on pages 56–57.

Summer

Not that one would make an "entire salad" of them, but the mizuna and mibuna leaf greens have an extraordinary flavor. These Japanese varieties are cultivated in Saint-Vincent-la-Commanderie in the Drôme (by the producer Fleur Délice). Mizuna has a gentle understated bitterness that is much smoother than rocket, and, not surprisingly, it has attracted the interest of many restaurateurs. Jean-Luc Raillon devotes his talent, which is keen, and his time, which he does not waste, to cultivating rare salad varieties, herbs, and edible flowers. While visiting his greenhouses, recipe ideas will come to you, and dreams of harmonious wines and delicacies (one imagines a Barsac wine, full of Sémillon freshness, in response to the flavor of pineapple sage). You can create an entire culinary culture exploring the pelargonium (aromatic geranium) or biting into a borage leaf (with its undertones of oysters and cucumber) or the more modest nasturtium. Jean-Luc would forgive Régis Marcon if he didn't order chickweed from him, as the plant — also dear to fellow chef Michel Bras — is bountiful in the fields and thickets around Saint-Bonnet. In every way, the quality of Jean-Luc's greens is undeniable, and he has never had any complaints about them.

Jean-Luc is also a character well worth knowing. His great success with chefs and greengrocers has not kept him from cultivating paradoxes along with plantain. "I never eat salad myself," he says, mischievously, as he watches you sample a sprig of his lovage or lemon balm or an off-season cherry tomato or baby eggplant from his greenhouses.

Crisp Foie Gras and Almonds with Green Lentils and Wheat Vinaigrette

Appetizer 🌲 🌲 🌲
A festive dish.
Pears may be substituted
for the radishes.
Serves 12

Ingredients
3 lbs. (1,2 kg) foie gras
2/3 cup (100 g) flour
3 large (100 g) egg whites
1 cup (100 g) slivered almonds
Fresh bread crumbs
7 tbsp. (100 g) clarified butter for cooking

Vinaigrette
1 tbsp. dijon mustard
1/3 cup sherry wine vinegar
2/3 hazelnut oil
1 shallot, finely chopped
2 tbsp. parsley, chopped

Grains
1/2 cup (100 g), green du Puy lentils
1 medium onion
1 clove
1 sprig thyme
1 bayleaf
salt, to taste
1/4 cup (50 g) bulgur or wheat
1 shallot, finely chopped

Radishes
10 oz. (300 g) young radishes
4 tbsp. (6 cl) grape seed oil
2 tbsp. brown sugar
2 vanilla bean pods, split
4 tbsp. (6 cl) balsamic vinegar
1/2 cup (100 g) shelled walnuts

The foie gras
Prepare 2 to 3 days in advance.

Remove the nerves from the foie gras. Roll in plastic wrap to form a "fat sausage" about 2 in. (5 cm) wide. Soak in warm water, 150°F (65°C), for 8 minutes. Chill with ice and refrigerate.

The vinaigrette
In a small bowl whisk the mustard with the sherry vinegar. Add the hazelnut oil in a steady stream while whisking. Add the shallot and parsley. Season with salt and pepper.

The lentils
Blanch the lentils. Cook in lightly salted water with an onion studded with the clove, the thyme, and bay leaf. The cooked lentils should be slightly crunchy. Drain. While they are still warm, toss with the vinaigrette.

The bulgur
Cook in salted water. Mix with the lentils and add the shallot.

Sweet and sour radishes with vanilla
Brown the radishes in the grape seed oil. Add the brown sugar, vanilla bean pods, and the balsamic vinegar. Reduce and set aside.

The radishes may be prepared several days in advance.

The sauce
Caramelize the honey in a pan and deglaze with the sherry wine vinegar. Reduce to form a syrup. Add the chicken jus.

The crisp medallions of foie gras
Cut 3 oz. (80 g) medallions of foie gras. Sprinkle with a little salt and roll in sifted flour. Dip each one into the lightly beaten egg whites, then roll in a mixture of crushed almonds and bread crumbs. Refrigerate.

Heat the clarified butter over high heat. Lay the foie gras in the pan and brown on both sides. Finish cooking in a 350°F (180°C) oven for 3 to 5 minutes.

Check for doneness by inserting a skewer into the center of the foie gras. If the skewer is hot when removed, the foie gras is cooked. Season with salt.

Presentation

Place some lentil and bulgur wheat salad in the center of each plate. Arrange the radishes, walnuts, mizuna leaves, and borage flowers around it. Lay the warm foie gras on the salad and cover each medallion with sauce.

Serve immediately, sprinkled with fine sea salt and freshly ground black pepper.

I am always dismayed to see hot foie gras dissolve in a pan—perhaps because of my frugal instincts, for which the people of Auvergne are known. So, I had the idea to coat it in egg whites, then in crushed almonds and bread crumbs. This way, the foie gras does not melt when it's fried, and it has a crisp, delicious crust.

Sauce
2 tbsp. (60 g) honey
4 tbsp. (6 cl) sherry wine vinegar
1 cup (25 cl) chicken jus, (p. 290)
Salt and pepper

Decoration
Mizuna leaves
Borage flowers

103

Crique with Langoustines

Traditional appetizer 🌲
Serves 4

Ingredients
1 lb. 2 oz. (500 g) potatoes
3 tbsp. (4 cl) crème fraîche
4 eggs

Herbs
2 tbsp. each of chopped chives,
chervil, flat-leaf parsley
1 onion, minced
7 tbsp. (100 g) melted butter

8 langoustine tails, peeled
2 cloves of garlic
7 oz. (200 g) mesclun salad
3½ tbsp. pistachio herb vinaigrette
(pg. 295)
Pinch of garlic

Salt and pepper

*T**he* **crique**

Peel and grate the potatoes. Press to obtain about 1 lb. (450 g) of pulp. Whisk the crème fraîche and eggs. Fold into the potato pulp with the fresh herbs. Season with salt and pepper.

Heat a small crêpe pan over high heat and add the melted butter. Cook the *criques* as you would cook pancakes, about ½ in. (1 cm) thick. The outsides should be crisp.

Heat a little butter in another pan and sear the langoustine tails. Season with salt and pepper.

Sort and wash the salad greens. Season with the pistachio herb vinaigrette and the pinch of garlic.

Presentation

Serve the hot *criques* with langoustines and a few salad greens on top. Drizzle with the langoustine cooking juices and the pistachio herb vinaigrette.

Crique is a specialty of the Ardèche region and is either cooked in olive oil or butter.

Just as everybody has their favorite way to prepare crique, *everybody also claims to have the true recipe. So, naturally, the method I present here is disputed.*

I particularly like the criques *that my fellow chef Marc Julliat prepares in Annonay. He makes them like a pizza, which he calls a* criqzza.

Pan-Fried Salmon
with Wild Sorrel

Fish
Serves 4

Ingredients
4 tbsp. (6 cl) olive oil
4 slices of salmon, 5 oz. (150 g)
each, with skin

Pearl barley
1 medium-sized onion, minced
2 tbsp. (30 g) butter
1 cup (150 g) pearl barley
4 tbsp. (6 cl) white wine
3 cups (75 cl) chicken stock
(pg. 290)
6 oz. (180 g) small
chanterelle mushrooms

Asparagus
12 wild asparagus or
green asparagus tips
4 tsp. (2 cl) hazelnut oil

Sorrel sauce
13 tbsp. (175 g) clarified butter
3 egg yolks
4 tbsp. (6 cl) cold water
Juice of 1/2 lemon
Handful of wild or garden sorrel

Salt and pepper

Wild sorrel is easily recognizable because of its pointed arrow tips. As children, my friends and I liked to chew the tart leaves that we found in the fields. I prefer the smaller leaves. In summer, they flower and produce small yellow seeds.

The pearl barley

Brown the onion in 1 tbsp. butter. Add the pearl barley and sauté until slightly golden. Add the wine and reduce by half. Add the chicken stock, season with salt and pepper. Cover and simmer gently for about 1 hour, stirring occasionally. Moisten with a little water as needed.

Heat 1 tbsp. of butter and quickly sauté the chanterelles. Add to the barley and keep warm.

The asparagus

In a sauté pan, brown the peeled asparagus tips in the hazelnut oil. Add a little water and season with salt and pepper. Half-cover the pan and cook gently. Keep warm.

The sorrel sauce

Keep the clarified butter warm so that it remains liquid. In a heavy stainless-steel sauté pan, whisk the yolks, water, salt, and pepper over low heat. Cook 3 to 4 minutes, until the mixture thickens enough to leave a ribbon trail. Be careful that it does not stick to the bottom of the pan and burn. Remove from heat and add the clarified butter little by little, whisking continuously. Add the lemon juice. The sauce should have a very light texture. Reserve one-third and keep warm.

Before serving, add the sorrel to 2/3 of the sauce, blending with an immersion blender. Adjust the seasoning.

The salmon

Preheat the oven to 250°F (120°C). Pour the oil in a frying pan and brown the salmon, skin side down. Finish cooking in the oven. The salmon flesh should be tender and warm inside.

Presentation

Arrange the barley and chanterelles in the center of each plate. Lay a slice of salmon on top. Place 3 tips of asparagus on top of the fish. Pour the sorrel sauce around it, and the reserved sauce is spooned onto the outer part of the plate.

Stuffed Truffole with Langoustines

Fish

Preparing the potato is a delicate process, so, to make the recipe easier, you can omit the potato.
Serves 4

Ingredients
4 large langoustines
6 medium-sized firm potatoes (allowing 2 extra in case some split while cooking)
2 cups (½ l) seafood stock (pg. 294)
½ cup (12 cl) white wine
2 medium shallots, minced
1 lb. 2 oz. (500 g) clams
4 oz. (120 g) mushroom duxelle (pg. 294)
1½ oz. (40 g) young carrots, sliced
5 oz. (150 g) gray chanterelles
3 tbsp. clarified butter

Herb butter
15 tbsp. (200 g) butter, creamed
2 tbsp. chopped parsley
1 tsp. dill
5 mint leaves
8 basil leaves
Several sprigs of thyme
1 clove of garlic, crushed and puréed
4 tbsp. (6 cl) olive oil

Salt and pepper

The seafood stock
Shell and refrigerate the langoustine tails. Use the langoustine shells to make the seafood stock (pg. 294).

The truffoles
Peel the potatoes. Cut them into pieces 3 in. (7 cm) long, 2 in. (5 cm) wide and 1 in. (2, 5 cm) thick. Carefully hollow out the centers with a melon baller. Butter a sauté pan large enough to fit all the potatoes and arrange them inside. Then, pour in enough seafood stock to half-cover the potatoes. Simmer and check for doneness with a knife.

The clams
Pour the white wine into a shallow, wide pan. Add the clams and finely chopped shallots. Cook for about 2 minutes, until all the clams have opened. Reserve the cooking juice.

The herb butter
Cream the butter in a food processor. Add the herbs, garlic purée, and olive oil. Turn the butter onto a sheet of plastic wrap and roll into a sausage shape. Refrigerate.

Of course, there is too much herb butter for this recipe. I suggest you freeze the rest for later use (with vegetables or escargots, for example).

The stuffed truffoles
Coarsely chop half of the clams and mix with the mushroom duxelle. Stuff each potato with the mixture.

The herb sauce
Brown the carrots in a tbsp. of butter over low heat. Moisten with the seafood sauce and the cooking juice from the clams. Cook about 15 minutes. Remove from the heat and blend with an immersion blender. The cooked carrot will thicken the sauce. Pass through a fine china cap strainer and keep warm.

The gray chanterelles

Clean the chanterelles and wash if necessary. Heat the pan, add 1 tbsp. of clarified butter, and sauté the chanterelles. Season with salt and pepper, keep warm.

Presentation

Preheat the oven to 400°F (200°C).

Heat a pan over high heat and add two tbsp. of clarified butter. Brown the langoustine tails and insert 1 into each potato. Bake for about 8 minutes, until very hot.

Reheat the remaining half of the clams in a little of the herb sauce. Place some on each plate and position a *truffole* in the center. In the meantime, boil the remaining herb sauce. Mix in 3 tbsp. (40 g) of the herb butter with an immersion blender until creamy. Add the chanterelle mushrooms.

Pour the sauce over the *truffoles*. Serve very hot.

Truffole *is the word used in the Ardèche region for potato. In fact, the potato first arrived in France in the Ardèche, in the small community of Saint-Alban-d'Ay. It was introduced by Pierre Sornas, a Franciscan monk from Toledo, Spain, in 1540.*

Vegetable and Mushroom Fricot

Vegetable
Serves 6

Ingredients
Boiled green vegetables
7 oz. (200 g) green beans
9 oz. (250 g) fresh
fava beans, shelled
5 oz. (150 g) garden peas, shelled
7 oz. (200 g) snow peas
5 oz. (150 g) fresh broad beans
Flat-leaf parsley

Braised vegetables
7 oz. (200 g) chard
9 oz. (250 g) young carrots
9 oz. (250 g) young turnips
7 oz. (200 g) small onions
4 cups (1 l) chicken stock (pg. 290)
14 oz. (400 g) firm potatoes
(ratte variety)
4 cloves of garlic
½ cup (12 cl) chicken jus (pg. 290)
2 tbsp. chopped parsley

Late spring mushrooms
Chanterelles
Porcini
5 oz. (150 g) slab bacon,
cut into large cubes

Olive oil
Butter
Salt and pepper

The green vegetables
Prepare and drain all the vegetables.
In a large pan of boiling salted water, boil each vegetable according to its size. The green beans and broad beans will take the longest to cook, then the fava beans, garden peas, snow peas, and parsley.
Refresh in iced water, drain, and refrigerate.

The braised vegetables
Peel the stringy threads from the chard. Place the leaves in cold water with a squeeze of lemon.
Peel the carrots, turnips, and onions.
Cook each vegetable separately in chicken stock, salt, and olive oil. Remove from heat and keep warm.
Peel the potatoes. Blanch them and sauté in a little butter with the cloves of garlic.

The mushrooms
Sort and clean the mushrooms. Heat a little olive oil in a nonstick pan and sauté the chanterelles. Season with salt and pepper, keep warm.
Do the same with the porcini. Season lightly and keep warm.

Presentation
Heat the cubed bacon in a casserole dish over medium heat.
Add the onions and stew gently to lightly brown.
Add the vegetables, mushrooms, chicken jus, and chopped parsley. Glaze the mixture with a tbsp. of butter and olive oil. Check the seasoning and serve very hot.

This dish may accompany roasted red meats, poultry, or game. Vegetable fricot is a Auvergne dish that combines different root vegetables (such as turnips, carrots, parsnips, and parsley root) with bacon cut into large chunks and straw-smoked bacon. All the ingredients are stewed slowly in stock.

Galette of Rabbit with Garden Herbs and Escargots

Meat
Serves 4

Ingredients
Saddles of rabbit
2 saddles of rabbit, with liver and kidneys
4 tbsp. (6 cl) olive oil
4 sprigs of rosemary
2 tbsp. (30 g) butter
24 large gris escargots
1 clove of garlic, halved
4 tbsp. (6 cl) pastis
10 oz. (300 g) flaky puff pastry (pg. 296)

Rabbit gravy
1 tbsp. (15 g) butter
1 onion, minced
1 carrot finely diced
4 tbsp. (6 cl) soy sauce
½ cup (12 cl) white wine

Herb stuffing
3 oz. (80 g) smoked slab bacon, cut into small cubes
4 shallots, finely minced
2 handfuls of spinach
2 handfuls of chard leaves
⅔ cup (15 cl) cream
10 sorrel leaves, chopped
2 tbsp. chopped parsley

Vegetables
2 tbsp. olive oil
3 stalks of chard
12 young carrots
12 new turnips
1 sugar cube

Salt, pepper, and nutmeg

The saddles of rabbit

Preheat the oven to 400°F (200°C). Brown the rabbit in oil in a frying pan. Season with salt and pepper. Roast in the oven for 10 to 12 minutes, basting frequently, and remove.

Slip a flexible knife between the central bone and the meat of each saddle to remove the 2 rabbit fillets. Keep warm.

Chop the bones and brown in 1 tbsp. butter in a sauté pan. Add and brown the onion and carrot.

Add the soy sauce to the pan. Deglaze with the wine and reduce by half. Add enough water to cover the bones. Cook for about 30 minutes, skimming the surface from time to time. Remove from the heat and let the flavors infuse for 10 minutes. Then, pass the sauce through a fine china cap strainer.

The garden herb stuffing

Brown the bacon in a heavy saucepan and add the shallots. When they are soft, add the coarsely chopped spinach and chard leaves. Let the vegetables wilt, then add the cream and sorrel. Boil and allow to gradually thicken.

Add the parsley and season with salt and pepper. Add a little grated nutmeg, check the seasoning, and keep warm.

The vegetables

Remove the stringy threads from the chard, cut the stalks into sticks, and wash. Brown in olive oil in a sauté pan. Add the carrots and turnips with a little of the rabbit sauce, salt, pepper, water, and the sugar cube. Cover and cook. When each vegetable is done, remove the cover to reduce the sauce and glaze the vegetables. Keep warm.

The brochettes

Sharpen the end of each rosemary sprig to form a point. Cut the liver in half and thread the livers and kidneys onto the sprigs. Season with salt and pepper. Heat 1 tbsp. of butter in a pan and brown the brochettes. Transfer to a plate and keep warm. In the same pan, sauté the escargots and garlic halves. Season with salt and pepper. Flambé with the pastis and keep warm.

Preheat the oven to 400°F (200°C). Roll out the pastry. Cut 4 rounds, each 4 in. (10 cm) diameter. Prick the rounds and let rest in refrigerator for 10 minutes. Then bake for 10 minutes. If the rounds begin to puff up while baking, place a small wire rack on top of them, reduce heat to 350°F (150°C), and cook about 20 minutes—watch that the pastry does not brown too much. Remove the rounds from the oven. Spread each one with herb stuffing and fan the thinly sliced rabbit around the edge.

Presentation

Place a *galette* in the middle of each plate. Arrange the escargots and vegetables around it. Crown with the sautéed liver and kidney brochette. Season with salt and pepper, drizzle with rabbit sauce.

This recipe does not require a trip to the market, but rather a hunt through the garden. This is why I vary the herb stuffing so often. This is a way I love to cook, in close relationship with the climate and seasons, an ever-changing cuisine.

White Peach Baba

Dessert 🌲 🌲

*It takes 2 days to
prepare this dessert, so use
just-ripened white peaches.*
Serves 8

Ingredients
Baba dough
*1 piece star anise
1 tsp. of cinnamon
½ vanilla bean pod, split
6 tbsp. (80 g) butter
¾ oz. (25 g) yeast
¾ cup + 2 tbsp. (20 cl) heavy cream
1 tbsp. honey
1⅔ cups (250 g) flour
8 eggs
1 tsp. salt*

Syrup and fruit
*3 tbsp. (30 g) raisins
6 white peaches
3¼ cups (80 cl) water
1¾ cups (375 g) sugar
10 peach leaves
¾ cup (18 cl) peach wine*

Garnish
*1 cup (250 g) pastry cream (pg. 297)
1 cup (25 cl) whipped cream
Zest of 1 lemon, chopped and
blanched*

*Peaches originated in China, and
there are two varieties: peaches
with yellow flesh and peaches with
more delicate white flesh, which
are sweeter and juicier. I prefer
fruit that has ripened on the tree.
The peaches that we use are from
the Eyrieux Valley in the nearby
Ardèche region, which has ideal
conditions for growing fruits such
as peaches and apricots.*

The baba dough

Prepare the babas one day in advance. Preheat the oven to 350°F (180°C). With a rolling pin, crush the star anise and add to the cinnamon and scraped vanilla bean seeds.

Soften the butter then beat until smooth. In a cup, mix the yeast with the cream and honey. Place the flour into a mixer with a dough hook. Add 3 eggs, salt, spices, and yeast mixture. Beat at medium speed until the dough pulls away from the sides of the bowl. Add in the remaining eggs, beat 5 more minutes, and add the creamed butter. Continue to beat until the dough forms a ball. Cover and let the dough rise at room temperature about 45 minutes.

Butter 8 individual baba molds (or 1 ring mold) and place in the freezer for 5 minutes. Divide the dough evenly and half-fill each mold. Let rise at room temperature until the dough reaches the rim of the mold.

Bake for 20 to 35 minutes, depending on the size of the mold you are using. Check for doneness by inserting a knife into the baba; the blades should come away smoothly. Remove the babas from the oven and unmold. Keep at room temperature to allow the pastry to dry slightly.

The following day: the peach syrup

Cover the raisins with warm water and let soak. Blanch the peaches in a pan of boiling water, refresh immediately, and remove the skins. Cut each peach into even quarters and set aside. Mix the water and sugar in a large sauté pan and boil. Add the peach leaves and quartered peaches. Simmer gently so that the peaches will not overcook. Remove the leaves and peaches from the pan. Add the soaked raisins, return to a boil, then remove from heat.

Allow the syrup to cool to room temperature. Set each baba on a skimming ladle and pour syrup over it. Sprinkle with peach wine.

Mix the pastry cream with the whipped cream and lemon zests. Slice each baba in half horizontally. Slightly hollow out the center and fill with the cream mixture. Replace the tops.

Presentation

Place the baba in the center of the plate. Fan the peach quarters around it and pour on the raisins and syrup.

Rose Shortbread with Wild Strawberries

Dessert 🌲
Handle the pastry carefully.
It is very delicate.
Serves 4

Ingredients
Rose shortbread
3 hard-boiled egg yolks
¾ oz. (20 g) dried rose petals
3 tbsp. (50 g) confectioners' sugar
1⅔ cup (250 g) flour
4 tbsp. (50 g) almond paste
10⅔ tbsp. (150 g) softened butter
Several drops of rose water

Strawberry cream
3½ oz. (100 g) strawberries
⅔ cup (125 g) sugar
¾ cup (200 g) milk
1 vanilla bean pod, split
3 egg yolks
3 tbsp. (25 g) cornstarch
¾ oz. (20 g) butter, cut in pieces
Confectioners' sugar
2 tbsp. (25 g) whipped cream

Decoration and fruit
Fresh roses, wild strawberries
Egg white, for brushing
Superfine sugar, to glaze

The rose shortbread

Mash the hard-boiled egg yolks with a fork and chop the rose petals. In a food processor, mix the confectioner's sugar, flour, almond paste, butter, hard-boiled yolks, and rose petals. Flavor with several drops of rose water. Stop the processor as soon as the dough forms a ball.

Turn the pastry dough onto parchment paper and roll it out to a thickness of ⅛ in. (4 mm). Refrigerate for several hours.

The strawberry cream

Remove the strawberry stems and blend the fruit to make a coulis, sweeten half of the mixture with ⅓ cup (75 g) of the sugar and set aside.

Pour the milk into a saucepan. Add the vanilla bean pod split with seeds removed. Boil.

In a mixing bowl, mix the egg yolks, cornstarch, unsweetened strawberry coulis, and the remaining sugar. Add the boiled milk.

Transfer the mixture to a stainless-steel saucepan and bring to a boil, whisking constantly. Cook only 30 seconds after the cream starts to boil. Pour into a bowl and add the pieces of butter.

Sprinkle with confectioners' sugar to prevent the cream from forming a skin. Refrigerate.

As soon as the strawberry cream has cooled, whip it again until smooth. Fold in the whipped cream to lighten the texture. (For convenience, whip 1 cup (25 cl) of cream. Use ¼ of it for this recipe, and the rest for something else.)

The dried roses

Brush each fresh rose petal with egg white to moisten. Coat with superfine sugar and place on a baking tray. Dry in the oven for 2 hours at 150°F (70°C).

The baking

With a pastry cutter, cut eight 3 in. (8 mm) rounds of dough. Sprinkle with sugar. Place on a baking tray and bake at 325°F (160°C) for about 30 minutes, until they turn a golden color.

Presentation

Fit a pastry bag with a ½ in. (15 mm) round tip. Fill the bag with the strawberry cream.

Pipe a teaspoon of cream into the center of each plate. Place a shortbread on the cream. Pipe a tbsp. of cream, in a spiral, on each shortbread—don't let it spill over the sides.

Arrange wild strawberries on top of the cream.

Gently place another shortbread on top of the strawberries. Be careful—the pastries are very delicate.

Apply a little caramel or almond paste to the top of the shortbread to attach the dried rose petals and cut pieces of the vanilla bean pod.

Decorate the plate with several drops of the sweetened strawberry coulis. Serve the remaining coulis on the side.

I discovered this pastry recipe in an old book. It is made with hard-boiled egg yolks, which makes it very crumbly.

This dessert may be flavored with flower essences or natural flowers, such as roses and cowslips.

117

Chocolate Fondant and Cherry Cakes

Dessert 🌲
Serves 8

Ingredients
Cherries in red wine
1 cup (¼ l) red wine
*9 oz. (250 g) cherries (several with
stems for garnish)*
¾ cup (150 g) sugar
1 clove
1 stick cinnamon

Chocolate cakes
7 tbsp. (100 g) butter
3½ oz. (100 g) bittersweet chocolate
⅓ cup + 1 tbsp. (80 g) sugar
2 eggs
5 tbsp. (40 g) cocoa powder
½ tsp. (2 g) baking powder

*This recipe is very easy to prepare.
The cherries may be replaced
by raspberries, pears in syrup,
or flambéed bananas.*

The cherries in red wine

Boil the wine over high heat and reduce to one-third its volume. Rinse the cherries and add to the wine.

Add the sugar, clove, and cinnamon.

Boil for 5 minutes. Reserve several cherries with stems to use as decoration. Pit the remaining cherries and set aside.

The chocolate cakes

Melt the butter and chocolate in a double boiler. The melted chocolate should not be too hot. Stir in the sugar with a spatula. Next, add the beaten eggs, then the cocoa powder and the baking powder, mix well.

Presentation

Butter 8 ramekins and sprinkle with sugar. Half-fill each ramekin with the chocolate batter and spoon some of the pitted cherries on top. Add more batter so that the ramekin is three-quarters full.

Presentation

Preheat the oven to 350°F (180°C). Place the ramekins in the oven and bake about 5 minutes. The cake centers should be barely cooked.

Serve with vanilla ice cream and almonds.

Green du Puy Lentil Tuile

Dessert 🌲
Serves 6

The tuile cookies

Cream the butter with a wooden spoon. Add the sugar, lentil flour, and finally the egg whites. Mix well and let rest for 1 hour.

Place small spoonfuls of the lentil dough on a buttered baking sheet, spacing them evenly. Roll out the dough to form tuiles. Bake at 400°F (200°C) for 15 minutes, until the edges of the cookies brown.

Presentation

Remove the tuiles from the oven. While they are still hot, shape each cookie around a bottle (for example) to give them their characteristic cresent shape.

Ingredients
Tuile cookies
9 tbsp. (125 g) butter
1 cup (200 g) sugar
1 cup (160 g) green du Puy lentil flour
10 large (300 g) egg whites

If you do not have lentil flour, grind green lentils in a coffee grinder and sift the grounds. The result will be the same.

Green lentil flour is being used more and more in our region to make breads and pastries. It lends a certain iron flavor to recipes.

There is no market friendlier than the Victor Hugo market in Saint-Etienne. A relaxed humor bounces from stall to stall—as if the local soccer team beat Marseilles every day 5–1, or as if the Soulas family's excellent ratte potatoes were being served with cavier every day. Régis Marcon loves the spirit of this market, especially first thing in the morning, and regularly buys his vegetables there. He even met his good friend Pierre Gagnaire there, several years ago.

In the marketplace, there's no time to dawdle. Three times a week, the Soulas family wakes at 4 in the morning to carry freshly hand-picked cardoons, chard, spinach, peas, and beans to the market. They, too, are enamored by the congenial place, where people with so many affinities and differences meet. Courtesy abounds, as customers compliment the merchants on the quality of their produce. The praise warms the heart, like a welcome coffee break or an aperitif taken in a café when the bus stops.

Terrine of Vegetable Confit and Lamb

Appetizer
Serves 10

Ingredients
Lamb jus
1 saddle of lamb
2 carrots, finely diced
1 large onion, finely diced
6 cloves garlic, crushed
3 sprigs of thyme
½ oz. or 6 sheets of gelatin, soaked in cold water

Vegetable confit
2 lb. 2 oz. (1 kg) tomatoes
½ tsp. sugar
2 red peppers
2 fennel bulbs
4 zucchinis
4 eggplants
1 sprig of fresh thyme, leaves picked
½ tsp. crushed coriander seed

Mustard cream
1 cup (25 cl) whipping cream
1 tbsp. whole grain prepared mustard
2 cornichon pickles, finely chopped
2 tbsp. chopped parsley
Salt, pepper, and paprika

Salt and pepper

The lamb jus

Prepare the terrine one day in advance.

Ask the butcher to debone the saddle of lamb and retain both the 2 top loin filets and the 2 bottom filets.

Heat oil in a small sauté pan and brown the crushed bones and lamb trimmings. Add the carrots and onion, then add the crushed garlic. Brown the vegetables and skim the fat from the pan. Add enough water to cover, a little salt, and the thyme. Boil, skim, and simmer for about 1 hour.

Pass the cooked mixture through a medium china cap strainer. Reduce to ¾ cup (18 cl) of liquid.

Add the softened gelatin and keep warm.

The lamb filets

Over high heat, heat a pan and pour in a little olive oil. Quickly brown the loins and filets on both sides. Refrigerate.

The vegetable confit

Peel the tomatoes, quarter them lengthwise, and remove the seeds with a small knife. Season each quarter with salt, pepper and sugar.

Arrange the tomatoes on an oiled baking sheet. Dry in the oven at 175°F (80°C) for 2 to 2½ hours. Transfer to a small container.

Peel and quarter the peppers. Peel the fennel bulbs and remove any stringy threads. Partially peel the eggplants and zucchinis and cut into ¼ in. (1 cm) strips. Remove some of the seeds.

In a covered pan, sauté each vegetable separately in olive oil with the fresh thyme leaves and crushed coriander. Add a little water if necessary. Allow 10 to 15 minutes for each vegetable. Season with salt and pepper.

Line a small terrine with plastic wrap, to make it easier to unmold and serve later.

Preheat the oven to 325°F (160°C).

Layer the eggplants, zucchinis, pieces of lamb, baked tomato, fennel, and peppers in the terrine, pouring a little warm jellied jus between each layer. Bake in a water bath for 1 hour.

Presentation

At the end of cooking, place a weight on top of the terrine to press it. Refrigerate for 24 hours before serving. Slice the terrine with a knife that has been dipped in warm water.

Whip the cream and add the mustard, gherkins, parsley, a pinch of paprika, salt, and pepper. Serve with the terrine.

I am very partial to vegetable terrines with large chunks of vegetables. This recipe also features lamb, but it may be made without the meat. Just substitute a little gelatin for the lamb jus between each layer of vegetables.

123

Crayfish Crab Cake on Tomato Jelly and Lovage Cream Sauce

Appetizer
Serves 6

Ingredients
Crayfish crab cake
4 cups (1 l) court bouillon
32 crayfish
1 crab, 1 lb. 12 oz. (800 g),
spider or dungeness
½ cup (60 g) quinoa
1 grapefruit, halved
½ green apple, with skin, diced
½ stalk of celery, peeled and diced
1 tomato, diced
¼ bunch of chives, finely chopped
4 tbsp. (6 cl) olive oil

Tomato jelly
1 tsp. or 3 sheets of gelatin
1 onion, chopped
1 tbsp. of tomato purée
1 sprig of thyme
6 fresh tomatoes, chopped
1 clove of garlic, crushed
4 cups (1 l) chicken stock (pg. 290)

Celeriac and lovage cream sauce
½ medium celery root, diced
8 leaves of lovage
2 cups (½ liter) crème fraîche

Garnish
Salmon eggs

Salt and pepper

Cooking the seafood
Boil the court bouillon and drop in the crayfish. Cook 2 minutes, remove, cool, remove the shells, and refrigerate. Add the crab to the stock and simmer about 18 minutes. Remove the crab from the stock, cool and remove the meat from the shell.

Preparing the quinoa
Pour the quinoa into a saucepan of boiling salted water, stir and simmer till cooked about 15 to 20 minutes, drain, and set aside.

The tomato jelly
Soften the powdered or sheets of gelatin in cold water.

Brown the onion in olive oil. Add the tomato purée, thyme, tomatoes, and garlic. Stew for about 5 minutes, then moisten with the chicken stock. Boil, skim the surface, and simmer gently for 20 minutes.

Filter the mixture though cheesecloth so that the liquid is clear. Adjust the seasoning. Reduce the liquid to 2 cups (½ l). Add the gelatin and set aside.

The celery root and lovage cream sauce
Heat a little olive oil in a pan. Add the celery root and several leaves of lovage. Add enough water to cover, season with salt and pepper. Cover and cook about 10 minutes. Add the crème fraîche and return to a boil until the sauce is smooth and creamy. Blend in a food processor and then pass through a fine china cap strainer.

This sauce should not be too thick, so dilute with water if necessary. Refrigerate.

The crayfish crab cake
Peel the grapefruit with a knife to remove the pith. Separate between the segments and finely dice.

In a bowl, mix the crabmeat, quinoa, grapefruit, diced apple, celery, tomatoes, chives, and olive oil. Check the seasoning. Form the mixture into cakes with a ring mold or coffee cup. Arrange the crayfish tails on top and decorate as you like.

Presentation

Portion the jelly into 6 large plates. Refrigerate, making sure the plates remain level.

When the jelly has set, slice it at the center and remove half. The plate will then have a half circle of jelly. With a pastry cutter, cut another semicircle of jelly, 2 in. (6 cm) wide, in the center of the plate.

Pour the lovage cream sauce into the empty side of the plate.

With a spatula, place a cake in the center of each plate. There should be tomato jelly on one side of it, and lovage cream sauce on the other. Serve chilled.

Lovage has long been believed to be an aphrodisiac, and the Greeks used it like laurel leaves to crown their athletes. In the sixteenth century, it was used in place of celery, although it has a more peppery flavor. In my region, lovage is frequently used in soups.

Rolled Sole with Crisped Bones, Braised Artichoke Barigoule with Olives

Fish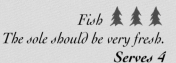
The sole should be very fresh.
Serves 4

Ingredients
Sole
2 tsp. honey
1 tbsp. soy sauce
Juice of ½ lemon
4 fillets of sole, each 9 oz. (250 g),
plus 9 oz (250 g) bones for the
sauce
2 tbsp. (3 cl) oil
2 tbsp. (30 g) butter

Honey-roasted bone crisps
4 cups (1 l) peanut oil
Bones of 4 sole from the top fins
1 tbsp. honey
3 tbsp. soy sauce
1 tsp. sesame seeds

Sauce
4 tbsp. (60 g) butter
4 large shallots, finely chopped
½ cup (12 cl) dry white wine
2 sprigs thyme, leaves picked
4 cloves of garlic, crushed

Braised artichoke barigoule
4 fresh baby artichokes
Juice of ½ lemon
6 tbsp. (8 cl) olive oil
½ onion, finely sliced
4 cloves garlic, unpeeled
10 black olives, pitted
½ cup (12 cl) white wine
1 sprig of thyme, leaves only

Salt and pepper

The Sole

Preheat the oven to about 225°F (110°C).

Mix the honey, soy sauce, and lemon juice.

Roll the fillets and tie with string. Marinate the fish in the honey soy mixture.

The honey-roasted bone crisps

Heat the peanut oil to 350°F (150°C) in a deep pan. Rinse and dry the sole bones. Deep-fry for 2 to 3 minutes and dry again with paper towels.

Mix the honey and soy sauce. Brush the bones with the mixture and dry in the oven at 175°F (80°C) for about 1 hour. Brush again every 15 minutes until very crisp.

The Sauce

Rinse the 9 oz. (250 g) of uncooked sole bones in cold water. Drain and dry with paper towels.

Heat 2 tbsp. of butter in a heavy casserole and brown the bones. Stir and scrape the bottom of the casserole often to keep them from browning too much.

Sweat the shallots in the casserole and deglaze with white wine. Reduce the liquid by three-quarters, then add enough water to cover.

Add the thyme and crushed garlic. Bring to a boil and then simmer for 30 minutes.

While the sauce is simmering, cover the casserole with plastic wrap or parchment paper to retain the flavors of the fish. Remove from heat. Let the flavors infuse for 10 minutes, then pass the sauce through a fine china cap strainer, pressing the contents. Skim the surface of fat. You should have about ⅔ cup (16 cl) of sauce; if you have more, reduce.

In a small saucepan, heat 2 tbsp. (30 g) of butter until it is hazelnut brown. Deglaze the butter with the sauce. Season with salt and pepper to taste. Keep warm.

The braised artichoke barigoule

Trim the artichokes, leaving only the heat and part of the stem. Place the hearts in cold water with lemon juice. Cut into quarters.

Heat the olive oil in a heavy sauté pan. Add the onion and allow to sweat before adding the artichokes garlic and olives. Brown gently.

Deglaze with the white wine. Salt lightly and add the thyme. Cover and cook. Remove the garlic, set aside and keep warm.

Cooking the sole

In a nonstick pan, heat the oil and butter. Brown the rolled sole fillets, basting often.

Cook for 10 to 15 minutes.

Presentation

Place 2 rolled fillets on each plate. Insert a honey-roasted fish bone between them. Surround with the artichoke *barigoule* and blanket with the sauce.

I would have never dared to eat fish bones before. I discovered this tradition in Japan, thanks to my fellow chefs and Harumi Osawa, in particular. In Japan, honey-roasted eel bones are served as a delicious starter.

Red Mullet Fillet on a Cod Mousseline with du Puy Lentil Ratatouille

Fish 🌲 🌲
*The diced vegetables are
an optional garnish.*
Serves 4

Ingredients
Mullet
3 oz. (80 g) salt cod
2 cups (½ liter) milk
1 sprig of thyme
¾ cup (18 cl) olive oil
½ medium-sized onion, minced
1 clove of garlic, finely chopped
½ cup (12 cl) crème fraîche
Pinch of Espelette pepper or
cayenne pepper
8 fillets of red mullet, each about
3 to 3½ oz. (80 to 100 g), (with
livers, optional)
basil leaves

Green lentil ratatouille
2 yellow peppers
2 red peppers
2 zucchinis
2 eggplants
4 tbsp. (6 cl) olive oil
1 sprig thyme, leaves picked
1 onion, minced
1 tomato, cubed
1 clove of garlic, crushed
7 oz. (200 g) cooked du Puy lentils
(pg. 142)

See pages 156 and 157 for
step-by-step photos.

The cod
One day in advance, soak the cod under slow running water to remove the salt.

The next day, cube the cod into large pieces and place in a pan. Cover with milk and cold water. Add the thyme and boil for 8 minutes. Remove from heat and drain.

In a sauté pan over medium heat, heat the olive oil. Sweat the onion and garlic, then add the cod pieces. When the fish absorbs the oil, add the crème fraîche and Espelette pepper. Adjust the seasoning. Process in a food processor to obtain a fine purée. Set aside.

The vegetables
Peel the peppers. Dice half of the peppers, zucchinis, and eggplants into small cubes. Reserve the scraps for the sauce. Set aside.

Cut the remaining peppers, zucchini, and eggplants into medium dice. Cook each vegetable separately, covered, in olive oil, several drops of water, and a pinch of salt. Set aside.

In a pan, sweat the onion over low heat. Add the small diced pepper, zucchinis, eggplants, and thyme. Sauté, uncovered, for 2 minutes.

Add the tomato and the garlic. Season with salt and pepper, mix in the cooked lentils. Adjust the seasoning and keep warm.

The ratatouille sauce
In a heavy sauté pan with olive oil, brown the onion and garlic. Add the medium dices from the peppers, zucchinis, eggplants, and tomatoes. Add the white wine.

Reduce the liquid by half, then add the fish stock. Add a little salt and the fresh thyme.

Cover and cook for about 30 minutes over low heat.

Remove from heat and let the flavors infuse. Pass through a fine china cap strainer into a sauté pan, pressing the contents. Reduce if necessary. Keep warm.

Presentation
Preheat your broiler.

In the center of each large, warm plate, arrange a rectangle of the cod mousseline—about 3 in. by 1 in. (7 cm × 3 cm) and ¼ in. (6 mm) thick.

Carefully spoon on the cubed vegetables, alternating the colors.

Pour a tbsp. of olive oil in a nonstick pan. Arrange the mullet fillets, skin side down.

Cook the fillets over high heat. The fish should be cooked cold to preserve its color. As soon as the fish sizzles, baste it with the pan juices. The center of each fillet should be just cooked.

Place the plates under the broiler or in a hot oven to warm.

Arrange the mullet fillets on top of the vegetable mosaic. Whisk the sauce with an immersion blender, adding a little olive oil, the mullet livers, and—at the last moment—some finely chopped basil.

Pour the sauce around each serving of fish. Serve with du Puy lentil ratatouille separately.

Ratatouille sauce
1 onion, minced
2 cloves of garlic, chopped
1 sprig thyme
¾ cup (18 cl) olive oil
½ cup (12 cl) white wine
2 tomatoes concassé (pg. 293)
1 cup (25 cl) fish stock
4 basil leaves
Several threads of saffron

Salt and pepper

The gustatory qualities of the green du Puy lentil are widely recognized—delicate flavor, soft skins, with a firm texture that is not starchy and does not require pre-soaking.

du Puy lentils are rich in vegetable protein, just as rich in protein as meat. I use them here as a summer vegetable.

Photograph of the recipe shown on the next two pages.

129

Lamb Baked in Bread Crust with Hay and "Wolf Spices"

Meat 🌲
Serves 10

Ingredients
Bread crust
2³/₄ cups (70 cl) water
2 handfuls of fresh hay
3 cups (1 kg) flour
2 tbsp. (35 g) yeast or leaven
2 tsp. (10 g) salt
7 tbsp. (100 g) mixed grains (wheat, oats, and rye)

Leg of Lamb
14 oz. (400 g) lamb's neck-bones
2 tbsp. (30 g) butter
1 onion, minced
1 carrot, finely diced
4 cloves of garlic, smashed
1 sprig of wild or fresh thyme
1 fresh tomato, quartered
2 handfuls of fresh hay
1 leg of lamb, 4 lbs. (1,8 kg)
4 tsp. olive oil

2 tbsp. of "wolf spices" (pg. 293)

Salt and pepper

This type of preparation requires that the lamb cook for a long time. The hay from our mountain plateaus both absorbs moisture and flavors the meat. My good friend Gérard Truchetet is fond of cooking whole hams this way.

The bread crust

Heat the water and, just as it boils, add the hay. Boil and immediately remove from heat. Cover and allow the flavors to infuse until cool.

Combine the flour, yeast, and salt in a mixing bowl. Add the water and hay, mix by machine with a dough hook or by hand until the dough comes away from the sides of the bowl.

Add the mixed grains. Let stand for at least 2 hours in a cool place. The dough will increase a bit in volume.

The lamb jus

Heat a sauté pan over high heat and brown the lamb's neck on all sides in butter. Drain the fat and add the onion, carrot, garlic, thyme, and tomato.

Deglaze with a little water, then add more water to just cover the pan contents. Season lightly with salt and pepper. Bring to a boil and simmer gently for 30 minutes.

At the end of cooking, add a small handful of fresh hay. Bring to a boil, immediately remove from heat, and cover. Allow to infuse for 10 minutes, then pass through a fine china cap strainer.

Reduce to 1 cup (25 cl) of jus.

The lamb

Preheat the oven to 475°F (240°C).

Heat a little oil in a pan and brown the leg of lamb on all sides. Season with salt and pepper.

Roll out the dough to about ½ in. (1,5 cm) thick. Place a handful of hay in the center and lay the leg of lamb on top. Wrap the lamb in the dough and place onto a floured surface.

With the palm of your hand, moisten the surface of the dough with water. Sprinkle with flour. Bake for 15 minutes at 450°F (230°C), then for 1 hour at 200°F (100°C).

Presentation

Allow to rest for 15 minutes. Cut and lift the top of the crust to remove the lamb. Slice the lamb. Serve with the "wolf spices" and a potato-porcini gratin or vegetable *fricot*.

Rabbit and Saint-Verny Wine Ragout
with Peaches and Wild Mountain Thyme

Meat 🌲 🌲
The Saint-Verny wine maybe replaced with any other dry white, and the wild thyme with garden thyme.
Serves 4

Ingredients
Rabbit
¾ oz. (20 g) ginger
1 large piece caul of pork, to wrap rabbit
1 rabbit, 3 lb. (1,4 kg), cut into 8 pieces
4 tbsp. (55 g) butter
1 large carrot, sliced
1 large onion, finely minced
6 prunes pitted
4 tbsp. (6 cl) cider vinegar
½ cup (12 cl) Saint-Verny white wine
2 cups (50 cl) chicken jus (pg. 290)
2 cloves of garlic

Yellow peaches with wild thyme
4 yellow peaches
12 to 15 stalks of asparagus
2 tbsp. (30 g) butter
2 tbsp. sugar
Several sprigs of wild thyme, leaves and flowers picked

Salt and pepper

Rabbit ragout

Peel and julienne the ginger. Place in a small pan and cover with cold water. Boil for 2 minutes, drain, and set aside. Cut the caul into 8 squares. Season the rabbit with salt and pepper. Roll each piece of rabbit in a square of caul, and tie with butchers twine.

Melt the butter in a casserole to hold all the rabbit. Brown the wrapped rabbit on all sides and remove.

Add the carrot and the onion to the pan. Sweat and brown slightly. Add the rabbit, 1 chopped peach, and the prunes. Caramelize the mixture and deglaze with vinegar.

Cover the pan 1 to 2 minutes to allow the vinegar to infuse the meat. Add the wine and reduce by half. Then add the chicken jus or water. Add the ginger and season lightly with salt and pepper. Simmer, covered, for about 40 minutes. Remove from heat and let rest for about 15 minutes. Remove the rabbit and ginger and cover with a damp cloth so that the meat does not dry out.

Reduce the sauce, crushing the prune and peach pieces in the pan so that they gradually blend into the sauce. Pass through a fine china cap strainer, pressing well. Refrigerate. Skim the fat and reduce again until the sauce coats the back of a spoon.

The garnish

While the ragout is cooking, boil the asparagus in salted water for about 2 minutes. Refresh and drain on paper towels.

Peel and quarter the remaining peaches. Heat the butter in a pan and caramelize the peaches, sprinkling them with the sugar and the wild thyme.

Presentation

Arrange the rabbit and ginger in a serving casserole. Coat with the sauce. Lay the asparagus and caramelized peaches on top.

This dish may be served with goat's cheese ravioli or fresh pasta made with lemon zest.

The breeding of rabbits, known as cuniculture, is an ancient practice. It is an expensive business, and the price of feeding them represents 40 to 50 percent of the cost.

For this recipe, select a hutch-raised or free range rabbit. These rabbits are four to five months old, so they are richer in fat and more tender.

I make this summer dish during the yellow-peach harvest in the Eyrieux valley. The flavor of the peaches is enhanced with wild thyme flowers.

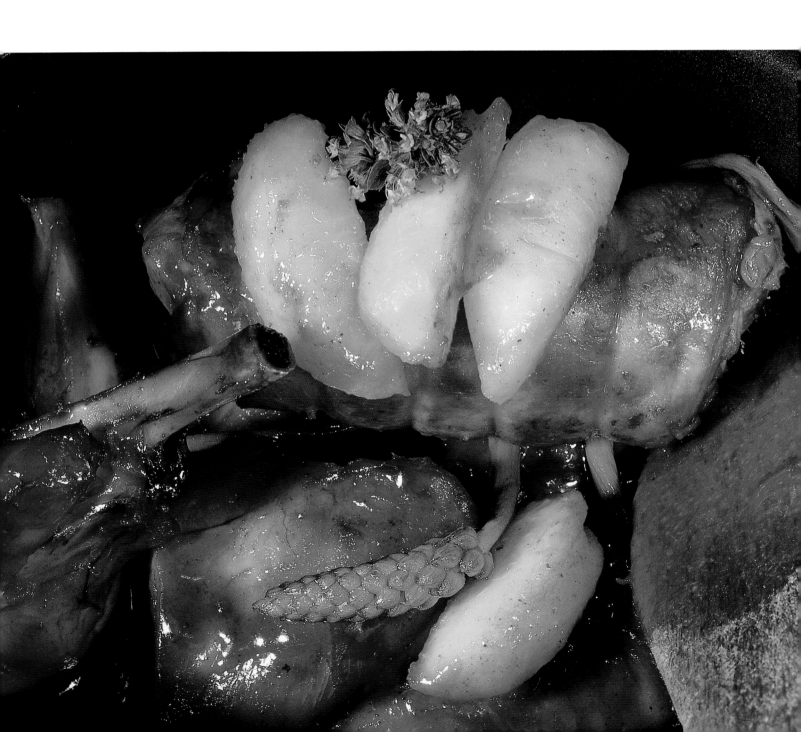

Charente Melon and Rhubarb
with Wild Balm and Mountain Honey

Dessert 🌲
You may substitute cantaloupe or Cavillon melon. The wild balm may be replaced with peppermint.
Serves 4

Ingredients
2 Charente *melons*
6 leaves of *wild balm, chopped*
6 tbsp. (8 cl) pastis
2 tsp. honey

Syrup
1 cup (¼ l) water
5 oz. (150 g) sugar
1 vanilla bean pod, split and seeds scraped
6 stalks of rhubarb

Paul Aulagnon supplies us with our wild balm. The plant exudes a strong licorice and mint scent. I like the aroma of this herb in infusions, and it is not volatile.

Above all, select the melons carefully. They should feel heavy, the stalk should be easy to remove, and you should be able to smell the fruit through the skin. Selecting melons is an acquired skill. Ask your grocer for assistance.

Split the melons and check the quality. Remove the seeds and strain them through a medium china cap strainer to recover the juice. Cut slices from the melon and set aside in a bowl.

Scrape the melon skins, and blend this pulp with the juice from the seeds in a food processor. Add the chopped balm, pastis, and honey. Pour the mixture over the melon slices and marinate for 4 hours.

The syrup
Boil the water, sugar, and vanilla pod and seeds. Cook 5 minutes to make a syrup.

Peel the rhubarb and cut into 3 in. (7.5 cm) sticks. Place the sticks in the hot syrup, return to a boil, and immediately remove from heat. Cover and refrigerate.

Presentation
Serve in individual dishes or on a serving platter. Drain the rhubarb and arrange in the center with the melon slices around it. Drizzle with the balm-flavored marinade.

136

Baked Crème Scented with Spignel Flowers

Dessert 🌲
This dish requires rather careful cooking. The spignel may be replaced with fennel seeds.
Serves 12

Ingredients
3 cups (75 cl) whole milk
1½ oz. (50 g) spignel flowers

10 egg yolks
½ cup (100 g) sugar
1 cup (25 cl) crème fraîche

Should you walk the paths bordering our prairies in early July, you will discover that the heat accentuates the honey aroma of the spignel. Cows are very fond of this plant, and the spignel flower is the emblem of the Mézenc marbled-beef producers' cooperative, In fact, spignel is one of the required ingredients in the animals' fodder.

The custard

One day in advance, boil the milk in a saucepan. Add the white spignel flowers. Return to a boil and remove from heat. Cover with plastic wrap and refrigerate for 6 hours.

The scent of the spignel flower depends on its quality and the time of harvest, so it is difficult to specify the exact amount you'll need.

Preheat the oven to 200°F (100°C). Whisk the yolks and sugar until light and creamy. Add the cream. Pour the scented milk into the mixture through a fine china cap strainer. Whisk and pass through the strainer again. Let rest for several minutes, then remove the froth on the surface.

Pour no more than 1 in. (2 cm) of batter into each ramekin. Bake for about 20 minutes.

To check for doneness, tilt one of the ramekins. The crème should just hold its shape and the center should be barely cooked. Remove from the oven and refrigerate.

Presentation

Just before serving, sprinkle with light brown sugar, removing any excess. Caramelize immediately with a salamander or—less elegant but equally as effective—a blowtorch. Serve immediately and enjoy the surprise!

Pistacho Cakes with Flowing Berry Centers

The fruit filling

Clean the fruit by rinsing it quickly under cold water. Dry on a clean cloth. Heat the butter in a nonstick or sauté pan. Toss in the fruit and sprinkle with sugar. Bring to a boil and add the raspberry eau-de-vie. Drain the fruit through a fine sieve, reserving the juice. Keep half of the juice warm. Add the drained fruit to the other half of the juice and divide into 6 molds, 1¾ in. (45 mm) in diameter. If you don't have individual molds, pour into a rimmed dish. Freeze.

Lining the molds

Cut 6 sheets of parchment paper, 2½ by 8 in. (6 × 20 cm). Brush the sheets with melted butter. Butter a set of stainless-steel molds, 2 in. (5.5 cm) in diameter and 1½ in. (4 cm) deep. Line with the paper strips. Refrigerate.

Unmold the fruit fillings and refreeze. If you placed the filling in a dish, cut circles about 1½ in. (45 mm) in diameter with a pastry cutter before refreezing.

The pistachio cake and assembly

Warm the pistachio paste in a double boiler. Add the creamed butter, powdered almonds, and cream of rice. Mix with a spatula.

Separate the eggs. Pour the yolks into the pistachio mixture. Beat the whites in a bowl with a pinch of salt. When the whites begin to froth, add half the sugar. Continue beating briskly to form stiff peaks. Add the rest of the sugar and continue beating until the whites stiffen to the consistency of meringue. Fold the whites into the pistachio mixture to obtain a smooth, even cream. Fill a pastry bag with the batter. Pipe a little batter into each lined mold, place a round of frozen fruit in the center, and then fill the mold with batter. Freeze for several hours.

Cooking and presentation

Preheat the oven to 375°F (180°C). Bake the cakes on a baking sheet for 18 to 20 minutes. Remove and let rest for 30 seconds.

Carefully unmold the cakes. Place one on each plate and surround with the remaining fruit juice.

Dessert 🌲 🌲
The cooking should be exact.
Serves 6

Ingredients
Fruit fondant and sauce
7 oz. (200 g) wild strawberries
7 oz. (200 g) raspberries
7 oz. (200 g) blueberries
7 tbsp. (100 g) butter
¼ cup (60 g) sugar
3 tbsp. (4 cl) raspberry eau-de-vie

Pistachio cake
*4 oz. (120 g) pistachio cream
or paste*
4 tbsp. (60 g) creamed butter
½ cup (50 g) powdered almonds
½ cup (50 g) cream of rice
2 eggs
Pinch of salt
½ cup (100 g) superfine sugar
1 tbsp. (15 g) butter, for the molds

This warm cake is inspired by the famous "molten chocolate" cake created by my friend Michel Bras. His dessert was so successful that it has since been adopted by chefs around the world and even by cake manufacturers. In this recipe, the cake is pistachio, and the chocolate in the center is replaced with the wild fruits that grow in abundance around our pine forests.

I n the old days, lentils were treated like dirt! "Too labor greedy," says Pierre Ambert, and they had no clout in the marketplace. So, the majority of Haute-Loire farmers were returning to milk production, and the future looked bleak for the lentil. Since ancient times, however, the region's attributes have favored the lentil (three gallo-roman vases have been excavated in the Saint-Paulien site, the capital of Velay): the land, the altitude, and the abundance of summer sun, which shines here for more hours each year than it does on even Toulouse and Bordeaux. Other producers in France and Canada could not aspire to such heights.

When it comes to lentils, quality is all-important—despite the fact that the French government took its time awarding the AOC, the origin-specific certificate of quality, to the du Puy lentil. Pierre Ambert and others showed great perseverance as they worked to get distributors and producers around the table to determine a strategy and build confidence before taking up the cause. When all was said and done, it was agreed that the lentil was just as photogenic as any other product on television. In the AOC-certificate battle, Pierre Ambert received tactical support from fellow chef Régis Marcon. The lentil is always welcome at Saint-Bonnet-le-Froid, particularly in Marcon's delicious lentil tuile cookies.

Pierre Ambert says he will retire in the next two years, but his diverse activities—farmer, chairman of the lentil producers' cooperative, CilverPuy; member of the government's AOC research commission and supporter of many bed and breakfasts—are as rich and hearty as the salted pork and lentils dish that he enjoys so much.

141

Salmon Tartare with "Poor Man's Caviar" (du Puy Green Lentils)

Appetizer 🌲
Serves 4

Ingredients

Lentils

¾ cup (150 g) du Puy green lentils
1 onion, studded with a clove
1 bouquet garni
½ cup (12 cl) mustard vinaigrette
(pg. 295)
6 tarragon sprigs

Tartare

Zest and juice of 1 lemon
Zest of 1 orange and juice for
the orange vinaigrette
3½ oz. (100 g) smoked salmon
11 oz. (320 g) fresh salmon
1 tsp. dill
1 shallot, finely choppped
3 medium-sized gerkins
12 small capers
10 tbsp. (14 cl) olive oil
several drops of Tabasco
1½ oz. (50 g) mayonnaise, optional

1 sprig of dill, to decorate

Salt and pepper

In the Haute-Loire, green du Puy lentils are often called "Poor man's caviar." The black pearl shapes resemble real caviar. Obviously I am very fond of both, but if I had to give a preference, I would choose the lentils. Not only are they less costly, they are also an excellent source of vegetable protein.

The tartare

Remove the zest from the lemon and orange with a potato peeler. Julienne into fine strips, then cut crossways for a very fine dice. Blanch the zests separately in cold water and drain. Refrigerate in separate bowls.

The lentils

Wash the lentils in cold water. Pour into a saucepan and cover with cold water. Bring to a boil and drain immediately.

Cook the lentils in twice their volume of water. Add a teaspoon of salt, the onion studded with clove, and the bouquet garni. Bring to a boil, skim the surface, and simmer gently for about 20 minutes. Taste a few lentils to check for doneness—they should remain firm.

Drain and place in a bowl. When cooled but still warm, add the mustard vinaigrette and tarragon.

Don't add too much salt during cooking, as it will toughen the lentils.

The tartare

Cut the fresh and smoked salmon into ¼ in. (5 mm) cubes. Chop all the ingredients for the garnish: the dill, shallot, gherkins, and capers. Combine the salmon, the garnish, and the lemon and orange zests in a bowl. Drizzle with the 4 tbsp. (6 cl) olive oil. Add the lemon juice, several drops of Tabasco, and a sprinkle of salt. Check the seasoning.

The orange vinaigrette

Heat the orange juice to reduce by three-quarters. The juice will be syrupy. Whisk in the lemon juice and 6 tbsp. (8 cl) olive oil. Season with salt and pepper.

Presentation

In the center of each plate, mound tartare into a 1 in. (3 cm) circle. Surround with the lentil salad and press down, without disrupting the tartare circle. Spoon on some orange vinaigrette and sprinkle with a little orange zest. Decorate with the feathery dill sprig.

Tomatoes Stuffed with Green du Puy Lentil Tabbouleh

The lentils

Blanch the lentils in twice their volume of lightly salted water, then simmer for about 20 minutes. They should remain slightly crunchy. Drain and keep warm.

The bulgur

Cook the bulgur in salted water, as you would rice. Drain and cool. Set aside.

The tomatoes

Remove some zest from the limes and finely dice. Blanch, drain, and set aside.

Quarter the tomatoes. Press in a colander to extract the juice.

Combine the lentils and warm bulgur in a large bowl. Add the lime zest and juice, the tomato juice, olive oil, red pepper, raisins, mint, onion, and a few drops of Tabasco.

The vinaigrette

Squeeze the juice from the lemon. Season with salt and pepper. Whisk in the olive oil, little by little. Flavor with a few drops of Tabasco.

Presentation

Hollow out the small tomatoes. Salt the insides, dry, and stuff with the tabbouleh. Serve as an appetizer with the lemon vinaigrette. Garnish with citrus zests and mint leaves.

Legumes and grain cereals have grown alongside each other for 10,000 years. In France, however, people tend to avoid legumes. The combination of lentils and grains in the same meal provides the nutritional equivalent of a good steak, in terms of vitamins and proteins. This is what gave me the idea to stuff tomatoes with bulgur and lentils.

Appetizer
Serves 4

Ingredients
⅔ cup (100 g) green lentils
⅔ cup (100 g) bulgur
2 limes
1 lb. 2 oz. (500 g) ripe tomatoes
5 tbsp. (7 cl) olive oil
1 red pepper, peeled and diced
2 tbsp. (20 g) raisins, soaked
10 fresh mint leaves, chopped
1 onion, finely chopped
Tabasco
16 small tomatoes

Vinaigrette
1 lemon, with zest
4 tbsp. (6 cl) olive oil

Salt and pepper

Photograph of the recipe shown on the next two pages.

Steamed Salted Hake on Cabbage Leaves

Fish 🌲
Serves 4

Ingredients
Hake
*1 hake fillet 1½ to 2 lbs. (from
the thickest part of the fish)
7 oz. (200 g) slab bacon,
blanched and diced
1 onion, minced
1 curly green cabbage
(in spring, use oxheart
cabbage), coarsely shredded
1 clove of garlic, minced
1 tbsp. (15 g) butter*

Sauce
*4 tsp. (2 cl) sweet Banyuls
white wine
1 tsp. tomato paste
4 tsp. (2 cl) Banyuls wine vinegar
4 tsp. (2 cl) soy sauce
6 tbsp. (85 g) butter, cut
into small cubes*

Coarse and fine salt, pepper

*In French, there are two words for
hake:* merlu *and* colin. *The real
name is* merlu; *the name* colin
*was invented to make it easier
to sell.*

The hake
Cut the fillet into slices 1 in. (3 cm) wide. Cover with coarse salt, let rest for 10 minutes, then remove the excess salt. Rinse under running water, dry, and refrigerate.

The bacon and cabbage
Dice the bacon, reserving 4 whole slices.

Heat a pan and fry the bacon slices, pressing them with a weight.

Heat a pan of salted water.

Sort and clean the cabbage leaves, retaining only the most tender. Wash the leaves in water with a few drops of vinegar. Drain.

Boil only a few leaves at a time. Refresh them, in turn, in a bowl of iced water. Drain and dry each leaf.

The sauce
In a small sauté pan, add all the ingredients for the sauce, except the butter. Whisk well and bring to a boil. Reduce the liquid to one-quarter of its volume.

Cooking the hake
Lay the fish slices in a food steamer. Cook over low heat to gently steam, checking frequently. The fish should be just cooked (about 8 to 10 minutes).

Presentation
Heat the butter in a pan. Add the diced bacon, onion, and cabbage leaves. Add a pinch of garlic and check the seasoning. Let stew. Whisk the sauce with 6 tbsp. (80 g) of butter.

Arrange a layer of cabbage in the center of the plate.

Lay the fish on top of the cabbage and pour sauce around it. Stand the crisp bacon on the steamed fish.

Vegetable Gratin from the Two Ardèches

The eggplants
Peel and thickly slice the eggplants. Dredge in flour. Sauté in olive oil with 1 clove of crushed garlic. Transfer to paper towels and add salt.

The zucchinis
Slice the zucchinis and dredge in flour. Sauté in a little olive oil and the remaining clove of garlic. Transfer to paper towels and add salt.

The tomatoes
In the meantime, peel the tomatoes, cut into slices, and remove the seeds.

Presentation
Preheat the oven to 325°F (165°C).

Butter a gratin dish. Alternate layers of eggplant, zucchini, and tomato. Cover with the crème fraîche. Sprinkle with the bread crumbs and bake 20 minutes.

Vegetable
Serves 4

Ingredients
Gratin
2 eggplants
2 tbsp. flour
2 cloves of garlic, crushed
Salt
2 zucchinis
6 ripe tomatoes
½ cup (12 cl) olive oil
¾ cup (18 cl) crème fraîche
2 tbsp. bread crumbs

In our part of the world, people say that the region of the Ardèche is, in fact, composed of two regions. The lower plateaus of the Bas-Vivarais mountains to the south, where the farmers with their thick accents crush olives to extract the fragrant oil, is the "Ardèche à l'huile" ("made with oil"). The upper plateaus of the Haut-Vivarais in the north, ascending to its highest point at the Gerbier-de-Jonc, with its pastures and grazing herds, is the "Ardèche au beurre" ("made with butter"). For this gratin, I use olive oil and cream and butter.

Verbena Chicken Casserole with Potatoes

Meat 🌲
Be sure to select good-quality free-range chicken.
Serves 4

Ingredients
Verbena butter
1 large bunch of verbena
16 tbsp. (200 g) butter
Juice of 1 lemon
2 bunches of 6 green onions

1 lb. 5 oz. (600 g) small new potatoes

Chicken
1 free-range chicken, 4¼ lbs. (2 kg)
4 cloves of garlic, crushed
¾ cup (20 cl) chicken jus (pg. 290)
10 oz. (300 g) flaky puff pastry (pg. 296)
1 egg yolk
Cream
4 tbsp. (6 cl) verbena liqueur

Salt and pepper

For this recipe, I use a 4¼ lb. (2 kg) chicken from the Allier or Ardèche. The chicken should be raised in cages on a diet of plants, grain flour, and milk, so that the meat is more tender.

The verbena butter

Pick the verbena leaves from their branches, trim away any tough sections, and chop with the green onions. Combine in a bowl with the butter, lemon juice, salt, and pepper. Cream the mixture in a food processor and set aside at room temperature.

Fill a pastry bag, with a ¼ in. (5 mm) tip, with verbena butter. As you run your index finger under the skin of the thighs and breast, pipe butter beneath the skin.

Evenly distribute the butter by pressing the outside surface of the skin. Refrigerate for 30 minutes.

The potatoes

Peel the potatoes and blanch in salted water. Drain.

The chicken

Heat a pan over high heat and place in the chicken. First brown the breast and thigh on one side, then turn and brown the other side. Season the inside of the chicken with salt and pepper.

Preheat the oven to 400°F (200°C).

Place two small ovenproof saucers upside down in a heavy casserole. Arrange a verbena branch, the potatoes, garlic, and chicken jus around the saucers. Place the chicken on top of the saucers and cover the casserole.

Roll the dough into a strip about 2 in. (6 cm) wide and long enough to wrap around the circumference of the casserole. Lightly moisten the dough and press it around the top edge of the casserole. Mix the egg yolk with a little cream and brush onto the dough. Place the lid on the dough to seal the casserole.

Bake for 1 hour. Remove the casserole from the oven.

Presentation

Break the pastry-crust seal and remove the chicken. Cut into 8 pieces: 4 from the thigh, 2 from the wings, and 2 from the breast. Remove the potatoes. Skim as much fat from the sauce as possible, add the verbena liqueur, and reduce to obtain ¾ cup (18 cl) of sauce.

Serve hot. Season each of the pieces and the potatoes with salt and pepper.

Guinea Fowl Stew with Blueberries and Saint-Joseph Wine

Meat 🌲
Select the guinea fowl carefully.
Serves 4

Ingredients
Guinea fowl
2 medium-sized onions, diced
1 large carrot
1 bottle red wine (preferably from the Cornas region)
4 tbsp. (6 cl) olive oil
3½ oz. (100 g) smoked slab bacon, diced
1 young guinea fowl, cut into 8 pieces
4 tbsp. (6 cl) Armagnac
1 tbsp. flour
1 bouquet garni
2 cups (½ l) chicken stock (pg. 290)
7 oz. (200 g) fresh blueberries
½ cup (12 cl) rabbit blood

4 tbsp. (6 cl) balsamic vinegar
Salt and pepper

The guinea fowl

Slice the onions and carrots into thin rounds. Boil the red wine to reduce to 1⅔ cups (40 cl). Set aside.

Heat the oil in a good-sized sauté pan and add the diced bacon. Brown the pieces of guinea fowl on all sides. Season with salt and pepper, then flambé with the Armagnac.

Add the carrots and onions and brown slightly. Sprinkle with the flour and cook for 1 minute. Moisten with the reduced red wine, then add enough chicken stock to just cover the pan contents. Add some of the blueberries, a bit of salt, and the bouquet garni.

Cover and simmer gently. After 15 minutes, remove the breast pieces. After 20 more minutes, remove the wings. About 25 to 30 minutes later, remove the legs.

Place the guinea fowl pieces on a plate and cover with a damp cloth.

Presentation

Pass the sauce through a fine china cap strainer, pressing the ingredients well. Reduce to obtain 1¼ cups (30 cl) of sauce. Strain again. Add the pieces of guinea fowl and the remaining blueberries to the pan. Pour a little blood into the sauce and heat without boiling. Correct the seasoning with a little pepper and balsamic vinegar if necessary.

The squawking guinea fowl is of African origin. It was already on the menu for the Egyptians, Greeks, and Romans (who called it Numidian chicken or Carthagian chicken, depending on the region). In Eastern Europe, it is sometimes called Bohemian pheasant, because of the Gypsies who made it popular in the fourteenth century.

The guinea fowl has always been difficult to domesticate as it lays only rarely. Its flesh is dry, so I use bacon in this recipe. I like the smoked flavor, too, which combines well with the blueberries.

I would recommend serving this dish with grain cereals, such as bulgur wheat, quinoa, or millet.

Blueberry and Pistachio Tart

Ingredients
9 oz (250 g) short pastry dough
(pg. 296)

Pistachio pastry cream
1 cup (¼ l) milk
1 tbsp. pistachio paste
3 egg yolks
3 tbsp. (40 g) sugar
3 tbsp. (20 g) cornstarch
4 tbsp. (50 g) butter
Confectioners' sugar

Other ingredients
2 tbsp. (30 g) confectioners' sugar
9 oz. (250 g) fresh blueberries
2 tbsp. (20 g) superfine sugar
1½ oz. (50 g) stale brioche,
for crumbs

Blueberries and huckleberries are from the same family as cranberries. The huckleberry is larger and grows in North America whereas the smaller blueberry, grows wild here in France. As a child blueberry picking was a real treat. Later in life while I was in the alpine chasseur corps of the army, we ate blueberries to improve our vision during nighttime marches through the mountains. In our region they are gathered by hand, or by machine — which is a benefit to some farmers. Unfortunately, the branches of the bush are often damaged.

The pastry
Prepare the short pastry dough. Set aside in refrigerator.

The pistachio pastry cream
Boil the milk and add the pistachio paste. Whisk the yolks, sugar, and cornstarch together in a bowl until light and creamy. Add the boiling milk.

Transfer the mixture into a stainless steel saucepan and return to a boil whisking constantly. The custard will gradually thicken. Pour back into the bowl and add the butter. Sprinkle with some confectioners' sugar to prevent the custard from forming a skin.

The tart
Preheat the oven to 375°F (180°C). Roll the pastry into a 12 in. (30 mm) circle and press into a 10 in. tart pan, or make 6 individual tarts. Prick the pastry with a fork, line with a sheet of parchment paper and weight with dry beans.

Bake "blind" about 15 minutes. Remove the pastry shell from the oven. Remove the parchment paper and dry beans.

Rinse the blueberries quickly in cold water. Drain and dry them.

Spread a thick layer of custard into the pastry shell. Sprinkle the brioche crumbs and cover with a generous layer of blueberries. Sprinkle with sugar.

Bake about 20 to 25 minutes. During the cooking the blueberries will burst and release their juices.

Presentation
Sprinkle with confectioner's sugar. The tart can be served at room temperature.

Without a doubt, the wines from Gérard Chave Hermitage are among Régis and Michèle Marcon's favorites. They are well balanced and rounded, elegantly mature, and smooth on the palate. The complicity between the chef and wine grower comes from the interweaving of their passions. Gérard Chave loves to visit Saint-Bonnet-Le-Froid for the mushroom festival, among other things. He is also handy in the kitchen (there are few wine growers with such a knack for foie gras or game), so he knows a virtuoso chef when he tastes one, especially one who plays such sweet sonatinas to the mushroom as does Régis Marcon. For his part, Marcon feels privileged to spend time at Gérard and Jean-Louis' estate, before the bottling, tasting all the nuances of the varying climates of the Hermitage hillside. There are always magic moments in the cellar, when they uncork a bottle of fine old ambrosia or release a *vin de paille* (straw wine) that is so filled with sunshine that it could melt all the snows of Kilimanjaro.

France is a country of many great vintage wines, it goes without saying. The secret of the Chave family's Hermitage is its longevity, the wisdom passed down from generation to generation, and the abundant generosity of spirit. . . .

Fresh Mushroom Pizza

Appetizer
Serves 4

Ingredients
Pizza dough
1 oz. (30 g) yeast
2 tbsp. olive oil
1½ cups (37 cl) warm water
4 cups (600 g) flour
2 tbsp. dijon mustard
4 tbsp. (6 cl) white wine

Mushrooms
*5 oz. (150 g) black chanterelles or
trumpet mushrooms*
4 tbsp. (6 cl) olive oil
*6½ oz. (180 g) bleeding milk cap
mushroom*
6½ oz. (180 g) hedgehog mushrooms
7 oz. (200 g) cauliflower mushrooms
6½ oz. (180 g) blue foot mushrooms
*6½ oz. (180 g) fairy ring
mushrooms*
1 clove of garlic, finely chopped
6 basil leaves
1 sprig of fresh thyme

Tomato sauce
*1 lb. 8 oz. (700 g) tomatoe concassé
(pg. 293)*
1 onion, chopped
1 tsp. chopped marjoram

Chili oil
*3 tbsp. freshly grated vintage Comte
cheese (or provolone)*

Salt, pepper, and sugar

The pizza dough

Mix the yeast and olive oil in tepid water. On a clean work surface, form the flour into a well. Pour in the yeast mixture and work into the flour. Shape the dough into a ball and knead for 10 minutes until elastic. Cover the dough with a damp cloth and set aside.

The mushrooms

Clean each mushroom separately and cut the largest into quarters. Blanch the black trumpets in boiling salted water for 1 minute. Drain and dry on paper towels.

Heat the olive oil in a nonstick pan and sauté the mushrooms, adding them to the pan in the following order: the milk cap, hedgehog, cauliflower, blue foot, and, finally, the fairy ring mushrooms without their stems.

At the end of cooking, add the chopped garlic, basil, and a little fresh thyme. Season with salt and pepper.

Drain in a colander.

The tomato sauce

In a heavy saucepan, brown the chopped onion in olive oil. Add the tomatoes and reduce. Season with salt and pepper. Add the chopped marjoram at the end of cooking.

Presentation

Preheat the oven to 400°F (200°C).

Divide the dough into 4 balls. Press each with the palm of your hand, then roll into 4 pizza rounds with a rolling pin. Mix the mustard with wine and lightly brush onto the dough.

Cover each pizza with the tomato sauce.

Arrange an attractive layer of mushrooms on top. Drizzle with chili oil and sprinkle with the Comte cheese.

Bake 15 to 20 minutes.

There is nothing quite like the sight of a kitchen table covered with mushrooms after a good morning of picking!

When I am out walking with Gilles Liège, we like to gather all the mushrooms we can find, and then sort them when we return.

By identifying, tasting, and analyzing them, each time we learn something new about nature, and about the undergrowth of the wood's edge.

Mushroom and Tansy Consommé

Appetizer 🌲
Serves 4

Ingredients
Handful of quality dried porcini
2 lbs. 2 oz. (1 kg) porcini
mushrooms, fairy ring mushrooms,
and chanterelles
1 leek
1 fennel
2 cloves of garlic, halved
4 tansy (or basil) leaves
Salt and pepper
Olive oil

Consommé, usually beef or chicken, is always pleasant to have at the beginning or middle of a meal. In this recipe, I wanted to create a type of mushroom consommé. The tansy adds a hint of aniseed and mint. (Pregnant women, however, should avoid tansy and substitute basil.)

One day in advance, soak the dried porcini in warm water.
Wash and quarter the fresh mushrooms.
Finely slice the leek and fennel.
Brown the leek and fennel in olive oil, then add the garlic. Add the fresh mushrooms and let sweat for 10 to 15 minutes.

Add just enough water to cover and reduce until dry. Gently brown the mushrooms.

Moisten with some of the soaking water and then add the porcini mushrooms. Bring to a boil, skim, and very gently simmer for 1 hour.

Remove from heat and let rest for 10 minutes. Filter slowly through a fine china cap lined with a damp cloth. Strain the consommé without pressing. Adjust the seasoning.

Presentation
Pour the piping hot consommé into a teapot. Add the tansy leaves and let the flavors infuse for several minutes before serving.

Braised Mediterranean Sea Bass on a Bed of Grapes

The sea bass
Preheat the oven to 350°F (180°C).

Gut wash and dry the sea bass. Season the cavity with salt and pepper. Heat 1 tbsp. of butter in a heavy bottomed pan and add the smoked bacon, onion, and garlic. Let sweat for 3 to 4 minutes. Add half of the fresh grapes and half of the grape bunches with stalks. Press down to pack. Lay the bass on top and cover with the remaining grapes and grape bunches. Add the red wine.

Bring to a boil, cover, and bake about 20 to 30 minutes. Check for doneness by slipping the point of a knife into the thickest part of the fish. The blade should come away slightly warm.

The red wine sauce
Remove the pan from the oven. Reduce the cooking juices to ¾ cup (18 cl) of sauce. Add the veal jus and red wine, and reduce again. Thicken the sauce slightly, if necessary, by adding a teaspoon of cornstarch dissolved in a little cold water. Whisk in the butter.

Check the seasoning.

Presentation
Present the whole bass to your guests so they can savor the sweet aroma of this dish. Serve with small new potatoes sautéed in butter.

Fish 🌲
Serves 4

Ingredients
2 lbs. 8 oz. (1,2 kg) sea bass
1 tbsp. (25 g) butter
5 oz. (150 g) smoked slab bacon,
cut into large cubes
1 onion, finely diced
8 cloves of garlic, unpeeled
4 oz. (120 g) fresh green grapes
4 oz. (120 g) fresh black grapes
9 oz. (250 g) grapes in bunches
3 cups (75 cl) red wine

Red wine sauce
½ cup (12 cl) veal jus (pg. 292)
1 cup (25 cl) Cote du Rhone red wine
4 tbsp. (50 g) butter

Salt and pepper

This cooking method reminds me of the days my father would descend into the valley to distill the local marc with the farmers I remember the eau-de-vie, steaming hot as it came out of the vat.

Pan-Fried Lake Pike Fillet with Potato Porcini Purée and Onion Sauce

Fish 🌲 🌲
*Good-quality dried porcini
are essential for this dish.*
Serves 4

Ingredients
Onion Sauce
*3 tbsp. (40 g) butter
3 medium-sized onions, thinly sliced
1 tsp. sugar
1 tsp. fennel seeds
4 tbsp. (6 cl) dry white wine
¾ cup (18 cl) veal jus (pg. 292)*

Potato porcini purée
*1½ oz. (50 g) dried porcini
10 oz. (300 g) potatoes
¾ cup (18 cl) cream
4 tbsp. (60 g) butter*

Fried onion
*1 large onion
½ cup (12 cl) milk
Handful of flour
4 cups (1 l) peanut oil for frying*

Lake pike
*14 oz. (400 g) fresh porcini
2 sprigs of thyme
1 clove of garlic, chopped
1 lb. 6 oz. (600 to 700 g) lake pike
fillet, with skin
4 tbsp. (60 g) clarified butter
4 tbsp. (6 cl) olive oil
4 cloves of garlic, unpeeled*

Salt, pepper, and porcini powder

The onion sauce

Melt the butter in a heavy sauté pan over gentle heat. Add the sliced onions, sugar, and a pinch of salt. Cook, covered, for about 40 minutes until the onions are soft and lightly caramelized.

Add the fennel seeds and deglaze with the white wine. Reduce again, then add the veal jus. Season with salt and pepper. Gently simmer about 10 minutes. Remove from heat and let the flavors infuse 10 minutes before passing through a fine china cap. Press the onions well to extract the juices.

The potato porcini purée

One day in advance, soak the dried porcini in warm water. The following day, steam the potatoes in their skins. Peel, and then pass the pulp through a food mill. Set aside.

Drain the mushrooms, reserve the soaking water. Strain the water into a deep saucepan and reduce by three-quarters over low heat. Add the crème fraîche, boil to reduce again.

Meanwhile, clean the soaked porcini and sauté over high heat in a tbsp. of butter. Turn the mushrooms onto a cutting board and finely chop. Add some of the mushrooms to the reduced cream. Reserve the rest for other recipes (for example, mushroom duxelle). Gradually add the potato pulp to the porcini-cream mixture. Mix well with a spatula and add butter to taste. Lightly season with salt and pepper. Cover and keep warm.

The porcini

Wash and brush the fresh porcini. Cut into thick slices. Heat the oil in a pan and add the garlic and thyme. Brown the porcini slices on each side. Season with salt and pepper.

Skim some of the fat from the onion sauce, add several spoonfuls to glaze the mushrooms.

The fried onion

Heat the oil in a deep casserole over medium heat. With a slicer or mandoline, slice the onion into very fine slivers. Soak them in milk, drain, and dip in flour. Heat the oil to about 350°F (170°C) and drop in the onion slices. Fry until brown and crispy. Keep warm on paper towels. Sprinkle with salt.

The lake pike

Preheat the oven to 325°F (160°C).

Cut the fish fillet into 4 slices. Heat the clarified butter and olive oil in a large nonstick pan. Add the fillets, skin side down. Add the garlic cloves and thyme leaves. Brown the skin and finish cooking in the oven, basting often. Season with salt and pepper. Check for doneness by inserting a skewer or needle into the center of the fish, it should come away slightly warm.

Presentation

Arrange some porcini slices in the center of each plate. Lay a fillet and clove of garlic on top. Place 2 small quenelles of potato porcini purée to one side. Drizzle with the onion sauce and decorate with several fried onions. Sprinkle powdered porcini around the edge of each plate.

The soaking water for the dried porcini is so fragrant and flavorful that I combined it with potato purée in this recipe. Ever since, it has been a specialty of the house.

The sauce made by reducing the porcini juice and cream can also be served with pasta, rice, or grains.

171

Two Mushroom Ragout

Main dish or vegetable 🌲
accompaniment
Serves 4

Ingredients
Mushrooms
14 oz. (400 g) each of
russula mushrooms and
man on horseback mushrooms
(substitute girolles)
1 tbsp. olive oil
3 tbsp. (50 g) butter
3 shallots finely chopped
½ cup (12 cl) dry white wine

The parsley butter
7 tbsp. (100 g) softened butter
1 clove of garlic, finely chopped
¼ cup (50 g) minced parsley
1 tbsp. flour

Salt and freshly ground pepper

This dish reminds me of
my mother's autumn cooking
when my brothers and sisters
and I would help her
in the kitchen.
At the restaurant, we serve
this mushroom ragout in soup
tureens, ladleful after ladleful.

The mushrooms
Remove the mushroom caps. Pull the skin from the edge of the caps and peel them. Clean thoroughly.

Heat the olive oil in a sauté pan. Add the butter and sweat the shallots. Add the mushrooms and brown for 5 minutes. Season with salt and pepper. Add the white wine, cover, and cook gently for 20 minutes. The mushrooms will release moisture.

The parsley butter
Meanwhile, prepare the parsley butter by mixing together the butter, garlic, parsley, and flour.

Presentation
Drain the cooked mushrooms over a saucepan. Return the mushrooms to the sauté pan. Boil the cooking juices and whisk in the parsley butter.

Continue whisking for 3 to 4 minutes, until the sauce begins to coat the back of a spoon.

Pour the sauce over the mushrooms. Serve immediately.

Venison Noisettes with Caramelized Quince Charlotte and Celery Mousseline

Meat

A time-consuming recipe.
Begin 2 days in advance.
Serves 4

Ingredients

Venison
1 lb. 5 oz. (600 g) venison fillet
(reserve the bones for
the venison sauce)
1 strip of fatback
¾ cup (18 cl) venison or
pepper sauce (pg. 292)
4 tbsp. (55g) butter

Quince charlotte
1–3 in. piece (20 g) fresh ginger root
4¼ lbs. (2 kg) quinces
2 lemons
1 star anise
1 vanilla bean pod
4 cups (800 g) sugar
3 tbsp. (40 g) butter
¼ tsp. ground cinnamon

Celery root mousseline
10 oz. (300 g) celery root
3 cups (75 cl) milk
3 tbsp. (30 g) short grain rice
3 tbsp. (4 cl) hazelnut oil

Potato chips
7 oz. (200 g) potatoes
(purple variety, optional)
4 cups (1 l) peanut oil for frying

Salt and pepper

The venison

One day in advance, marinate the venison bones in the wine for the venison sauce recipe.

The following day, cut 2 fillets from each side of the central bone. Use all the bones to make the venison sauce.

Cut each fillet into 6 *noisettes* so that there are 3 per serving. Slice the fatback very thinly and wrap each venison piece, securing it with a wooden toothpick.

The quince charlottes

Peel and finely slice then dice the ginger. Place in a pan of cold water and boil for 3 minutes to blanch. Set aside.

Peel and quarter the quinces. Remove the core and seeds. Place in a bowl of cold water with lemon juice.

Pour 8 cups (2 l) of water into a deep saucepan. Add the juice of 1 lemon, the star anise, vanilla pod, and sugar. Bring to a boil and add the quinces. Cover with parchment paper and cook for 12 to 15 minutes.

Drain the quinces in a colander. Reserve the syrup for other recipes. Dice half of the stewed quinces.

Brown the diced quinces in the butter. Drizzle with lemon juice and the cinnamon.

With a slicer or mandoline, finely slice the remaining quinces. In a nonstick pan, brown each slice over medium heat until it is a rich amber color. Set aside on a plate.

Butter 4 small charlotte molds. Line each with quince slices and fill with the diced quince. Press down to pack well.

The celery root mousseline

Peel the celery and cut into large cubes. Boil the milk in a deep saucepan. Add the rice and a little salt. Simmer, covered, for 25 to 30 minutes. Drain and purée in a food processor until smooth. Add the hazelnut oil and keep warm.

The potato chips

Wash the potatoes but do not peel them. With a slicer or mandoline finely slice them. Rinse with cold water to remove any excess starch and pat dry.

Heat 4 cups (1 l) of the peanut oil in a deep pan to 350°F (170°C). As soon as the oil starts to steam slightly, fry the potato slices in small quantities at a time. They should be crisp but retain their original color.

Set aside on paper towels and sprinkle with salt.

Cooking the charlottes and venison
Preheat the oven to 350°F (180°C). Place the charlottes on an baking sheet and bake about 15 minutes. Heat a 2 tbsp. of butter in a pan and brown the venison on each side. Season with salt and pepper. Cook until medium rare, or to your taste.

The sauce
Thicken the sauce by whisking in 2 tbsp. of butter, and optional rabbit or pork blood.

Presentation
Arrange a quince charlotte in the center of each plate and top with a bit of remaining diced quince. Pipe 3 small mounds of celery mousseline around the charlotte and crown each with a potato chip. Lay venison noisettes between the mounds of mousseline and surround with sauce.

Young game is always the most flavorful. Traditionally, the meat was marinated before cooking to tenderize it and mellow the strong flavor. Today, however, only the meat of older animals is marinated.

On the other hand, venison should be barded, wrapped in fatback, because it is very lean — five times less fatty than beef.

Veal Kidneys à l'Orange with Juniper Berries

Meat
Serves 4

Ingredients
Veal kidneys
2 pink veal kidneys, with fat
8 shallots
Juice and zest of 1 orange
3¼ cup (18 cl) veal jus (pg. 292)
1 tsp. juniper berries
1 tbsp. (20 g) butter
4 tbsp. (6 cl) Grand Marnier

Salt, pepper, and grated nutmeg

My butcher, René Chatelard, always sets aside for me some nice pink veals kidneys from milk fed calves. I like to serve them whole with a plate of small macaroni tossed in the kidney cooking jus.
This dish is delicious, particularly if you don't trim away the fat around the kidneys.

The kidneys

Prepare the kidneys and remove the nerves. Leave about ¼ in. (½ cm) of fat around them.

Heat a heavy pan over high heat with 2 tbsp. of butter, brown the kidneys and let them finish cooking over low heat in the oven at 400°F (200°C) about 10 minutes.

Remove the pan from the heat and transfer the kidneys to a plate. Reserve all the cooking juices and blood. Add 2 tbsp. of butter to the pan, add the shallots and slowly cook them until soft.

Skim the fat from the casserole and the shallots. Add the orange juice, some of the zest and nutmeg. Reduce by half. Add the veal jus. Crush the juniper berries and mix into the sauce with the kidney juices. Check the seasoning.

Pass the sauce through a fine china cap. Whisk in the 1 tbsp. butter and Grand Marnier.

Presentation

Trim the fat from the kidneys, according to taste. Coat the kidneys with the sauce and glaze under the broiler. Arrange in a serving casserole and cover with a little more sauce.

Decorate with orange zest and juniper berries. Serve in thick slices and season with fine sea salt and black pepper.

Braised Wild Duck in Cranberry Wine

with Caramelized Onion Polenta

Meat
The cranberries may be replaced by blueberries.
Serves 4

Ingredients
Ducks
*2 mallard ducks, each 2 lb.
(900 g to 1 kg)
1 tbsp. butter
4 tbsp. (6 cl) peanut oil*

Cranberry wine
*1 orange
2 cups (50 cl) red wine
4 tsp. (2 cl) sherry wine vinegar
1 onion
1 carrot, finely sliced
4 juniper berries
2 star anise
1 clove
3½ tbsp. (5 cl) crème de cassis
(black currant liqueur)
½ cup (60 g) cranberries
1 bouquet garni
1 tbsp. flour
2 tbsp. butter*

Polenta
*1¼ cups (30 cl) milk
1 cup (150 g) polenta
4 tbsp. (6 cl) crème fraîche*

*2 medium-sized onions,
finely chopped
2 tbsp. (30 g) butter
1 tsp. honey
2 tbsp. (3 cl) balsamic vinegar
2 tbsp. of freshly grated vintage
Comte or Parmesan cheese*

Salt, pepper, and grated nutmeg

The ducks
One day in advance, remove the zest from the orange. Place in a pan of cold water and boil to blanch. Refresh in cold water.

Remove the duck thighs. Leave the breast fillets on the carcass for roasting later.

The marinade
Pour the red wine into a casserole. Add the zest, vinegar, onion, carrot, juniper berries, star anise, clove, crème de cassis, half the cranberries, and the bouquet garni.

Boil for 2 to 3 minutes and remove from heat. When the marinade is cool, add the duck thighs. Refrigerate.

Cooking the thighs
The following day, drain the thighs and dry with paper towels.

In a very hot sauté pan, brown both sides of the thighs in a tbsp. of butter, skin side first. Season with salt and pepper.

Add the onion and carrot garnish from the marinade. Brown again, then sprinkle the thighs with the flour.

Stir the flour into the pan ingredients with a wooden spatula and cook gently. Add some wine marinade while scraping the bottom of the pan.

Add enough wine marinade to just cover the pan contents and bring to a boil. Simmer gently 1½ hours.

Skim the surface from time to time. Check for doneness by pressing the thighs with your fingers; the meat should yield easily.

When the cooking is done, let the thighs rest and then transfer to a plate. Pass the cooking juices through a fine china cap lined with cheesecloth.

Skim the fat and reduce to obtain a slightly thicker sauce.

The breast fillets
Brown the duck breasts still on the bone in the peanut oil. Season with salt and pepper. Reduce the heat and cook slowly until medium rare. Keep warm.

The polenta

Boil the milk with salt, pepper, and nutmeg. Add the polenta in a steady stream and reduce the heat. Cook about 15 minutes, stirring constantly with a wooden spatula.

Add a little cream to smooth the polenta.

Meanwhile, in a sauté pan, brown the finely sliced onions in butter and honey over medium heat.

Cover and cook for about 20 minutes, until the onions start to caramelize.

Deglaze with the balsamic vinegar and add a little of the reduced sauce. Reduce again and add to the polenta. Sprinkle with the grated cheese and check the seasoning.

Presentation

Sauté the cranberries in 1 tbsp. of butter 2 to 3 minutes.

Pour in the duck sauce and whisk in 1 tbsp. of butter. Check the seasoning.

Place a duck thigh in each plate. Remove the breast fillets from the bone and set a fillet on top of each thigh.

Serve the polenta and caramelized onions separately.

Coat the duck with sauce and serve remaining sauce on the side.

Cranberries are more acidic than blueberries and slightly bitter. This fruit goes well with mallard and other game birds. Cranberries grow nearby us, at an altitude of 4,265 ft. (1,300 m) on Felletin mountain, "the mountain of the three suns," near Saint-Julien-Molhesabate.

Quince Tarte Tatin
with Honey and Gentian Ice Cream

Dessert
Serves 8

Ingredients
Quince tarte tatin
*9 oz. (250 g) flaky puff pastry
(pg. 296)
7 quinces
Juice of ½ lemon
½ cup + 2 tbsp. (120 g) sugar
4 cups (1 l) apple juice
6 tbsp. (80 g) butter*

Syrup
*4 cups (1 l) water
1½ cups (300 g) sugar*

Honey and gentian ice cream
*12 egg yolks
4 cups (1 l) whole milk
⅔ cup (250 g) mountain
wildflower honey
Lemon zest
½ cup (12 cl) heavy cream
4½ tbsp. (7 cl) gentian liqueur*

*The quince, which originated in
Iran, was enjoyed by the ancient
Greeks and Romans. Like the
pear, the quince does not ripen well
on the tree. Instead, it should be
left to ripen in temperatures of 60
to 70°F (14 to 19°C), and its
fragrant aroma will fill the room.
Quince is not eaten raw because it
is very bitter and full of tannin,
which is dispersed during
cooking.*

The quince tarte tatin
Preheat the oven to 400°F (200°C).

Roll the pastry into a circle 9 in. (22 cm) by ⅛ in. (3 mm) thick. Bake between two baking sheets until crisp.

Peel and quarter the quinces, toss with lemon juice, and cook them in the syrup. In a separate pot caramelize the sugar and deglaze with the apple juice. Reduce by half and add the butter. Reduce again until syrupy.

Add the drained quinces and cook 15 to 20 minutes.

Cool.

Arrange the caramelized quinces in a nonstick 8 in. (20 cm) round mold. Bake about 10 minutes. Place the baked pastry round on top of the quinces and turn upside down carefully.

The honey and gentian ice cream
Separate the eggs and pour the yolks into a bowl. Boil the milk in a saucepan, add the honey. Pour the milk over the yolks, stirring with a whisk. Return the mixture to the saucepan and cook, stirring constantly, until the sauce coats the spatula—about 180°F (85°C). Add the lemon zest and refrigerate for 10 hours. Add the cream and gentian liqueur and process in an ice-cream maker.

Presentation
Heat the *tarte tatin* in the oven. Serve with the honey and gentian ice cream.

Mushroom Ice Cream

inely dice the porcini and candy it in the 1 cup of sugar and ½ cup (1 dl) water.

Heat the milk to boiling and add the powdered mushrooms. Allow the flavors to infuse for 3 to 4 hours. Add the glucose and powdered milk, reheat. Whisk the egg yolks and ½ cup sugar until light and creamy and pour the hot milk on top. Return the mixture to the saucepan and cook as you would a soft custard.

Pass through a fine china cap, cover, and let cool for several hours.

Add the lightly whipped cream and process in an ice-cream maker. Gradually add the candied diced porcini.

Dessert 🌲
Serves 12

Ingredients
2 tbsp. finely diced fresh porcini
1 cup (200 g) sugar
6 cups (1.5 l) of milk
2 tbsp. mushroom powder (pg. 293)
¼ cup (90 g) glucose
½ cup (60 g) powdered milk
12 egg yolks
½ cup (100 g) sugar
1 cup (25 cl) cream

The idea of mushroom ice cream always raises a few eyebrows. This recipe, however, is typical of my approach, which is to work with a theme or product in every possible way—provided the result is good.

When Gilles Liège is not tasting apples, he is hunting for mushrooms. Although it is easy to be overwhelmed by the many varieties, Gilles Liège does not miss a step. He can identify apples the way others can name butterflies. An enduring science, as the many types of apple are becoming lesser known in these monotonous days, when people assume that the only apple in the Garden of Eden was the Golden Delicious. Yet, Gilles Liège can talk endlessly about Paradise and *la pomme*. "These days, no one is interested in the complexity of the apple, the subtle blend of tart and sweet that varies with every variety. There is the *Sainte-Germaine*, an apple that is longer than it is wide, with its distinctive musky flavor. Then there is the *Goutte d'or*, which is an integral part of our Haute-Loire heritage"—and it keeps no secrets from him. In an orchard one day, Gilles Liège saw a farmer cutting down his old apple trees to plant Golden Delicious. It's easy to imagine Gilles trying to restrain the man's swinging arm, like the hero of a French folk tale. Equally passionate about mushrooms, he has a particular interest in the russulas, the "outcasts" of the mushroom family. He has developed a fine palate for their distinctive aromas. Despite his claim that he is "more curious about things than people," he has a certain affinity with Régis Marcon and the chef's "technical approach to the mushroom" and its flavors and textures, which Régis has been perfecting for the past seven years. "When Régis chooses a particular mushroom variety to accompany shellfish, he confirms my own intuition. He has a remarkable sense of harmony." From the orchard or the forest to the kitchen, their shared interest is not in danger of subsiding anytime soon. One day, Gilles Liège brought some white haricot beans, called *Duchesse de Chambord*, from his home in Poitou. Régis Marcon set them to music right away.

183

Chicken Liver Salad with Apples, Chestnuts and Flambéed Porcini

Appetizer 🌲
Serves 4

Ingredients

Mushroom vinaigrette (pg. 295)
10 oz. (300 g) mesclun salad,
chickweed, garden herbs,
and other greens
10 oz. (300 g) porcini or
milk cap mushrooms
1 apple (Reine de
Reinette variety)
2 tbsp. each chopped fresh herbs
(parsley, tarragon, chives)
5 oz. (150 g) fresh chicken livers,
nerves removed
3 tbsp. hazelnut oil
Dash of sherry wine vinegar
18 chestnuts, toasted
1 tsp. pear eau-de-vie
1 tbsp. butter

Salt and pepper

I perfected this recipe after a conversation with fellow chef Jean Delaveyne, whom I had the plea-sure to meet one evening in Cannes at the Escoffier Foundation cookery demonstrations. He makes his salad with porcini and cranberries, flambéed with kirsch.

The salad

Prepare the mushroom vinaigrette and wash and dry the salad greens.

Clean and quarter the mushrooms.

Wash the apple, remove the seeds, and cut into thin slices.

Toss the salad greens, herbs, and vinaigrette. Set aside.

Brown the chicken livers in 1 tbsp. hazelnut oil until medium rare. Deglaze with the sherry wine vinegar. Keep warm.

Heat 2 tbsp. of hazelnut oil in a pan, add the mushrooms. Brown for 3 to 4 minutes. Add the chestnuts and apple slices. Brown slightly.

Pour on the eau-de-vie and flambé. Season with salt and pepper and whisk in 1 tbsp. of butter.

Presentation

Arrange the chicken livers in the center of the plate.

Cover the chicken livers with salad and sprinkle the hot mushrooms, chestnuts, and apples on top. Serve immediately.

Escargot and Savory Herb Shortbread

Appetizer
Serves 4

Ingredients
Shortbread dough
4½ oz. (125 g) butter, creamed
1⅔ cups (250 g) flour
2 oz. (60 g) cheese (Cantal or
Salers), freshly grated
1 egg
Pinch of sugar
½ tsp. fennel seeds, ground

Mixed herbs
3½ oz. (100 g) smoked slab bacon,
finely diced
1 medium-sized onion, chopped
Handful of spinach, shredded
¾ cup (18 cl) crème fraîche
3 tsp. chopped parsley
8 leaves of sorrel, chopped
½ bunch of burnet or chervil, chopped
Garlic purée

Chanterelles and escargots
36 large escargots (gros gris)
¾ oz. + ¾ oz. butter (20 g + 20 g)
4 tsp. (2 cl) pastis
7 oz. (200 g) chanterelle mushrooms
1 shallot, chopped
Salt and pepper

*The success of this recipe has
more to do with the herbs than
with any particular technique.
You may use any type of wild
herb, such as wild sorrel and
spignel—or garden weeds
such as chickweed or purslane.
The flavors in this recipe will
change with the seasons.*

The shortbread dough
Mix the creamed butter with the flour and grated cheese. Add the egg, sugar, and ground fennel seeds.

Knead the dough to form a ball, knead the dough, and roll back into a homogeneous ball. Cover with plastic wrap and refrigerate.

The mixed herbs
Sauté the bacon and onion in butter for 2 to 3 minutes. Add the shredded spinach and wilt for several minutes. When the spinach is cooked, add the cream. Boil to reduce. Add the chopped herbs and season with salt and pepper.

Reduce the mixture until it begins to caramelize. Add a pinch of garlic purée and adjust the seasoning. Transfer to a bowl and keep warm.

The chanterelles and escargots
Drain the mushrooms. Sauté the escargots in a nonstick pan with 1½ tbsp. (20 g) of butter. Salt lightly, then flambé with the pastis. Keep warm.

Clean the chanterelles. Rinse quickly under running water if necessary and dry with a cloth. Sauté the chanterelles in the remaining butter over high heat. Add the chopped shallot. Season with salt and pepper, keep warm.

Baking the dough
Preheat the oven to 300°F (150°C). Remove the pastry from the refrigerator and roll out to a thickness of about ⅛ in. (4 mm). Prick the pastry with a fork and cut into 4 rounds with a 3 in. (8 cm) pastry cutter. Arrange the pastry rounds on a baking sheet and bake about 20 minutes. While baking, the pastry will swell because of the cheese. Place another baking tray on top to keep the pastries flat. Remove from the oven and keep warm.

Presentation
Spread some of the herb mixture on each pastry and arrange the escargots around the edge. Mound the chanterelles in the center. Place in the oven for 5 minutes. Serve hot, with a mixed salad of greens, herbs, and a touch of garlic.

Scallops and a
Discovery of Mushrooms

Fish
Serves 4

Ingredients
*12 scallops (good-sized, in the shells
if possible)
4 tbsp. (55 g) melted butter*

Mushrooms
*5 oz. (150 g) blue foot mushrooms
5 oz. (150 g) common chanterelles
½ cup (12 cl) olive oil
2 medium shallots, finely minced
5 oz. (150 g) violet St. George's
mushrooms
5 oz. (150 g) chanterelles or black
trumpet mushrooms
7 oz. (200 g) saffron milk cap
mushrooms*

*Rosemary and
mushroom butter sauce*
*4 tbsp. (6 cl) dry white wine
1 large shallot, thinly sliced
¾ cup (18 cl) mushroom stock
1 sprig of rosemary
4 tbsp. (50 g) butter
1 tsp. chopped garlic*

*You should make this recipe
only if you have a good mushroom
harvest of several different
varieties. It's a good way to
discover the flavors and aromas
of each.*

T*he mushrooms*
Clean all the mushrooms, rinse in water if necessary. Blanch the blue foot mushrooms for 1 minute in boiling salted water, then refresh. Blanch and refresh the black chanterelles. Dry with paper towels.

Heat 1 tbsp. of olive oil in a nonstick pan. Sauté each mushroom variety separately, adding minced shallot.

Drain each variety in a colander and reserve the cooking juices. Keep warm.

The rosemary and mushroom butter sauce
Pour the white wine into a small sauté pan. Add the minced shallot and reduce by three-quarters. Add the mushroom stock and rosemary and return to a boil. Remove the rosemary sprig after 1 minute (or to your taste), as its flavor should not dominate. Keep warm.

The scallops
Heat the melted butter in a nonstick pan. Quickly brown the scallops and season with salt and pepper.

Preheat oven to 400°F (200°C)

Arrange the scallops in a baking dish. Crown each scallop with some of each type of mushroom. Finish cooking in the oven, about 10 minutes.

Presentation
Whisk the butter into the sauce, season with salt, pepper, and the chopped garlic. Adjust the seasoning.

Just before serving, whisk the sauce again with an immersion blender.

Arrange the scallops and mushrooms on a very hot plate.

Place the extra mushrooms in the center. (In a optional wrapped and fried potato curl).

Pour sauce around the mushrooms and scallops.

Decorate with a sprig of rosemary if you wish.

Baked Sea Bass with Mushrooms and Shellfish

Fish
Serves 4

Ingredients
Fish
1 lb. 5 oz. (600 g) sea bass fillet without skin
¾ cup (18 cl) fish stock (pg. 291)

Stuffing
4 tbsp. (60 g) butter, creamed
7 oz. (200 g) mushroom duxelle (porcini-based if possible) (pg. 294)
1 egg
1½ oz. (40 g) fresh white bread, without crusts
3 tbsp. finely chopped parsley

Shellfish
2 large shallots minced
¾ cup (18 cl) dry white wine
30 plump mussels
24 cockles

Vegetables
2 medium-sized carrots
5 oz. (150 g) green beans

Butter sauce
2 tbsp. (30 g) butter
4 tbsp. (6 cl) olive oil
1 tbsp. minced chives
2 tbsp. diced tomato

Salt pepper, and saffron

Discard any open mussels that do not close when you tap them with a finger. In this recipe, my idea was to combine mushrooms with the ocean flavor of shellfish.

The stuffing
Mix the butter, mushroom duxelle, egg, bread, finely chopped parsley, salt, and pepper. Set aside.

The shellfish
Divide the shallots between 2 small sauté pans. Add the white wine and mussels to one pan and put the cockles and a pinch of saffron into the other.

Cover and boil for 1 to 2 minutes, depending on the size of the shellfish. They should be open but not overdone.

Reserve the cooking juices.

The steamed vegetables
Boil 2 saucepans of salted water. Cut the carrots into sticks. Trim the green beans and remove the stringy threads. Cook the vegetables separately. Allow 2 minutes for the beans and 4 minutes for the carrots. Refresh in ice-cold water.

The fish
Cut the sea bass into 4 slices of 5 oz. (150 g) each. Season. Spread a ¼ in. (8 mm) layer of the stuffing on one side of each fillet.

Arrange the fillets in a buttered oven dish and pour fish stock around them. Bring to a boil, then bake for about 12 minutes at 300°F (150°C).

Remove from oven. Drain the fish slices, reserving the cooking juices, and transfer to another baking dish. Return to the oven to brown.

The butter sauce
Combine the cooking juices from the sea bass and shellfish. Whisk with the butter and olive oil. Reduce slightly. Add the chives and the diced tomato. Check the seasoning and add a squeeze of lemon juice if necessary.

Presentation
Lay a fillet on each plate and arrange vegetables and shellfish around it. Whisk the butter sauce before serving so that it is foamy and smooth. Pour the sauce around the fish and vegetables.

Pumpkin Gnocchi and Swiss Chard

Vegetable 🌲 🌲
Serves 4

Ingredients
Gnocchi
9 oz. (250 g) squash puree,
(pumpkin, buttercup,
butternut or hubbard)
1 egg
6 tbsp. (60 g) flour
1½ oz. (50 g) Cantal, Comte, or
Parmesan cheese, grated
Salt and freshly ground pepper
Nutmeg

Chard cream sauce
4 large stalks of Swiss chard
1 large onion, minced
4 oz. (100 g) smoked slab bacon,
finely diced
4 tbsp. (6 cl) olive oil
½ cup (12 cl) double cream

Presentation
4 tbsp. (50 g) melted butter
4 tbsp. (50 g) cheese, freshly grated

This Italian-style recipe was inspired by the different types of squashes provided by our good friends the Prades.

The gnocchi
Preheat the oven to 400°F (200°C). Wash the squash and bake it whole for about 1 hour 30 minutes.

Slice open the pumpkin, remove the seeds, and purée the flesh. For this recipe, you'll use 9 oz. (250 g) of purée.

Mix the purée with the egg, flour, and grated cheese. Season with salt, pepper, and grated nutmeg. Mix thoroughly until the dough is smooth. Refrigerate.

Cooking the gnocchi
Boil a large pot of salted water. Mold the dough into 1½ in. (3.5 cm) long *rissoles*. Cover well with flour. Cut each *rissole* into ½ in. (1 cm) slices and roll between the palms of your hands so that they taper at the ends. Coat again with flour so that they will not stick together. Cook in boiling water until they float to the surface. Remove the gnocchi with a skimmer. Drain on paper towels and refrigerate.

The chard cream sauce
Wash the chard and remove the stalks from the leaves. In a sauté pan, brown the onion and diced bacon in a little olive oil 1 to 2 minutes. Cut the chard stalks into a small dice, add to the pan. Cover and cook 1 to 2 minutes. Shred the chard leaves and add to the pan. Cover and cook to soften. Season with salt and pepper. Add the cream and bring to a boil. Adjust the seasoning.

Presentation
Pour the cream sauce into a heavy baking dish (a gratin dish, for example). Arrange the gnocchi on top. Add the melted butter and sprinkle with grated cheese.

Heat in a 400°F (200°C) oven 15 minutes.

Serve immediately.

Anchovy Studded Pork Loin
with Cauliflower Mushrooms and Chanterelles

The pork loin

Peel the garlic, remove the green sprouts, and cut lengthwise into 4 to 6 slices, depending on their size. Blanch in cold water and continue to boil for 2 minutes. Repeat this blanching process two more times.

With the point of a knife, make several slits in the sides of the loin. Stud the meat with the anchovies, the silvers of garlic, and sage leaves. Brush the loin with olive oil and season with salt and pepper. Rub with a little thyme. The surface of the meat should be well covered with a coating.

Cooking the loin

Preheat the oven to 250°F (120°C). Brown the loin on all sides over high heat and remove from pan. In the same pan, brown the pork trimmings and bones. Add the onion and carrot. Transfer to a heavy casserole braiser.

Add the bouquet garni, 2 crushed cloves of garlic and the juniper berries. Add the pork loin, a glass of water, and the pork jus. Roast about 1 hour, basting frequently. The temperature at the center of the meat should be at least 150°F (68°C).

The cabbage

Remove the outer cabbage leaves, cut in quarters, and cut out the center rib. Julienne the cabbage into 1 in. (2.5 cm) strips. Bring a large pan of salted water to a boil and add the cabbage. Blanch, refresh in cold water, drain, and set aside. Clean the mushrooms. Blanch the chanterelles in boiling water for 30 seconds. Refresh, drain, and dry.

The sauce

Remove the pork loin from the oven and wrap the meat in aluminum foil. Keep warm. Skim the fat from the cooking juices in the casserole. Pass the juices through a fine china cap, pressing well, to obtain ¾ cup (18 cl) of sauce. Reduce if necessary. Keep warm.

Presentation

Heat 2 tbsp. of butter in a sauté pan. Brown the blanched cabbage for 3 to 4 minutes, stirring with a fork. In a separate pan, sauté the cauliflower mushrooms and the chanterelles in 2 tbsp. of butter. Stir the mushrooms into the cabbage. Season with salt, pepper, and a pinch of cumin. Adjust the seasoning. Slice the pork loin into thick slices. Arrange the cabbage and mushroom garnish around the slices. Whisk the anchovy butter into the sauce and serve in a sauceboat.

Meat 🌲🌲
The preparation of this dish is a delicate process.
Serves 4

Ingredients
Pork loin and sauce
6 cloves of garlic
2¼ lbs. (1 to 1.2 kg) pork loin, ribs removed (reserve trimmings)
10 anchovies in oil
10 leaves of fresh sage
4 tbsp. (6 cl) olive oil
1 small bunch of fresh thyme
½ cup (12 cl) pork jus (pg. 290)
1 medium-sized onion, thinly sliced
1 large carrot, thinly sliced
1 small bouquet garni
2 cloves of garlic, crushed
10 juniper berries
Anchovy butter: 1½ tbsp. (20 g) butter, 2 crushed anchovy fillets, ½ clove of garlic

Garnish
4 tbsp. (60 g) butter
1 small curly savoy green cabbage
7 oz. (200 g) cauliflower mushrooms
7 oz. (200 g) black chanterelles

Salt, pepper, and ground cumin

The cauliflower mushroom grows in mountain pine forests in summer and autumn. It is an edible mushroom, much loved for its hazelnut flavor. It is best to eat them young as they become tough later. The black chanterelle, otherwise known as the "black trumpet," "trumpet-of-death" or "horn of plenty," has a slightly bitter flavor and a mild aroma reminiscent of mirabelles.

Père Montchal's Woodcock Pâté Toasts

Meat 🌲
You will need a meat grinder
with a fine blade. This recipe
is dedicated to the memory
of Monsieur Montchal.
Serves 4

Ingredients
1 woodcock
4 tbsp. (6 cl) olive oil
3 oz. (80 g) fatback
1 gray shallot, quartered
2 to 3 sprigs of fresh thyme
4 cloves of garlic, unpeeled
and crushed
6 tbsp. (8 cl) Armagnac
6 tbsp. (80 g) butter
4 juniper berries
1½ oz. (40 g) foie gras (optional)

Garnish
rye bread, garlic, and hazelnut oil

It is against the law to serve woodcock in restaurants in France. Hunting the bird is permitted, however. If you have a friend who is a keen hunter, ask him about the sport and the fascinating relationship between dog, hunter, and prey. With this recipe, I wanted to pay homage to the late Monsieur Montchal, a friend from Lyons who would often visit the house. Every autumn, he would prepare woodcock in his own special way.

The woodcock

On returning from the hunt, hang the woodcock by its feet at room temperature and let it mature, although it should not become gamy.

Each day, check the odor of the bird beneath its wing. After 3 to 4 days, depending on the bird and the room temperature, you should notice a difference. Now the woodcock has gained flavor and is ready to be cooked. If you are not going to prepare it immediately, wrap and freeze it.

Carefully pluck the woodcock, starting with the tail. Remove all the feathers (if you are a hunter, you will want to keep the "painter's quill"). Clip the ends of the claws and remove the eyes, crop, and gizzard. Leave the white, fatty intestines—they are edible and very tasty because the woodcock expels its excrement before flight. Singe the bird with a direct flame.

Preheat the oven to 400°F (200°C).

Heat the olive oil in a small casserole. Brown the bird on all sides. Remove and season with salt and pepper. Bard the woodcock with the fatback and tie carefully.

Return the woodcock to the casserole. Add the shallot, thyme, and garlic. Add 2 tbsp. of butter and the juniper berries. Roast 12 to 15 minutes, basting and turning every 5 minutes.

Remove from the oven and flambé with the Armagnac. Cut the string, peel the garlic, and remove the thyme.

Quarter the bird. In a meat grinder with a fine blade, grind the bird, including the bones but not the beak. Add the remaining butter and the foie gras if desired. Mix to form a smooth and even pâté. Adjust the seasoning, adding a little extra pepper if necessary.

Presentation

Toast several slices of rye bread. Rub lightly with garlic and drizzle with hazelnut oil.

Spread each slice with the woodcock pâté and serve.

Spiced Figs in Flaky Pastry Square

Dessert
Serves 8

Ingredients
Flaky pastry
10 oz. (300 g) flaky puff pastry
(pg. 296)

Fig marmalade
½ tsp. fennel seeds
½ tsp. cumin
¼ tsp. pepper
½ tsp. cinnamon
Pinch of sugar
1 lb. 5 oz. (600 g) fresh purple figs
5 oz. (150 g) dried figs

Garnish
8 fresh figs
6 tbsp. (80 g) semi-salted butter
¼ cup (60 g) brown sugar

For this recipe, I use violet figs, which, in my opinion, are the most flavorful.

The fig marmalade

Grind the spices, sift through a metal sieve, and add the sugar. Peel the fresh figs and chop the dry ones.

Place the figs in a heavy saucepan and sprinkle with the spiced sugar. Simmer over low heat to create a marmalade. Stir frequently to keep the figs from sticking to the bottom of the pan. Transfer into a bowl.

The flaky pastry

Preheat the oven to 400°F (200°C). Remove the flaky puff pastry dough from the refrigerator. On a lightly floured work surface, roll into a 6 in. (15 cm) square by ⅛ in. (3 mm) thick. Place on a baking sheet and refrigerate for 15 minutes to relax the dough.

Remove from the refrigerator, prick with a fork, and spread with the fig marmalade.

Halve the fresh figs lengthwise and arrange decoratively on top of the marmalade.

Presentation

Cut the butter into 16 small cubes. Place a cube in the center of each fig. Sprinkle with brown sugar. Place the baking sheet in the oven. After 15 minutes, reduce the heat to 300°F (150°C). Cook about 40 minutes.

Serve with fennel ice cream.

Apple Pompe, Auvergne Style

Dessert 🌲
Serves 10

Ingredients
2 lbs. 2 oz. (1 kg) Granny Smith
apples
3 lb. 5 oz. (1.5 kg) Reine de
Reinette apples (substitute
macintosh or empire)
Lemon juice
7 tbsp. (90 g) butter
1/2 cup sugar
Apple eau-de-vie
3 vanilla bean pods, split
and seeds scraped
1 stick of cinnamo
1¼ lbs. (500 g) flaky puff pastry
(pg. 296)
1/2 cup (150 g) apricot marmalade
1 egg
1 egg yolk
4 tsp. (2 cl) cream

This apple cake is called a pompe
("pump") because it swells during
cooking. I used to bake this cake
every year when the Monte-Carlo
rally passed through Saint-
Bonnet. Vatanen, Saby, Biason,
Icks—and other great rally
drivers—loved this dessert, which I
served with vanilla ice cream. This
is my own version of a traditional
Auvergne recipe. The original
recipe uses lard instead of butter.

The apple filling

Peel, halve, core and seed the apples, then toss with lemon juice.

Cut the Granny Smiths in half again. Heat 3 tbsp. of butter in a pan and, when it foams, add the Granny Smith wedges. Brown on each side. Add ¼ cup (50g) of sugar. Make sure the apples do not disintegrate. Flambé with eau-de-vie, then refrigerate.

Cut the *Reine de Reinette* apples into large dice. Heat 3 tbsp. of butter in a sauté pan. Add the apples, ¼ cup of sugar, the vanilla, and cinnamon. Cook, uncovered, and stew the apples into a pulp to make an applesauce. Reduce slowly over low heat to dry. Add the 1 tbsp. of butter, transfer to a bowl, and refrigerate.

The pompe

Preheat the oven to 400°F (200°C). Divide the flaky pastry dough into 2 parts. Roll out the dough into a 12 in. (32 cm) square and a 13 in. (34 cm) square.

Lay the small square on a baking sheet. Spread apricot marmalade on the surface of the dough, to within 1 in. (2 cm) of the edges. Cover with the stewed apples and layer the Granny Smith wedges on top.

Presentation

Brush the edges of the dough with an egg wash. Place the large square of dough over the apple filling.

Press the edges well to so that the filling does not seep out during cooking.

Brush the top of the cake with an egg wash. Bake 15 minutes at 400°F (200°C), then at 350°F (180°C) for 45 minutes. Beat the egg yolk and cream, toward the end of the cooking, brush onto the cake.

Remove from oven. Allow to cool on a dollie and serve warm.

Chanterelles Steeped in Peach Liqueur

lean the mushrooms thoroughly.
Boil the vermouth in a saucepan. Add the mushrooms and spices. Simmer for 4 minutes. Pass through a fine china cap and remove the spices. Cool.

Presentation

Put the mushrooms into a bowl and add the peach liqueur and plum eau-de-vie. Cover and refrigerate. You may conserve them for 3 to 4 months. Serve after coffee, as you would cherries steeped in eau-de-vie.

This dessert is served after coffee, just as one would serve raspberries and cherries steeped in eau-de-vie. It is one way to tell your guests that the party is by no means over. In this recipe, I substitute mushrooms for the fruit—and the results is surprising. Prepare this liqueur only if you have small, firm chanterelles that are not too plump.

Dessert 🌲
This recipe may be made with small common chanterelles.
Serves 10

Ingredients
3 cups (75 cl) Vermouth
1 lb. 2 oz. (500 g) common chanterelles (small and firm as possible)
¼ stick of cinnamon
2 cloves
2 star anise
1 vanilla bean pod
3 cups (75 cl) peach liqueur
1 cup (25 cl) plum eau-de-vie

Jean-Baptiste Prades has learned a thing or two about squash. He shares his incredible knowledge of the subject with enthusiasm and eloquence—as in his book, *Grand Livre des Courage* (*Big Book of Squash*), co-written with his wife, Nicole, and Victor Renaud and published by Rustica. Jean-Baptiste helped Régis Marcon delve into a new inexhaustible encyclopedia of flavors. Some extremely flavorful varieties, such as white Horn of Plenty, may be grated, and prepared like celery. Others, like Winter Luxury, are delicious enough to be included in desserts. Since he has met Jean-Baptiste and Nicole Prades, Régis has produced more squash recipes than he could ever have imagined—gnocchi, crêpes, and more. The tireless couple also cultivates a hundred or so varieties of tomato and has already drawn Régis's attention to the incredible diversity of the fruit—we may soon see changes in the menu at the Auberge!

It all began at an evening meal with the Prades in Saint-Bonnet, six years ago. Dinner was a great success, and Jean-Baptiste praised Régis's artistry ("Finally," exclaimed the former teacher of applied sciences, "a cuisine with a soul!"). Régis, for his part, was delighted by the curiosity that his friends, who lived on the other side of the region, had delivered to his door. The fact is, enthusiasm for squash must be contagious, because the conversation returned to it, time and again, opening up new culinary perspectives. Not only does the versatile cucurbit inspire the masks of Halloween (the Jack O'Lantern), it can inspire every moment of a meal as well.

Porcini Mushroom Pâté en Croute

Appetizer 🌲 🌲
Begin 2 days in advance.
Serves 10

Ingredients
10 oz. (300 g) veal top round
1 tsp. of ground cumin
1½ cups (35 cl) crème fraîche
1 tbsp. mushroom powder (pg. 293)
12 porcini, each about
2 in. (5 cm) diameter
4 oz. (120 g) chanterelles
4 oz. (120 g) black chanterelle or
black trumpet mushrooms
4 tbsp. (6 cl) olive oil
1 clove of garlic
1 sprig of thyme
3 egg yolks
6 tbsp. (80 g) butter, creamed
1¼ lbs. (500 g) flaky puff pastry
(pg. 296)
1 tbsp. chopped flat leaf parsley
8 tarragon leaves, chopped

Salt and pepper

*To make this recipe you must use
a cast-iron or metal mold. The
results with porcelain or glass
molds are disappointing because
the pastry does not brown.
This is a good recipe to serve
to a large group of guests. Slice
the pâté into slices at least ½ in.
(12.5 cm) thick with a serrated
knife. This can be served with
a salad of porcini or other
mushrooms and can be kept warm
on top of your stove. You may also
serve it with a mushroom sauce.*

The mousseline filling

Remove the nerves from the veal and cut the meat into small cubes. Season lightly with salt and pepper and sprinkle with ground cumin. Refrigerate.

Boil the crème fraîche and mushroom powder. Remove from heat and refrigerate. Clean all the mushrooms.

Heat the olive oil in a pan. Sear the chanterelles and porcini with the garlic and thyme. Refrigerate. Next sear the black chanterelle mushrooms, season with salt and cook covered, 2 to 3 minutes. Drain and refrigerate.

Place the cubed veal in the chilled bowl of a food processor. You will have good results if the meat is very cold when you begin. Purée to a smooth paste. Gradually add the mushroom cream and the egg yolks. Finish by adding the creamed butter. Check the seasoning. The mousseline filling should be smooth and glossy. Refrigerate.

The pastry crust

Preheat the oven to 400°F (200°C).

Roll the dough into a rectangle 18 in. (45 cm) long, 10 in. (25 cm) wide and ¼ in. (4 mm) thick. Reserve the remaining dough.

Butter a mold and line it with parchment paper, as you would for a cake. Lay the dough rectangle into the mold allowing it to hang over the edges slightly.

Add the chopped herbs, chanterelles, and black chanterelle mushrooms to the filling. Fill the bottom of the dough lining the terrine with the mixture. Stand the porcini mushrooms in a line in the center of the filling, packing them tightly against each other. Fill the mold with mousseline. Cover the filling by joining the ends of the dough in the center of the mold. Brush with an egg wash. Cover the upper surface of the pâté with another rectangle of dough and brush again with an egg wash.

To create a decoration, score the surface of the pastry with the back of a knife. Make 3 small incisions to let steam escape while baking.

Bake 10 minutes at 400°F (200°C). Then reduce heat to 350°F (180°C), and bake another 30 to 35 minutes. Let cool and rest 1 day before serving.

Presentation

Remove from the mold and slice with a serrated knife.

Hare Terrine with Prunes

Appetizer 🌲 🌲

Begin 2 days in advance. May also be made with other game, such as venison and wild duck
Serves 12

Ingredients
Hare marinade
Zest of 1 orange
2¼ lbs. (900 g) pork jowl,
half fat, half lean
14 oz. (400 g) hare meat, from a
6½ lb. (3 kg) hare with nerves
removed (from thigh and shoulder)
8 juniper berries, crushed
6 tbsp. (8 cl) Auvergne marc
(substitute cognac or armagnac)
14 oz. (400 g) saddle of hare
1 tbsp. butter
1 cup (20 cl) cup venison sauce
(pg. 292)

Seasoning
1 tbsp. sugar
2 tbsp. (30 g) salt
1 tsp. ground pepper
1 tsp. of quatre epice
(French 4-spice)

Filling and terrine
5 oz. (150 g) dried prunes, pitted
1 tea bag
7 oz. (200 g) chicken liver and
juniper mousse (page 40)
6 to 8 thin slices of fatback

I use pork jowl in this recipe because its fat does not melt as much during cooking. This terrine may also be made with mallard, venison, or wild boar. The terrine should be baked gently so that it is soft. This dish is best eaten a week after cooking.

The hare marinade

One day in advance soak the prunes in hot tea. Blanch and drain the orange zest. Julienne the zest, dice finely and set aside. Remove the bones from the thigh and shoulder of the hare. Cut the pork jowl and hare into strips. Mix the orange zest, juniper berries, seasoning ingredients, and marc, pour over the meat to marinate. Cover with plastic wrap and refrigerate at least 12 hours.

The following day remove the bones from the saddle of hare. Remove the hare fillets and cut off the silver skin.

Heat the butter in a pan and brown the fillets. Season with salt and pepper. Skim the fat from the pan and remove the fillets. Add ½ cup (2 cl) of the venison sauce and reduce until the sauce coats the back of a spoon. Remove from heat. Place the fillets back into the pan, coating them with sauce. Set aside.

The filling and terrine

Drain and dry the prunes. Finely chop the marinated meat with a knife or grind in a meat grinder with a medium blade. Mix the meat with the prunes and chicken liver parfait until smooth. Add ½ cup (12 cl) of venison gravy.

Line the bottom and sides of the terrine with fatback strips.

Fill half the terrine with the forcemeat. Place the hare fillets on top, then finish filling the terrine with the forcemeat. Press the contents.

Leave the terrine at room temperature for several hours. The color will change.

Cooking the terrine

Preheat the oven to 250°F (120°C).

Place the terrine in a baking dish and half fill the dish with hot water. Bake at 250°F (120°C) 1½ hours. The temperature at the center of the terrine should be 150°F (65°C) when done.

Presentation

When finished cooking, remove the terrine from the oven. Lay a plastic wrapped board on top to pack it down and let cool at room temperature about 1 hour. Refrigerate.

If you cover the entire surface with hot fat, the terrine will be protected from the air and will keep longer.

Sea Bass with Chestnut Scales
and Vanilla Fish Sauce

The sea bass

Cut the fillet into 4 slices.

In a food processor mix 4 tbsp. (50 g) of the creamed butter 1 oz (30 g) of the bread and 2 oz. (60 g) of chestnuts to form a smooth paste.

Brush the skin side of the fish with egg yolk. Spread a thin layer, about ¹⁄₁₆ in. (2 mm), of the chestnut paste on top.

Thinly slice the chestnuts—again about ¹⁄₁₆ in. (2 mm) thick—and arrange them decoratively on each fillet in a scale pattern. Sprinkle with the remaining bread crumbs and dot with small cubes of butter. Set aside.

Reserve the remaining chestnuts for serving.

The chestnut purée

Cook the chestnuts in milk with a split vanilla bean pod. Drain and purée in a food processor. Add the butter, salt, pepper, and rum.

The vanilla fish sauce

Very lightly caramelize the sugar in a saucepan. Deglaze with balsamic vinegar and add the fish jus. Scrape the seeds from the split vanilla bean pod, add them to the sauce. Boil and let the flavors infuse several minutes. Pass through a fine china cap.

In another saucepan heat 1 tbsp. of butter until nut brown. Add to the strained sauce.

Cooking the sea bass

Preheat the oven to 325°F (160°C). Butter the bottom of a heavy baking dish. Arrange the fillets and bake about 15 minutes.

To check for doneness, prick the center of each fillet with a knife. The blade should be hot when withdrawn.

Place the dish under a hot broiler for a short time to brown the chestnuts and bread crumbs.

Presentation

Brown the reserved chestnuts in a pan. Drain the fillets and arrange in the center of a serving dish.

Place the chestnut purée alongside the fish with several roasted chestnuts. Pour the vanilla fish sauce around the fish and purée.

Fish 🌲 🌲
Serves 4

Ingredients
Sea bass
1½ lbs. (about 600 to 700 g) thick fillet of sea bass, without skin
6 tbsp. (80 g) butter, creamed
1½ oz. (50 g) soft white bread, without crusts
7 oz. (200 g) chestnuts
1 egg yolk

Chestnut purée
7 oz. (200 g) chestnuts
1 cup (¼ liter) milk
1 vanilla bean pod
2 tbsp. (30 g) butter
4 tsp. (2 cl) rum

Vanilla fish sauce
1 tbsp. (20 g) superfine sugar
4 tbsp. (6 cl) balsamic vinegar
¾ cup (20 cl) fish jus (pg. 291)
1 vanilla bean pod
3 tbsp. (40 g) butter

Salt and pepper

Peeling chestnuts is a process that requires patience, as you have to remove the shell and the brown skin.

To make it easier, nick the edges with a knife, boil in small quantities, and peel the chestnuts while they are still very hot.

Grilled Scallop and Porcini Rosemary Brochettes
with Potato Peanut Mousseline

Fish 🌲
The recipe may also be served with a plain potato purée with butter.
Serves 4

Ingredients
Brochette
12 plump scallops
4 branches of rosemary
12 porcini
½ cup (12 cl) peanut oil

Potato peanut mousseline
4 oz. (120 g) roasted peanuts, chopped
6 tbsp. (8 cl) peanut oil
4 tbsp. (6 cl) vinegar balsamic
6 tbsp. (8 cl) crème fraîche
10 oz. (300 g) potato purée
1 tbsp. butter

Salt and pepper

The scallop inhabits Atlantic and Mediterranean waters, particularly on the European side, and is abundant along French and Spanish coastlines. In France, the scallop is known as the coquille Saint-Jacques. *In the Middle Ages, the pilgrims that traveled along the Saint Jacques de Compostelle, a popular pilgrimage route, used scallop shells to eat or beg with. The shells became the symbol of the route.*

The scallops
Clean and rinse the scallops thoroughly in cold water. Drain and dry on a cloth.

Brush the porcini, cleaning the stems well. Sharpen the ends of the rosemary branches. Thread porcini and scallops onto them alternately.

Marinate the brochettes in peanut oil. Season with salt and pepper, refrigerate.

Preheat the grill, making sure it is very clean. Toast the chopped peanuts in a pan with peanut oil.

When the grill is very hot, place the brochettes on it, positioning them on the diagonal.

When slightly browned, reposition them on the opposite diagonal — so that they have a crisscross pattern across the surface.

Grill both sides, allowing 3 to 4 minutes for each side. Sprinkle with a few drops of balsamic vinegar.

The potato mousseline
Pour the cream into a small sauté pan, boil and whisk in the potato purée.

Reheat slowly, gradually adding most of the roasted peanuts and 1 tbsp. of butter. Keep warm.

Presentation
Arrange the mousseline in the center of each plate and lay a brochette on top. Drizzle with the remaining peanut oil and peanuts.

Fresh Cod Roulade with Baked Parsnips, Squash, and Squash Fries

Ingredients

1¼ lbs. (600 g) fillet of cod
4 tbsp. (50 g) clarified butter
4 tbsp. (6 cl) olive oil

Baked parsnips and potimarron squash

7 oz. (200 g) potimarron squash
(substitute Hubbard, Butternut, or
Buttercup)
2 parsnips
4 tbsp. (60 g) butter
1 large onion, finely sliced
1 sprig of fresh thyme
1 clove of garlic, chopped
1 cup (25 cl) chicken stock (pg. 290)

Potimarron squash purée

5 oz. (150 g) potimarron squash
(substitute as above)
2 tbsp. (30 g) butter

Butternut squash fries

9 oz. (250 g) piece of
butternut squash
4 cups (1 l) peanut oil

Red wine sauce

1 cup (25 cl) red Bordeaux wine
2 shallots, minced
2 tbsp. crème de cassis
½ cup (12 cl) veal jus (pg. 292)
3 tbsp. (40 g) butter

Salt, pepper, and nutmeg

The baked parsnips and potimarron squash

Preheat the oven to 350°F (180°C)

Peel the potimarron squash. Peel and wash the parsnips. Cut these vegetables into ⅛ in. (4 mm) thick slices. Heat the 2 tbsp. of butter in a sauté pan and lightly color the onion 5 minutes with a pinch of salt, thyme, and the garlic. In a buttered gratin dish, spread a layer of potimarron squash, next a layer of the cooked onions, and a layer of parsnips. Repeat, seasoning with salt and pepper between each layer.

Half-fill the dish with the chicken stock and down with 2 tbsp. of butter. Cover with buttered parchment paper and bake about 35 minutes.

The potimarron squash purée

Without removing the skin, quarter and steam the potimarron squash. Remove the flesh and press through a food mill. Season with salt, pepper, grated nutmeg and butter.

The butternut squash fries

Peel the butternut squash. The flesh is fairly firm. Cut several French fry sticks 2 in. (5 cm) long and ¼ in. (½ cm) wide. Wipe and set aside. Heat the peanut oil in a deep saucepan.

The red wine sauce

Boil the red wine and shallots over gentle heat to reduce by three quarters. Add the *crème de cassis* and veal jus. Whisk in a bit of the potimarron squash purée to lighten the texture, if necessary. Keep warm.

The cod

Cut the cod into 1¼ in. (3 cm) wide pieces. Roll and tie with string. Heat the clarified butter and oil in a pan and sear the fish. Brown each side, basting with the cooking butter.

208

Presentation

When the peanut oil is hot, fry the butternut squash sticks until golden. Drain on paper towels. Whisk cubes of butter and some salt and pepper into the sauce. Check the seasoning.

Place some of the baked vegetables in the center of each plate. Fill a pastry bag (with a fine tip) with the potimarron squash purée and pipe a ring around the inner edge of the plate. Drain the cod roulades and place on the baked vegetables. Fill the area between the fish and the purée ring with sauce. Crown the fish with butternut fries.

Nicole and Jean-Baptiste Prades helped me discover the world of squash.

In this recipe, I wanted to combine several squash varieties.

Roasted John Dory Fillet with an Anchovy, Black Olive, and Acorn Squash Sauce

Fish
Serves 4

Ingredients
4 lbs. (1.8 kg) John Dory fillet
4 tbsp. (6 cl) olive oil
2 tbsp. (30 g) clarified butter

Acorn squash sauce
1 acorn squash
Juice of 1 orange
2 anchovy fillets in oil
6 black olives
Juice of ½ lemon
2 tbsp. (30 g) butter

Spinach
3 tbsp. (40 g) butter
2 lbs. 2 oz. (1 kg) spinach
1 clove of garlic
Zest of 1 orange

Salt and pepper

This recipe features another variety of squash, an acorn squash called Cream of the Crop. The acorn squashes are so-called simply because they resemble acorns. The flesh is very juicy with a slight hazelnut flavor. The juice itself is not as sweet, so I've added a little orange juice. The overall flavor is enhanced by the anchovies, olives, and lemon juice.

The acorn squash sauce

Peel the acorn squash. Cut it into large cubes and place in a juicer to extract 1 cup (25 cl) of juice. Heat the squash juice and orange juice in a saucepan and reduce by three-quarters. Keep warm.

Drain and finely chop the anchovies. Pit and finely chop the olives. Place the anchovies and olives in a bowl and set aside.

The sautéed spinach

Heat the butter in a pan and add the spinach leaves. Stir constantly with a fork that you have skewered a clove of garlic with. Lightly season with salt and pepper. Add the orange zest and finish cooking the spinach.

Remove from heat and drain on paper towels.

The John Dory

Fillet the John Dory and cut into four portions. Heat a pan over high heat and add the clarified butter and olive oil. Carefully place the fillets in the pan. Season with salt and pepper. Brown both sides, turning with a spatula and basting with the cooking juices. Check for doneness by pricking the fish with a knife, but don't be fooled. John Dory flesh is always very firm.

Presentation

Whisk 2 tbsp. (30 g) of butter into the sauce, then add the diced anchovies and olives.

Check the seasoning, adding several drops of lemon juice if necessary. Arrange the spinach in the center of each plate and place a fillet on top. Pour the squash sauce around the fish.

Hare with Cardinal Chestnut Purée, Prepared Two Ways

Meat
Serves 8

Ingredients
Hare
Zest of 1 orange
15 shallots
10 cloves of garlic
6 cups (1,5 l) red Syrah wine
6½ lbs. (2,8 to 3 kg) hare, skinned
(with liver, heart, and blood)
Garden thyme and wild thyme
1 lb. 2 oz. (500 g) fatback strips,
for barding
8 juniper berries
1 bouquet garni
4 tbsp. (6 cl) olive oil
6 tbsp. (8 cl) Armagnac
12 pieces slab smoked bacon
2 tbsp. (60 g) butter

Cardinal purée and vegetables
14 oz. (400 g) red beets
2 medium-sized onions
3 tbsp. (30 g) butter
1 tbsp. (20 g) brown sugar
Orange flower water
8 brussels sprouts
3 Reine de Reinette apples
(substitute macintosh or empire)
24 pre-cooked chestnuts

Sauce (for presentation)
½ cup (12 cl) cream
1 tbsp. mustard
½ tbsp. red currant jelly

Salt and pepper

The hare
One day in advance, blanch the orange zests in cold water and set aside. Peel the shallots and garlic cloves, removing the green sprouts.

Boil the wine in a saucepan and flambé.

Set aside the saddle and cut the rest of the hare into pieces. Season with salt, pepper, and thyme. Carefully roll each piece with wild thyme and a strip of fatback. Tie securely.

Quarter 12 shallots. Line the bottom of a casserole with the shallots and 8 cloves of the garlic. Add the orange zest, juniper berries, and bouquet garni. Brown in olive oil over high heat 5 to 6 minutes.

Brown the pieces of hare, basting with the pan juices, and then flambé with the Armagnac.

Add enough flambéed red wine to just cover the pan contents. Lightly salt, bring to a boil and cover. Bake 10 hours at 250°F (120°C).

Meanwhile mix the liver, heart, kidney, remaining shallots and garlic in a food processor. Refrigerate.

The cardinal purée and vegetables
Peel and finely slice the beets and onions. Brown the vegetables in 1 tbsp. of butter in a heavy saucepan. Season with salt, pepper and the brown sugar. Moisten with a little water and roast in the oven about 1 hour.

Pass the cooked vegetables in a food mill to make a fine purée. Add several drops of orange flower water and keep warm.

The brussels sprouts
Peel the leaves from the brussels sprouts. Drop them into a pan of boiling salted water to cook, but do not let them lose their color. Refresh in cold water and set aside.

Peel the apples and cut into large wedges. Sauté in a pan with the 2 tbsp. of butter. Set aside.

The saddle of hare

Prepare the 2 saddle fillets, remove the silver skin and nerves. Cut the fillets into 24 noisettes and flatten slightly.

Roll each noisette in half a slice of smoked bacon. Skewer with a wooden toothpick to hold the bacon in place.

The hare

After 10 hours of cooking, remove the hare from the oven. Trim away the fat and bones and shred the cooked meat with a fork.

Keep warm in a covered casserole.

Pass the cooking juices through a fine china cap, pressing well to release all the flavors.

Pour this gravy into a large, shallow dish. Refrigerate so that the fat separates and solidifies, making it easier to remove.

Pour the skimmed juices into a deep, heavy saucepan. Whisking constantly, add the liver, heart, and kidney mixture. Bring to a boil, then quickly reduce heat and simmer about 45 minutes. Scrape the bottom of the pan frequently to prevent the sauce from sticking.

Pass through a fine china cap and then reduce the sauce, skimming the surface from time to time. Keep warm.

The sauce

Mix a little hare's blood with the cream, mustard, and red currant jelly. Stir into the sauce. Cook for 5 minutes and then pass through a fine china cap lined with cheesecloth. Keep warm, but do not boil.

Reheat the shredded meat, adding a little sauce. Season to taste with salt and pepper.

Heat 1 tbsp. of butter in a pan over high heat. Brown the noisettes on one side, season with salt and pepper, turn. Cook medium rare, or according to your taste.

Reheat the brussels sprouts in a pan in a tbsp. of butter. Cut the chestnuts in half and toss in a hot pan.

Presentation

Place noisettes on each plate. Add a quenelle of cardinal purée and arrange the chestnuts, apples, and brussels sprouts to add a little color to the dish.

Set a soup spoon of stewed hare on one side of the plate. Pour sauce over the noisettes.

This is a variation on the legendary dish "lievre a la cuiller" hare braised for 24 hours and so tender that it can be eaten with a spoon.

The flavors of the two cooking methods, for the pan-fried noisettes and the shoulder and thighs—complement each other well.

213

Spaghetti Squash
Spaghetti "for the Kids"

Vegetable
Serves 4

Ingredients
1 spaghetti squash
4 tbsp. (6 cl) olive oil
8 oz. (230 g) fresh spaghetti
4 to 6 tbsp. (60 to 80 g) butter

Salt

This was one way to make my son, Paul eat his vegetables. I added pasta to the vegetables, and he was turning his ears to suck in all the spaghetti.

Heat the food steamer.
Cut the spaghetti squash in half and steam until cooked.
With a fork, pull out from the vegetable all the spaghetti-shaped strands. Set aside.

Boil a pot of salted water, adding several drops of olive oil.
Add the fresh pasta and stir with a fork. Cook until *al dente*. Drain immediately.
Mix the pasta and the spaghetti squash strands in a sauté pan. Add the butter and heat.

Warm Chocolate Macaroons with Pistachio Cream and Gentian Caramel

The pistachio mousseline

Boil the milk in a saucepan and stir in the pistachio paste. Whisk the egg yolks and sugar until light and creamy, then add the flour. Add the boiling milk and stir. Return the mixture to the saucepan and bring back to a boil, whisking constantly to form a thick pastry cream. Transfer to a food processor, with motor running gradually add the butter, until the custard is smooth and glossy.

The gentian caramel

Caramelize the sugar in a saucepan and deglaze with the gentian liqueur.

The macaroons

Melt the chocolate and butter in a double boiler. Whisk the egg whites into stiff peaks, gradually adding the sugar in thirds. Mix the yolks and cornstarch into chocolate. Fold in the egg whites. Fill a pastry bag with a ½ in. (1 cm) tip and pipe the macaroon batter onto a buttered baking sheet. Freeze.

Preheat the oven to 350°F (180°C).

Presentation

About 10 minutes before serving, bake the macaroons 5 to 6 minutes. When they are ready (they should still be soft in the center), remove from the oven and gently lift the cookies off the tray with a spatula.

Put a little pistachio mousseline on the center of each plate and place a macaroon on top. Pipe a little more mousseline onto the macaroon and cover with another cookie.

Pour a generous amount of gentian caramel around the plate.

Dessert

Serves 4

Ingredients

Pistachio mousseline
2 cups (50 cl) whole milk
2 tbsp. (30 g) pistachio paste
8 egg yolks
7 tbsp. (80 g) sugar
⅓ cup (50 g) flour
14 tbsp. (200 g) butter

Gentian caramel
4 tbsp. (50 g) sugar
½ cup (12 cl) gentian liqueur

Macaroons
7 oz. (200 g) bittersweet chocolate
4 tbsp. (60 g) butter
6 egg whites
⅓ cup (70 g) superfine sugar
2 egg yolks
1 tsp. cornstarch

The roots of the gentian plant are used to make a slightly bitter liqueur and also to flavor pastries. In the Auvergne mountains, the plant is uprooted in mid-August and the roots alone may weigh as much as 22 lbs. (10 kg). They are washed, dried, and cut into small chips before being distilled into alcohol or liqueur.

I prefer fresh rather than dried roots because they are fruitier and exude the aroma of fresh citrus.

Winter Luxury Squash Crêpes

Dessert 🌲

This recipe may be prepared with other squash varieties, too.

Serves 12

Ingredients
Crêpe batter
4½ oz. (125 g) squash purée, cooked
4 eggs
¼ cup (40 g) flour
3 tbsp. (30 g) sugar
pinch of salt
2 tbsp. (30 g) butter melted
1 cup (25 cl) milk

Filling
4 oranges
1 lb. 2 oz (500 g) Winter Luxury squash
3 tbsp. (45 g) butter
½ cup (100 g) sugar
3½ oz. (100 g) prunes diced
3½ oz. (100 g) dried apricots, diced
Zest of 2 oranges, blanched
1 tsp. candied ginger
7 oz. (200 g) pastry cream (pg. 297)

Suzette sauce
4 tbsp. (50 g) butter
1 cup squash juice, reduced by ¼
1 cup orange juice, reduced by ¼
Zest of 2 lemons
4 tbsp. (6 cl) Grand Marnier

See pages 282 and 283 for step-by-step photos.

The crêpes
Mix the squash purée, eggs, flour, sugar, and salt in a bowl. Add the melted butter and the milk. Let rest for 1 hour.

The filling
With a knife, peel the oranges from top to bottom, removing the skin and the white membrane. Separate the segments.

Dice the squash. Lightly brown the cubes in butter. Add the sugar and caramelize for several minutes. Add the prunes, apricots, orange zest and candied ginger.

Mix in pastry cream.

Stuff the crêpes, wrapping them to form small parcels.

Presentation
Arrange the crêpes in a buttered gratin dish. Place in heated 300°F (150°C) oven for 10 minutes.

Add the reduced juices and lemon zest, reduce by half. Arrange the orange segments around the crepes.

Heat the Grand Marnier and flambé the crêpes.

Winter Luxury is a variety of squash that comes from Mexico and the southeastern United States. The skin is orange and has intricate patterns. The flesh is firm enough for this crepe recipe. This squash works very well in desserts, it has a fruity flavor and is not at all bitter.

Potato and Porcini Mushroom Gratin

1. One day in advance
Soak 4 oz. (120 g) of dry porcini mushrooms in 3 times their volume of tepid water.

2. The following day
Drain the mushrooms and boil the soaking liquid to reduce by three-quarters. Add ½ cup (120 g) of milk and 1 cup (250 g) heavy cream. Add 1 chopped garlic clove and 1 sprig of thyme. Season with salt, pepper, and some grated nutmeg.

3. The porcini mushrooms
Coarsely chop the porcini mushrooms.

Sweat 2 finely chopped shallots in 2 tbsp. (30 g) of butter. Add the mushrooms and brown the contents of the pan.

4. The gratin

Cut 3 lbs. 5 oz. (1,5 kg) of potatoes (preferably, the Bintje variety) into slices about ⅛ in. (3 mm) thick. Arrange a layer of potato slices in a buttered gratin dish. Add a layer of porcini and cover with another layer of potatoes. Salt lightly.

5.

Pass the mushroom cream sauce through a fine china cap onto the top layer of potatoes. Season with salt, pepper and a dash of nutmeg.

6. Presentation

Bake at 325°F (160°C) for 40 to 50 minutes, depending on the potatoes.

Remove from the oven and serve hot.

Winter

Grains

In many regions of the world, grains play an important part in each meal. Wheat, corn, rice, and lentils are the world's most harvested grains and legumes and take the place of animal proteins in regions where livestock is scarce.

Of the more than 8,000 varieties of grain, only a small number are actually used for cooking, and most have a fine, hard husk that needs to be removed. Grains have three distinctive sections: the bran (a protective fiber-rich layer); the germ (an embryo); and the protein-rich tissue around the germ that nourishes the plant.

To have the best flavor, grains should be as fresh as possible. Rinse them well in running water to remove all dust and dirt. Preferably, you should select whole organic grains that are free of pesticides and chemicals.

"The supermarkets in France," says Robert Celle, "often have aggressive names—*Atac, Géant* ("Giant"), *Mammouth* ("Mammoth"), and *Mousquétiares* ("Muske-teers"). "We like to think we have a gentler approach toward our clientele." The logo of his company, Celnat, with its sun beaming down on furrowed Earth, reflects this approach. The company has had great success specializing in organic grains, legumes, and seaweed—including "wakame" imported from Brittany and Japan.

Celnat's location is perfect—Saint-Germain-Laprade in the Haut Loire, the region with the highest average altitude in France. The work reaches nearly the same heights as the mountain plateaus themselves. The rice must be hulled, the organic credentials continually checked through sampling and soil analysis, the products sold to restaurateurs, the consumers enlightened about the nutritional and economic values of vegetable protein, and new innovations tested (such as the quick cooking method of steaming sliced, mixed grains and then toasting them in the oven). All in a day's work for Robert Celle, who sings songs of praise to the glorious barley, rye, spelt, and quinoa. Such enthusiasm strikes a natural chord with Régis Marcon, who has had an interest in grains for over 20 years.

Five Ways to Prepare Grains

How are grains cooked?

Simmering in water

Grains are cooked in two, three, even four times their own volume in boiling salted water or stock. The quantity of water varies with the type of grain. If the grain is cracked, add less water.

Slowly pour the grains into the liquid, so as not to stop the boiling too quickly. Add a little oil to the water to keep it from boiling over. Stir occasionally.

Rinse the cooked grains under cold running water.

Steaming

Cook the grains in a food steamer over boiling water until they are al dente. Let rest for 10 minutes before you "fluff with a fork."

The pilaf method

Brown the grains in oil, then add liquid. Cook in the oven or covered over low heat.

As when making risotto, the liquid is added little by little, and stirred constantly. The cooking is done when the grains are swollen and creamy.

Stirring frequently

This method is used to cook polenta and oatmeal. Allow 4 times the volume of liquid—boiling water, milk, or cream. Pour the grains into the boiling liquid and stir constantly, particularly when cooking oatmeal.

Let the grains swell at the end of cooking. To make pudding, sweeten with sugar.

Pre-cooked grains

In this new process (from the Maison Celnat), the grains are thinly cut, steamed, and lightly toasted to heighten their flavor.

These pre-cooked grains are cooked in 15 to 20 minutes. A very interesting product: organic, rich in fiber, and quick to prepare.

Cooking with grains

Grains have a very pleasant taste and are available year-round. They combine well with delicate dishes and all types of spices, herbs, and citrus and dried fruits. They are good accompaniments to meat, fish, and shellfish.

Grains combined with legumes are a completely balanced, nutritious meal.

You can vary your diet with millet, barley, oats, quinoa, wheat, rice, bulgur wheat, corn, and spelt.

Germinated grains and legumes

Germinating grains is an old technique. Even in ancient times, humans knew how to brew beer barley.

You can germinate millet, barley, rye, alfalfa, soy, and even bulgur (a wheat that is already germinated and pre-cooked).

You can also germinate lentils and other legumes.

Why germinate legumes and grains?

Cooking food alters its nutritional content, but we cannot eat raw grains and legumes. Germinating solves the problem.

From the first day of germination, enzymes begin to multiply, in a process similar to pre-digestion. The proteins are broken down into amino acids, and the vitamins increase tenfold. The result is a grain that is much easier to digest.

I eat germinated grains and legumes mixed into green salads, raw and cooked vegetables, potato, pasta and rice dishes.

Caramelized Fennel Tarte Tatin
with Marinated Vegetable Salad

Appetizer 🌲 🌲
You may replace the fennel with endives and the honey with sugar.
Serves 8

Ingredients
Tart
4 bulbs fresh fennel
2 oranges
1 tbsp. of acacia honey
1 tbsp. coriander seeds (or aniseed)
7 tbsp. (100 g) butter
*10 oz. (300 g) flaky
puff pastry dough (pg. 296)*

Salad
2 small artichokes
2 carrots
1 avocado
Juice of ½ lemon
3 tbsp. olive oil

Salt and pepper

This recipe recalls the international Tattinger competition of 1989, where, in the final test, we had to make three garnishes for game. As time was short, I prepared the vegetables and the garnish at the same time, with fennel in flaky pastry.

The tart
Clean, wash, and dry the fennel. Cut lengthwise into ½ in. (1 cm) thick slices. Remove the zest from 1 orange, julienne, and then finely dice. Blanch, drain, and set aside.

Pour the juice from both oranges into an 8 in. (20 cm) nonstick tart pan or cast iron fry pan. Add the zest and honey. Crush the coriander with a rolling pin and cut the butter into cubes. Add to the pan. Season with salt and pepper and boil 1 to 2 minutes to blend.

Arrange the fennel in a star shape pattern in the pan with the tops pointing toward the center. Cover with parchment paper. Simmer gently for 1 hour until the fennel has softened and is covered with the glaze. Add a little water from time to time if necessary.

Remove from heat and let the pan cool.

Roll the pastry dough into a 10 in. (24 cm) circle, ⅛ inch (3 mm) thick. Prick the dough with a fork and cover with plastic wrap. Refrigerate.

When the dough has relaxed, lay it over the fennel in the pan, pressing with your fingers. Trim the excess, leaving 1¼ in. (3 cm) of dough around the edge.

Butter a small round pastry ring mold and place it on top of the tart, pressing gently. The mold will prevent the pastry from shrinking too much. Heat the tart briefly over high heat.

The salad
Pare down the artichokes leaves and cut into slices, toss with lemon juice, and place in cold water. Peel the carrots and avocado. With a mandoline, slice the vegetables into very fine strips. Toss with the lemon juice and olive oil, and season with salt and pepper.

Presentation
Bake the tart for 10 minutes at 400°F (200°C), then for 20 minutes at 325°F (170°C).

Remove from oven. Pass the pan over a high flame to caramelize the contents and make the tart easier to unmold. Turn the tart onto a serving plate. The marinated vegetable salad is optional.

Trout Fillets with Citrus Fruits, Grapefruit Mousseline, Pink Field Mushrooms, and Herb Salad

Appetizer
Serves 4

Ingredients
4 trout fillets

Grapefruit mousseline
Juice of 3 pink grapefruits
3 oranges
1 sheet of gelatin
½ cup (12 cl) whipped cream

Salad
7 oz. (200 g) pink field mushrooms
(substitute oyster mushrooms)
4 oz. (120 g) garden peas
4 oz. (120 g) rocket or arugula
4 oz. (120 g) mache lettuce
8 flat-leaf parsley leaves, chopped
10 tarragon leaves, chopped
¼ bunch of chives, chopped
¼ bunch of chervil, chopped
3 tbsp. hazelnut oil
1 fresh tomato, peeled and diced
Dash of sherry wine vinegar

Citrus vinaigrette (pg. 295)

Salt and pepper

The grapefruit mousseline

Over gentle heat, reduce the orange and grapefruit juices with the zest of 1 orange to obtain 1¼ cups (30 cl) of liquid.

Reserve ½ cup (12 cl) of the juice. Reduce the remaining juice, adding a sheet of gelatin presoaked in cold water. Mix with a whisk. As the juice cools, it will begin to set. Gently fold in the whipped cream with a rubber spatula. Season with salt and pepper. Transfer the mousseline to a bowl, cover with plastic wrap, and refrigerate.

The salad

Clean the mushrooms and shell the peas. Cook these vegetables in salted water for 3 minutes. Drain and cool. Set aside.

Sort and wash the greens and herbs. Season with hazelnut oil, a dash of vinegar, and a little freshly ground pepper.

Sauté the mushrooms in hazelnut oil and season with salt. Add the peas and diced tomato. Heat for 2 minutes.

Cooking the trout

Heat a tbsp. of olive oil in a pan. When the oil is hot, season and brown the trout on each side for 2 minutes. The centers of the fillets should remain slightly under cooked.

Keep warm.

Combine all the vinaigrette ingredients.

230

Presentation

Arrange some salad, peas, and mushrooms in the center of each plate.

Cut each fillet into thirds and arrange the pieces around the salad. Place an orange segment between each piece.

With a warm tablespoon, scoop the orange and grapefruit mousseline onto the salad. Sprinkle with orange zest.

Spoon the warm citrus vinaigrette over each slice of trout.

This is a dish that I have adapted from a pastry recipe. I like playing with the contrast of hot and cold, as with the trout and cold grapefruit mousseline. I serve this with an herb salad and firm, early pink field mushrooms.

This recipe has a dominant acid flavor, which makes it a very refreshing starter.

231

Auvergne Style Lobster Hot Pot

Ingredients
2 Maine lobsters, each 1 lb. (450 g)
3½ tbsp. (5 cl) oil
¾ cup (20 cl) seafood stock (pg. 294)

Stuffed cabbage
½ curly green cabbage
1 carrot, diced
1 onion, minced
1 tsp. chopped parsley
1 clove of garlic, chopped
1 tsp. vinegar

Vegetables and garnish
4 oz. (120 g) slab bacon
(not smoked)
1 cervela sausage, plain or stuffed
with porcini or truffles
4 carrots, with tops
2 small turnips
2 small onions with shoots
7 tbsp. (100 g) butter
Pinch of sugar
4 tbsp. (6 cl) olive oil
12 small new potatoes

Olive oil
Basil
Salt and pepper

The lobster
Boil a pot of salted water, drop in the lobsters, and cook for 4 minutes. Refresh in cold water. Slice in half lengthwise. Remove the gravel pocket and reserve the coral. Shell the claws and knuckles. Set aside.

The stuffed cabbage
Preheat the oven to 350°F (180°C).

Boil a saucepan of salted water with a dash of vinegar. Cook 8 cabbage leaves, refresh in cold water, and drain. Reserve 4 whole leaves. Quarter and julienne the remaining 4.

In a heavy sauté pan, brown the carrot and onion in a tbsp. of butter over high heat. Add the cabbage and some seafood sauce, cook gently for 30 minutes over very low heat. Add the chopped parsley and a pinch of garlic.

Add the meat from the claws and knuckle. Check the seasoning. This garnish should be very flavorful. Roll the 4 reserved cabbage leaves with a rolling pin to soften them. Fill them with the cabbage lobster mixture and form into balls.

Place the stuffed cabbage in a buttered baking dish and bake for 20 minutes. Baste with seafood stock from time to time. As the sauce reduces, it will glaze the cabbages.

The vegetables and garnish
Heat a pan of water and gently poach the bacon and sausage. After ½ hour, remove the sausage and keep warm. Let the bacon cook another hour. Meanwhile, cook the carrots, turnips, and onions separately in 1 tbsp. of butter, salt, and sugar. Heat 2 tbsp. of oil and butter in a pan. Brown the potatoes and season with salt and pepper.

Cover and keep warm.

Presentation
Heat oil in a sauté pan. Add the lobster halves, skin side down. Season with salt and pepper. Lightly brown and finish cooking in the oven.

In a small sauté pan, reheat the vegetables with a little seafood stock. Reduce the remaining stock in a separate pan.

When the reduced sauce is fragrant, add some of the coral and 2 tbsp. (30 g) of butter. At the last moment, add several minced basil leaves. Check the seasoning and mix with an immersion blender.

Place the stuffed cabbage in a very hot casserole. Add the vegetables, lobster halves, sausage and bacon. Pour sauce generously over the contents. Cover the casserole dish. Serve immediately onto piping hot plates.

Sometimes I change a meat recipe into a fish recipe, or vice versa. Here, I followed a traditional recipe from Auvergne practically to the letter, but replaced the salt pork with lobster.

Monkfish à *la* Grenobloise with Artichokes and Quinoa

Fish
Serves 4

Ingredients

1½ lbs. (700 to 800 g) monkfish
fillet
4 tbsp. (6 cl) olive oil
4 cloves of garlic, unpeeled
1 sprig of fresh thyme
1 tbsp. butter

Braised artichokes with quinoa
6 small artichokes
1 lemon, zest and juice
1 large onion, minced
4 tbsp. (6 cl) olive oil
½ cup (12 cl) dry white wine
¾ cup (150 g) quinoa
1 tbsp. (15 g) butter

Grenobloise sauce
2 slices of white bread
5 tbsp. (60 g) butter, clarified
1 large tomato, diced
1 lemon
7 tbsp. (100 g) butter,
cut into small cubes
2 tbsp. capers
2 tbsp. soy sauce
1 tsp. of honey

Salt and pepper

The artichokes

Prepare the artichokes and halve them lengthwise. Place in a bowl of water with several drops of lemon juice.

In a sauté pan, sweat the onion in 2 tbsp. of olive oil over high heat. Brown the artichokes. Add the white wine and a little water. Salt lightly and simmer, covered, for about 15 minutes. Keep warm.

The quinoa

Heat 2 cups (50 cl) of salted water in a saucepan. Add the quinoa and boil for 10 to 15 minutes, stirring from time to time. The quinoa is cooked when each grain has doubled in volume and released its white germ.

The Grenobloise sauce

Cube the bread.

Heat the clarified butter in a sauté pan. Evenly brown the bread cubes.

Drain the croutons on paper towels and keep warm.

Finely dice the tomato. Peel the lemon, removing the pith. Separate the segments and remove the seeds. Dice the lemon segments, reserving the juice, and set aside.

The monkfish

Preheat the oven to 350°F (180°C). Skin and gut the monkfish. Tie it as you would a roast and place in a heavy baking dish. Brown the fish in olive oil over high heat. Season with salt and pepper. Add the garlic and thyme. Bake in the oven for 15 minutes, basting often.

Presentation

Reheat the quinoa in the tbsp. butter. Finely chop and add the lemon zest, reserving some for the presentation. Fill the cavities of each artichoke half with the quinoa. Drizzle with olive oil and place in the oven to keep warm.

In a sauté pan, heat the cubed butter until hazelnut brown.

Add the diced lemon segments, tomato, capers, and a dash of the caper juice. Add the remaining lemon juice, soy sauce, and honey. Whisk to blend.

Cut the monkfish into thin slices. Place some quinoa in the center of each plate and lay the fish slices on top.

Arrange the stuffed artichokes around the fish. Pour sauce over the fish and around the plate. Decorate with the reserved lemon zests.

Quinoa is a grain from South America (the high plateaus of Bolivia) and was worshipped by the Incas. It is known as "Inca rice" or "tears of the sun" in Colombia, and "Indian tongue" in Bolivia. Quinoa, one of the most nutritious grains in the world, was eatern by the builders of the great Inca empire. It is also very light and gluten-free. Quinoa is grown in place of poppies in many South American countries.

Baked Scallops
with Cabbage

Fish 🌲 🌲
*Make sure the shellfish
is fresh and firm.*
Serves 4

Ingredients
40 scallops

Cabbage garnish
*¼ large cabbage
4 oz. (120 g) smoked bacon,
finely diced
1 onion, minced
1 tbsp. butter*

Fish sauce with smoked bacon
*4 tbsp. (6 cl) white wine
1 large shallot
3½ oz. (100 g) smoked
slab bacon, diced
¾ cup (20 cl) fish stock (pg. 291)
4 tbsp. (6 cl) crème fraîche
2 tbsp. (20 g) butter
½ cup (12 cl) whipped cream*

Salt, coarse salt, and pepper

*In this recipe, the shellfish
are accompanied by green
cabbage, the signature
vegetable of the Auvergne.*

The cabbage
Boil a pan of salted water.

Shred the cabbage and boil 3 to 4 minutes. Refresh in cold water and drain.

In a sauté pan, brown the diced bacon and onion in the tbsp. butter. Stew for 3 to 4 minutes. Check the seasoning and keep warm.

The fish sauce with smoked bacon
Pour the white wine into a sauté pan. Add the minced shallot and reduce by half. Add the bacon and fish stock. Return to a boil.

Pass the cooking liquid through a fine china cap into another sauté pan. Reduce by three-quarters to obtain a syrupy sauce. Add the crème fraîche. Return to a boil and reduce until the sauce coats the back of a spoon. Whisk in the butter, then add the whipped cream, whisking gently so as not to lose the texture of the cream.

Set aside.

The scallops
Preheat the oven to 425°F (220°C) and preheat a broiler or salamander.

Open the scallops with a short knife, covering your hand with a cloth for protection. Wash the scallops if necessary. Scatter sea salt on a baking sheet and arrange the scallop shells, curved side down.

Remove the scallops from the shells. Place a little stewed cabbage into each shell and place a scallop on top. Cover with cream sauce.

Place the baking sheet under the broiler to bake and brown. After several minutes, remove the golden scallops from the oven.

Serve immediately.

Capon Stuffed with Truffles

Meat 🌲 🌲

This recipe does not necessarily require a garnish, but goes well with cardoons, mushrooms, or chestnuts.
Serves 8

Ingredients
Stuffing
5 oz. (150 g) fresh truffles (melanosporum Périgord black truffle)
6 tbsp. (80 g) butter
5 oz. (150 g) white mushrooms, sliced
3 shallots, minced
9 oz. (250 g) fatback, cut into small cubes
3 oz. (80 g) chicken livers
2 sage leaves, finely chopped
1 tbsp. chopped parsley
3 oz. (80 g) foie gras, cut into cubes
2 tbsp. (3 cl) Armagnac
2 oz. (60 g) soft white bread, diced
2 eggs

Capon
7 to 9 lb. capon (3 to 4 kg) (ask your butcher to prepare it for you, reserving the liver)
1 carrot, finely sliced
1 onion, finely sliced
6 cloves of garlic, unpeeled
¾ cup (20 cl) dry white wine
¾ cup (20 cl) chicken jus (pg. 290)
3 tbsp. (40 g) butter

Salt, pepper, and quatre epice (French 4 spice)

The stuffing

Wipe and finely dice the truffles. Set aside.

Heat the butter in a pan, and when it begins to foam, add the mushrooms.

Cook 2 to 3 minutes, add the shallots. Season with salt and pepper. Coarsely chop and refrigerate.

Chop the bacon and chicken livers in a meat grinder with a medium blade. Add the sage and parsley and mix well. Season with salt and pepper.

Add the diced truffle, chopped mushrooms, foie gras, Armagnac, bread, and eggs. Mix until smooth.

Season with salt, pepper, and *quatre epice*. Cover with plastic wrap and refrigerate.

The capon

Preheat the oven to 425°F (220°C).

Salt and pepper the inside, then stuff and truss the capon.

Boil a large pan of water, add the capon, and cook for 5 minutes. This process makes the poultry flesh firmer, ensuring that the stuffing remains inside. The boiled capon also loses some of its fat. Remove and carefully dry with a cloth.

Place the capon on its side in a large nonstick sauté pan and brown over high heat.

So as not to damage the meat, turn the capon with two wooden spatulas to brown the other side. Turn again to brown the back and then to color the breast. Season with salt and pepper.

Lay the capon in a heavy roasting pan. Arrange the carrot, onion, and garlic cloves around the bird.

Roast about 10 minutes, basting frequently, until golden.

Reduce the temperature to 200°F (100°C) and cook at least 2 hours. Baste every 15 minutes.

Check for doneness by inserting a needle or skewer into the thighs. The juice that flows out should be clear, without traces of blood.

Remove the capon from the pan. Skim the fat from the cooking juices, place the pan over high heat, and caramelize the vegetables. Deglaze with white wine and reduce again. Add a little water and the chicken jus. Pass the sauce through a fine china cap, pressing the vegetables well.

Presentation

Heat the butter until it is hazelnut brown and add to the sauce.

Serve the capon with cardoons, mushrooms, or chestnuts.

When you carve the bird, if you notice that the thighs are under cooked, serve the breast fillets first and return the thighs to the oven and cook with the pan juices until tender.

The capons I use come from Paul Michel's farm in Saint-Trivier de Courtes, in the heart of the Bresse region. After castration, they are allowed to range freely to fatten up and then are kept in dark wooden cages. Most of the poultry Michel breeds win prizes at the annual poultry fair, the Trois Glorieuses.

Barley Risotto with Porcini Mushrooms and Salers Cheese

Vegetable 🌲
Serves 6

Ingredients
Risotto
Handful of dried porcini
1 onion, chopped
7 tbsp. (100 g) butter
2 oz. (60 g) beef marrow
1½ cups (300 g) pearl barley
¾ cup (18 cl) of dry white wine
3 cups (75 cl) chicken stock
(pg. 290)
Vintage Salers cheese, grated

This is a variation on the world-famous dish, risotto. The rice is is replaced with pearl barley. I cook the barley in the soaking water for the dried porcini or with fresh porcini. If you do not have vintage Salers cheese, you can substitute Parmesan.

One day in advance, soak the dried porcini in 3 cups (75 cl) of slightly warm water.

The following day, gently sauté the onion in half the butter in a casserole, without browning.

Cut the beef marrow into small pieces and add to the pan to soften for 3 minutes.

Sprinkle in the pearl barley and mix well so that all the grains are well coated in marrow. Add the white wine and stir until well absorbed. Add the soaking water from the porcini.

Reduce heat and cook until all the liquid is absorbed.

Add the chicken stock and season with salt and pepper. Cook for a solid hour.

Coarsely chop some of the soaked porcini and add to the casserole 15 minutes before the barley has finished cooking.

Presentation
Mix in the remaining butter and the *Salers* cheese. Serve immediately.

Fresh Fruit Salad
with Szechwan Pepper, Verbena Curd Sorbet, and Iced Pastry Straws

The fruit salad

One day in advance, peel the fruit and cut into ¼ in. (½ cm) cubes. Coat with the lemon juice.

Mix the pear juice and syrup. Add to the fruit salad. Marinate overnight.

The verbena curd sorbet

Boil 3 cups (75 cl) of water. Add the verbena, allow to infuse, and strain. Add the sugar to make a syrup, boil 5 minutes more, remove from heat.

When the syrup cools, add the curds and lemon juice and pass through a fine china cap. Process in an ice-cream maker at 19°F (–7°C).

The royal icing

In a bowl, mix the egg white with a wooden spatula, gradually adding the sifted sugar, until the icing thickens. Add 2 or 3 drops of lemon juice.

The pastry straws

Preheat the oven to 350°F (180°C)

Roll the pastry dough to a thickness of ⅛ in. (3 mm). With a spatula, coat the dough with royal icing. Cut the dough into strips 4 in. (10 cm) long and ¼ in. (8 mm) wide. Arrange on a baking sheet.

Bake about 10 minutes at 350°F (180° C).

The snowflakes

Fill a paper pastry cone with the royal icing. Draw snowflake shapes and sprinkle with confectioner's sugar. Let harden at room temperature.

Presentation

Arrange some fruit salad in the center of each plate. Lay a scoop of verbena curd sorbet on top. Decorate with pastry straws and a snowflake.

Pastry straws remind me of my childhood. I would press my nose up against the window of Mlle. Feasson's bakery and devour the large iced straws with my eyes.

Dessert 🌲
The Szechwan pepper may be replaced with black pepper.
Serves 12

Ingredients
Fruit salad
3 pears in syrup
3 kiwis
10 litchis
2 mangoes
2 bananas
2 apples
Juice of ½ lemon
¾ cup (18 cl) fresh or pasteurized pear juice
2½ tbsp. (4 cl) pear syrup, flavored with Szechwan pepper

Verbena curd sorbet
3 cups (75 cl) water
2 bunches of verbena
1 cup (200 g) sugar
1 lb. 2 oz. (500 g) curds or fromage blanc, 20% fat
5 tbsp. (70 g) lemon juice

Royal icing (for the straws and snowflakes)
1 egg white
½ cup (60 g) confectioners' sugar
Several drops of lemon juice

Pastry straws
5 oz. (150 g) flaky puff pastry dough (pg. 296)

Photograph of the recipe shown on the next two pages.

Chocolate Dome with Exotic Fruits

Dessert 🌲
The fruit marinade should
be made one day in advance.
Serves 6

Ingredients
Exotic fruit marinade
4 passion fruits
16 litchis
1 ripe mango
½ ripe pineapple
⅔ cup (130 g) superfine sugar
4 leaves of fresh mint
½ vanilla bean pod, split in two and
seeds scraped

Chocolate mousse
13 oz. (380 g) dessert chocolate,
bittersweet
7 tbsp. (95 g) butter
13 large or 13 oz. (380 g) egg whites
⅔ cup (130 g) superfine sugar
3 egg yolks
Cocoa powder to sprinkle
mint leaves, to garnish

The fruit marinade (to be made 24 hours in advance)

Halve the passion fruits, remove the flesh, and set aside. Peel the other fruits. Dice the litchis, slice the mango and pineapple. Boil 2 cups (½ l) of water. Add the sugar, mint leaves, and vanilla bean pod. Add the mango and pineapple slices and the litchi. Return to boil, then set aside. Cover with plastic wrap and refrigerate.

The chocolate mousse

Drain one-third of the fruit salad and dab with paper towels to remove excess moisture.

Melt the chocolate in a double boiler. Add the butter and stir with a spatula.

Beat the egg whites into peaks, adding the sugar in thirds.

When all the sugar is added, whip the whites to form smooth, stiff peaks, as for a meringue.

Meanwhile, beat the egg yolks and add to the chocolate. Fold in only half of the egg whites at one time to be sure the mixture is smooth and even.

Fill a pastry bag, fitted with a single tip, with the chocolate mousse. Pipe a little mousse into individual demisphere molds (or coffee cups).

Spoon some of the drained fruit inside each mold and fill with mousse, pressing well. Freeze for 3 to 4 hours.

Presentation

Remove from the freezer and dip each mold in hot water for a few seconds. Unmold each mousse, sprinkle with powdered cocoa, and transfer to the center of a plate. Arrange the passion fruit and the remaining fruit marinade around the plate. Decorate with mint leaves and serve cold.

I f you want to know what makes bees tired or learn about the dreaded Varroa mite that decimates entire swarms—a creature right out of the goriest horror movie—you only have to ask Vincent Faure. Beekeeping has not inspired many fictional films (apart from Theo Angelopoulos's *The Beekeeper*, starring Marcello Mastroianni), but the passion for apiculture shapes Vincent Faure's day-to-day reality at his aptly named home, *Ferme des abeilles*, "The Bee Farm." When talking with Faure, his work seems cut and dried. "All you have to do is be at the right place at the right time," he says. But the "all" that you have to do includes a world of experiences, buzzing memories, sharp pleasures, and stung fingers.

Typically, he watches over about 800 hives ("Any less than that," he says, casually, "would be inefficient") to ensure that every new pot of liquid gold makes it into the family history book (Vincent's parents also wore the beekeeper's mask). Although bees appear to be controlled by the weather, the behavior of the swarms is often difficult to explain. Who knows why, in 1999, honey production in the region increased by 15,000 tons—the equivalent of national production in a lean year? Enough honey, indeed, for the breakfast tables at the Auberge des Cimes—and at many other tables, too.

Glazed Rabbit in Mead Gelée

Appetizer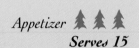
Serves 15

Ingredients
*1 free-range rabbit, with
liver and kidneys
1 celery root
½ lemon
8 slices of duck foie gras,
¼ in. (½ cm) thick*

Gelée
*1 pkg. or 7 sheets of gelatin
1 carrot, finely sliced
2 medium-sized onions
1 leek
1 stalk of celery
3 cups (75 cl) chicken stock
(pg. 290)
1 small bouquet garni
½ cup (12 cl) mead*

Accompanying salad
*7 oz. (200 g) mesclun salad
¾ cup (18 cl) hazelnut oil
vinaigrette (pg. 301)
3½ oz. (100 g) germinated grains
(lentils, alfalfa,
pearl barley, etc.)
Salt and pepper*

The gelée
Soak the gelatin in a small amount of cold water.

Separate the rabbit into its different cuts. Remove the saddle and reserve for later in the recipe. Place the rabbit and the vegetables for the *gelée* in a pan. Moisten with the chicken stock or cold water, add salt and the bouquet garni. Boil, skim the surface, and simmer gently for about 1 hour. This stock should remain clear. Remove from heat and allow the flavors to infuse for 10 minutes. Remove the meat.

Strain the stock through a fine china cap or a damp cheesecloth and return to the pan. Reduce again to strengthen the flavor and obtain 2 cups (½ l) of bouillon. Check the seasoning—it should be fairly salty. Add the softened gelatin, let dissolve, and bring to a boil. Cool. When the bouillon is still slightly warm, add the mead. Set aside at room temperature.

The celery root
Peel the celery root and cut into ⅛ in. (3 mm) thick slices. Boil salted water and several drops of lemon juice in a saucepan. Drop the celery root into the water and cook until just slightly crunchy. Refresh and drain. Place on paper towels to remove excess moisture.

Assembling the terrine
Line a triangular mold (or small terrine) with plastic wrap. Arrange the slices of celery root, cut into squares, so that the sides of the mold are completely lined and covered. Repeat with slices of foie gras, ⅛ to ¼ in. (4 to 5 mm) thick. Shred the rabbit meat, fill the mold, and ladle in the *gelée*. Refrigerate for at least 12 hours.

The brochettes and salad
Cut the rabbit saddle. Assemble the brochettes with the saddle, kidneys, and liver. Sort and wash the salad greens. Season with the vinaigrette and add the germinated grains.

Presentation
Unmold the terrine. Cut it into ¾ in. (2 cm) slices with a sharp knife that has been dipped in hot water. In a pan, brown the brochettes in a tbsp. of butter. Season with salt and pepper. Stand a slice of the terrine on each plate, with the salad and brochette to the side.

Serve with a small glass of mead.

Marie Christine's Green Lentil Ragout with Smoked Poached Eggs

Appetizer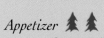
Serves 4

Ingredients
Green lentil ragout
7 oz. (200 g) green du Puy lentils
4 cups (1 l) chicken stock (pg. 290)
1 onion, studded with a clove
1 sprig of thyme
3 tbsp. (40 g) butter
3 oz. (80 g) lightly salted
slab bacon, diced
1 onion, diced
1 medium carrot, finely diced
2 oz. (60 g) celery root, diced
Several slices of truffle (optional for
garnish)

Poached eggs
3 tbsp. (4 cl) vinegar
4 to 6 very fresh eggs

Truffle sauce
2 shallots, minced
½ cup (12 cl) port
¾ cup (20 cl) slightly thickened
chicken jus (pg. 290)
1 tsp. chopped parsley
1 clove of garlic, chopped
1½ tbsp. (20 g) butter
1 tbsp. black truffles, chopped

Salt, pepper, and fine sea salt

*This recipe is dedicated to my
sister, Marie-Christine, who once
gave me this beautiful message:
"Forget yourself for the sake
of others."*

The lentils
Blanch the lentils in cold water and drain. Pour into a saucepan with the chicken stock, the studded onion, and thyme. Salt lightly.

Cook for about 20 to 25 minutes. Check the cooking, drain the lentils, and reserve the cooking stock.

Add a little of the cooked lentils to the stock and reduce. Blend in a food processor to obtain a thick sauce.

In a sauté pan, sweat the diced bacon, onion, carrot, and celery root in the butter. Cook, covered, for 5 minutes. Add the lentils and a little of the thickened sauce and cook for 5 minutes. Keep warm.

The poached eggs
Boil a large saucepan of water with a dash of vinegar. Break each egg into a cup. Pour them carefully, one at a time, into the boiling liquid. The egg whites will wrap themselves around the yokes. Allow 2 to 3 minutes for each egg. Check the cooking by pressing with a finger. Remove the eggs from the water with a skimming ladle and refresh in iced water.

If you have a food smoker, cold-smoke each egg for 10 minutes. Set aside.

The truffle sauce
Reduce the chopped shallots and port in a sauté pan. Add the chicken jus. Set aside one-third of this sauce. Add the lentils to the rest of the sauce. Mix in the parsley, garlic, butter, and the chopped truffles. Check the seasoning.

Presentation
Reheat the eggs in a pan of hot water. Carefully remove each one, dry carefully, and season. Arrange the lentil ragout in the center of the plate and place an egg on top. Surround the ragout with slices of truffle, sprinkled with a little fine sea salt. Serve hot with the reserved truffle sauce.

Skate with Endives and Chestnuts, Croutons with Caper Tapenade

Fish
Serves 4

Ingredients
Skate
2½ lbs. (1,2 kg) skate wing
¾ cup (18 cl) white wine
1 large shallot, thinly sliced
1 sprig of parsley

Tapenade croutons
2 tbsp. anchovy fillets
3 tbsp. capers
3 tbsp. olives, pitted
1 clove of garlic
½ cup (12 cl) olive oil
½ lemon
2 slices of country bread

Endives and chestnuts
3 tbsp. (40 g) butter
2 endives
1 Granny Smith apple
12 chestnuts
2 tbsp. olive oil

Sauce
1 tsp. honey
4 tbsp. (6 cl) sherry wine vinegar
4 tbsp. (6 cl) soy sauce
6 tbsp. (80 g) butter
1 tbsp. small capers
Several drops of lemon juice
Salt and pepper

The skate
Wash the skate and place in a large pan. Add the white wine, shallot, and parsley. Cover with water and simmer for 4 to 5 minutes. Take the skate out of the pan and remove the skin and cartilage. Wipe the fish with paper towels and keep cool.

The tapenade croutons
Finely chop the anchovies. Put the anchovies, capers, olives, and garlic into a food processor. Purée, adding the olive oil, lemon juice, and pepper.

Toast the slices of bread and spread with the tapenade.

The endives
Heat 1 tbsp. of butter in a pan. Peel the leaves from the endives and sauté them quickly. They should remain slightly crunchy. Season with salt and pepper and keep warm.

The apple
Peel and dice the apple.

Heat 1 tbsp. of butter in a pan and brown the apple. Set aside.

The skate and chestnuts
Heat the olive oil and 1 tbsp. butter over high heat in a large nonstick pan. Cut the skate into 4 slices and add to the pan.

Brown each side, turning carefully with a spatula. Add the chestnuts. Keep warm.

The sauce
Caramelize the honey in a sauté pan and deglaze with the vinegar. Reduce to a syrupy consistency. Add the soy sauce.

In another saucepan, heat the butter until hazelnut brown. Add the diced apple, honey sauce, and capers. Season with salt and pepper and add several drops of lemon juice.

Presentation

Arrange the skate in the center of each plate.

Cover with sauce. Arrange the chestnuts and endives around the fish and serve with the tapenade croutons.

Skate is at its best 2 to 3 days after being caught, as its odor is not strong.

Be sure to always rinse fish with cold water and lemon or vinegar before cooking.

Cardoon Gratin with Pig's Feet and Smoked Lavort Cheese

Vegetable
Serves 6

Ingredients

3 lbs. 5 oz. (1,5 kg) white cardoons
Juice of 1 lemon
4 cups (1 l) chicken stock (pg. 290)
4 tbsp. (6 cl) olive oil
2 tbsp. flour
Juice of ½ lemon
1 pig's foot, cooked
½ cup (12 cl) crème fraîche
1 clove of garlic
3½ oz. (100 g) Lavort cheese, freshly grated (substitute comté)

Salt, pepper, and nutmeg

This is a recipe from my former chef and now nephew, Gilles Roux. His family is from the mountains around Lyons, where people are very partial o cardoons, which are cultivated with great care and attention. The cardoon is related to the artichoke and has been on menus since the sixteenth century, when there were also red, yellow, and dark green varieties. Today, only the white cardoon is cultivated.

The cardoons

Clean the cardoons. Remove the stalks and leaves, retaining only the white part of the vegetables. Remove the stringy threads and cut into 3 in. (7 cm) sticks. As you work, place the sticks in a bowl of cold water with lemon juice. Cover with plastic wrap. The cardoons must not come into contact with the air.

Cooking the vegetables

Boil the chicken stock. Add a little water if necessary, depending on the quantity of cardoons. Add the olive oil, flour, a little salt, and several drops of lemon juice (too much lemon juice will keep the cardoons from cooking).

Place the vegetables in the stock. Cover with a sheet of parchment paper, with a small hole pierced in the center to allow steam to escape. Cook about 1 hour or more. Check for doneness—they should be tender. Drain, reserving the cooking juices.

The sauce

Debone the cooked pig's foot. If it is cold, reheat in the cooking juices to remove the bone more easily. Dice the meat.

Reduce the cardoon cooking juices to obtain a slightly thickened sauce. Add the crème fraîche and boil until the sauce coats the back of a spoon. Adjust the seasoning with salt, pepper, and a pinch of nutmeg.

The gratin

Coat the cardoons with the sauce. Butter a gratin dish, then rub it gently with the clove of garlic. Arrange the cardoons in the dish. Cover with sauce. Sprinkle with the diced pig's foot and grated Lavort cheese.

Presentation

Bake until the gratin is golden brown, in a preheated 400°F (200°C) oven, about 10 to 15 minutes.

Duck with Green du Puy Lentil Ragout and Bacon Garlic

Meat 🌲
Serves 4

Ingredients
Duck
2 duck thighs
½ tsp. (2 g) coarse salt
½ tsp. (2 g) sugar
1 clove of garlic
1 sprig of thyme
¼ bay leaf
2 lbs. 2 oz. (1 kg) duck fat
2 magrets duck breasts

Green lentil ragout
7 oz. (200 g) green du Puy lentils
1 carrot, finely diced
½ stalk of celery, finely diced
1 onion, chopped
1 chicken bouillon cube, diluted in
2 cups hot water or stock
3½ oz. (100 g) lightly salted slab
bacon, cut into cubes
1 sprig thyme
Bay leaf
Pinch of star anise
½ clove of garlic
2 tbsp. (30 g) butter

Sauce
Zest and juice of 1 orange
1 tbsp. light brown sugar
4 tbsp. (6 cl) vinegar
Chicken jus (pg. 290)
Cornstarch
3 tbsp. (4 cl) Grand Marnier
1 tbsp. (15 g) butter

Garlic bacon
8 cloves of garlic
¼ oz. (10 g) butter
7 oz. (200 g) salted bacon, thinly
sliced into 8 pieces
Pinch of sugar

Salt and pepper

The duck confit
One day in advance, season the duck thighs with the coarse salt, pepper, and sugar. Rub with the garlic, thyme, and bay leaf. Cover and set aside overnight.

The following day, heat the duck fat in a pan. Add the thighs and simmer gently for about 1 hour 30 minutes, until the meat is tender enough to pierce with the tip of a knife. Keep warm.

In a hot pan, without any oil, brown the skin sides of the duck breasts. Then roast in oven for 25 minutes at 250°F (120°C), until medium rare.

The lentils
Moisten the lentils with cold water and bring to a boil. Drain and cool.

Brown the carrot, celery, onions, and bacon in some of the cooking fat from the thighs. Add the lentils and moisten with the chicken stock. Add the thyme, bay leaf, star anise, and garlic. Cook 20 to 25 minutes.

Drain the lentils, reserving the cooking juices. Reduce the liquid with 2 tbsp. of cooked lentils to obtain ½ cup (12 cl) of sauce. Add 1 tbsp. of butter, blend the sauce until smooth and add to the remaining lentils.

The sauce
Remove the zest from the orange. Blanch in a pan of cold water, drain, and set aside. Caramelize the sugar and deglaze with orange juice and vinegar. Reduce to a syrupy consistency. Moisten with the chicken jus, add the orange zest, and reduce again.

Thicken with a little cornstarch (mixed with cold water). Add the Grand Marnier and a tbsp. of butter.

The garlic bacon
Blanch the garlic cloves in a pan of water for 2 minutes and drain. Repeat the blanching process two more times. Brown the garlic in butter and wrap each clove in a slice of bacon. Secure each with a wooden toothpick.

Reheat the lentils. Drain the thighs, wipe with paper towels, and brown in a pan. Heat the sauce and sauté the garlic bacon sprinkled with sugar until brown.

Presentation
Place some lentils in the center of each plate.

Halve the thighs and lay on top. Arrange slices of duck breast around the thigh. Add the garlic bacon and pour on the sauce.

I like this way of preparing lentils. Most are kept whole and delicious, enhanced by the flavors of the others that are blended with the cooking juices.

Pork Glazed in Spices with Apple Blood Pudding and Sweet Potato Purée

Meat
Serves 10

Ingredients

Pork
15 lb. (7 kg) piglet
4 tbsp. (6 cl) oil
6 tbsp. (80 g) butter

Herb stock
8 cups (2 l) of water
1 leek
1 carrot, finely sliced
1 bouquet garni
1 onion, studded with a clove

Mixed spices
1 vanilla bean pod
1 tbsp. black pepper
1 tbsp. fennel seeds
1 tsp. Espelette pepper
1 tbsp. ground cinnamon
2 tbsp. honey
2 cups (50 cl) pork jus (pg. 290)

Apple blood pudding
3 apples (Sainte Germaine variety
or substitute Granny Smith)
4 tbsp. (60 g) butter
1 tsp. mustard
1 lb. 2 oz. (500 g) blood sausage

Sweet potato purée
2 lbs. 2 oz. (1 kg) sweet potatoes
4 tbsp. (6 cl) cream
1 tbsp. butter
4 tbsp. (6 cl) toasted almond oil

**Seasonal mixed vegetables
(optional)**
2 lbs. 2 oz. (1 kg) Japanese
artichokes, carrots, snow peas,
salsify, etc., depending on season

Salt, pepper, and sugar

The pork

Debone the piglet. If you find the task daunting, ask your butcher to do it for you. Set aside the legs and loin. Save the shoulder for another recipe.

Cook the head and ears for 1 hour 30 minutes in the herb stock. Then you can easily remove the meat from the bone. The cheeks, ears, and tongue can be added to the mixed vegetables.

Preheat the oven to 325°F (160°C).

Add olive oil and butter to a hot pan. Brown the legs and loin. Season with salt and pepper.

In a baking dish, brown the vegetables from the herb stock in butter and oil. Add a cup of water, then add the legs and loin. Cook, allowing 25 minutes for the loin and 45 to 50 minutes for the legs. Baste the pork frequently. Remove the meat and let rest. Keep warm.

Grind the dry spices with a rolling pin or in a coffee grinder. Mix, adding the honey and slightly warm pork jus.

The apple blood pudding

Peel the apples and cut into small cubes.

Heat the tbsp. of butter in a pan and brown the apple cubes. Lightly season with salt and pepper.

At the end of the cooking, add the mustard. Keep warm.

In the same pan, gently heat the blood sausage, retaining the skin. Keep warm.

The sweet potato purée

Wash the sweet potatoes and boil in salted water. When thoroughly cooked, remove the skin and press the flesh through a food mill. Boil the cream and mix into the pulp. Add the butter and toasted almond oil. Keep warm in a water bath.

The mixed vegetables

Boil all the green vegetables in salted water, drain, cool, and set aside.

Steam the other vegetables, such as artichokes and carrots, with salt, a pinch of sugar, butter, and a little of the pork cooking juices. Combine all the vegetables, check the seasoning, and keep warm.

Finishing the pork

Preheat the broiler.

Arrange the legs and loin on a baking sheet. Brush with the mixed spices and place under the broiler. Remove and brush with the spices again. Repeat this process several times.

Presentation

Heat the pork gravy and add some of the spice mixture. Boil for 5 minutes, correct the seasoning, and pass through a fine china cap.

Cut the legs into slices and the loin into chops. Season with salt and pepper.

Arrange the meat on a dish. Crown the blood sausage with diced apple and pour sauce over the sweet potato purée. Serve hot.

The Sainte Germaine apple is a variety from the Limousin region. It is half-sour, half-sweet.

This apple is excellent when eaten raw, but even better in a blood sausage fricassee. One of my best chefs, Davy Tissot, once took this recipe to a major competition.

Warm Millefeuille with Chicory Pastry Cream and Ice Cream

Dessert 🌲 🌲
The chicory pastry,
sometimes difficult
to make, may be replaced
by the classic flaky pastry.
Serves 6

Ingredients
Chickory pastry
1½ lbs. (70 cl) butter
1⅔ cups (250 g) flour
1 tsp. (5 g) salt
½ c + 1 tbsp. (14 cl) of water
2 tsp. (10 g) chicory extract
confectioners' sugar, to sprinkle

Chicory pastry cream
2 cups (½ l) whole milk
3 tbsp. roasted ground chicory
6 egg yolks
½ cup (100 g) sugar
½ cup (50 g) cornstarch
6 tbsp. (80 g) butter
½ cup (12 cl) whipped cream

Chicory ice cream
2 cups (½ l) milk
2 tbsp. roasted ground chicory
6 egg yolks
½ cup (100 g) sugar
½ cup (12 cl) crème fraîche

The chicory pastry

The chicory pastry is made by flavoring classic flaky puff pastry with chicory extract. Rub 6 tbsp. (80 g) of the butter into the flour until the mixture has the texture of fine bread crumbs. Add the salt. Make a well in the middle and add the water and chicory extract. Knead and form a ball.

Score a cross on top of the dough. Wrap in plastic wrap to prevent it from drying out and let rest for 45 minutes. This dough is called the *détrempe*. Roll into an 8 by 10 in. (20 × 25 cm) square that is ¾ in. (2 cm) thick.

Knead the butter so that it is malleable enough to form a 5 by 5 in. (12 × 12 cm) square. Place the butter on the *détrempe* so that the butter square is at a 45° angle to the pastry square. Fold the corners of the pastry toward the center of the butter square, overlapping and sealing the ends. This folded dough is called the *pâton*.

Tap the *pâton* with a rolling pin to form a large, even square, again securely sealing the edges. Evenly roll the *pâton* to form a strip 18 in. (45 cm) long, 7 to 8 in. (18 to 20 cm) wide, and no more than ½ in. (1 cm) thick. Fold the dough back on itself, making 3 equal-sized folds, chill and let relax for 45 minutes.

Turn the dough a quarter-turn to change the direction in which you are working it. Roll, fold, and relax the dough again. Repeat the entire process a third time.

After the dough has relaxed, roll into a rectangle ⅛ in. (3 mm) thick. Prick with a fork, cover with a slightly damp cloth, and refrigerate for about 1 hour.

Baking the pastry

Preheat the oven to 400°F (200°C) Roll the dough onto a baking sheet. Bake at least 10 minutes, be careful to watch the cooking. Then reduce the heat to 300°F (150°C). After 20 minutes, the pastry will rise, so place a wire rack on top to prevent it from swelling unevenly.

After 10 more minutes, check that the underside of the pastry is cooked. Carefully turn the pastry onto another baking sheet so that the underside is now on top.

Bake for another 45 minutes, then remove and let cool. With a serrated knife, cut the pastry into 2 in. (6 cm) squares.

Generously sprinkle the squares with confectioners' sugar. Melt and caramelize the sugar under the broiler. The sugar glaze enhances the crisp texture of the pastry and protects it from the moisture of the pastry cream.

The chicory pastry cream *(method on pg. 303)*
Prepare the custard, infusing the milk with the ground chicory. You don't need to strain the milk, the ground chicory can remain in the pastry cream. When the cream is cool, gently add the whipped cream.

The chicory ice cream
Boil the milk and chicory grounds in a saucepan.

Whisk the egg yolks and sugar in a bowl until light and creamy. Stir in the chicory milk with a spatula. Return to the heat, stirring constantly. Do not let the mixture boil. As soon as it has thickened slightly, pass through a fine china cap and refrigerate.

When the mixture is cool, add the crème fraîche. Process in an ice-cream maker.

Presentation
Warm the pastry squares and pipe chicory pastry cream between 2 of every 3 layers.

To decorate, partially cover the top layer of pastry and sprinkle with confectioner's sugar. Serve with the chicory ice cream.

The chicory root is roasted to make a beverage. At home, at breakfast, we always added a little chicory to our coffee to help digestion. Since then, I have been very partial to chicory.

Mango, Red Banana, and Thyme Brochette with Quince Sauce

Dessert
Serves 4

Ingredients
Brochette
3 vanilla bean pods
1½ cups (40 cl) fruit syrup
3 mangoes
3 red bananas
Juice of 1 lemon
4 tbsp. (60 g) butter, melted
1 sprig of fresh thyme
Sugar
Quince custard sauce
2 cups (½ l) whole milk
6 egg yolks
¼ cup (50 g) sugar
4 oz. (120 g) quince paste

I think that everybody in France has an aunt or grandmother who makes a lovely quince paste. In my case, "Auntie" had a knack for picking the best wild quinces. She would wrap the paste in paper and, with her never-ending smile, bring it to our house.

The syrup

Split in half lengthwise and scrape the vanilla bean pods. Heat the syrup, add the vanilla bean pods, and boil for 2 minutes. Remove the pods, drain, and dry on a baking sheet in a 175°F (80°C) oven.

The fruit

Peel and quarter the mangoes. Let marinate in the syrup.

Peel the bananas, slice into rounds, and mix with the mangoes. Coat with syrup and add the lemon juice.

Marinate the fruit for several hours.

Quince custard sauce

Boil the milk in a stainless-steel saucepan. Whip the egg yolks and sugar in a bowl until light and creamy. Add the boiling milk and return the mixture to the saucepan. Heat while stirring with a spatula. When the custard begins to boil, remove from heat, pass through a medium china cap, and cool.

Cut the quince paste into small cubes, reserving a few for decoration. Put the rest into a bowl, add the sauce, and mix with an immersion blender.

Presentation

Heat a nonstick pan and add the melted butter. Pat the brochettes with paper towels and place in the pan. Brown and sprinkle with thyme. Turn the brochettes, adding a little sugar to caramelize them.

Coat the plates with quince sauce. Lay one brochette in the center of each plate and sprinkle with several cubes of the quince paste. Serve immediately.

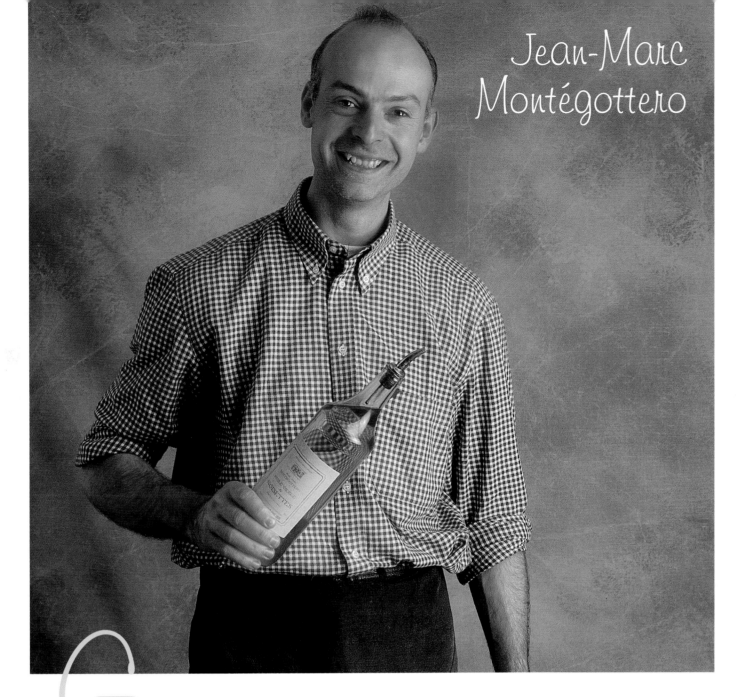

Generally, you don't just stumble across your vocation—unless your name is Jean-Marc Montégottero. One day, in 1979 or 1980, Jean-Marc found an old millstone that had once been used to press nuts and olives for oil. The spirit of the object instantly sent Jean-Marc on an (at first) imaginary voyage far beyond the family's hardware business.

The real journey was not exactly a smooth cruise on a sea of oil, so to speak. Jean-Marc had to rummage through backyards to uncover missing mill parts beneath gardens. He then had to find skilled masons and mechanics. It took months to "get the bits and pieces back together again," he said. The traditions of the region prompted him to produce walnut oil first. He then moved onto hazelnut, canola, peanut, toasted sesame seed, pecan, and others. Soon, he was producing a quintessential pine nut oil and rich, fragrant pistachio oil for Régis Marcon, Fredy Girardet, and other great chefs.

"First find what you want, then go looking for it," Picasso once said. Jean-Marc Montégottero found his vocation as easily as a next-door neighbor's front gate, but then tirelessly sought the best way to open it. He will continue to refine his experience, improve his materials, and fortify the texture and aroma of his oils. He is also getting ready to file a patent that would revolutionize oil manufacturing. The secret? Now that would be telling. The walls have ears.

Quail Gribiche with Warm Sage Pâté en Croûte

Appetizer 🌲
Serves 4

Ingredients
Quail
5 free-range quail, 8 oz. (220 g) each
4 bacon slices for wrapping
2 tbsp. (30 g) butter
4 tbsp. (6 cl) oil
2 cloves of garlic, halved
½ cup (12 cl) chicken jus (pg. 290)
Salt and pepper

Gribiche sauce and salad
2 hard-boiled eggs
4 small gherkins
8 capers
2 medium shallots
1 tsp. dijon mustard
6 tbsp. (8 cl) canola oil
6 tarragon leaves, chopped
7 oz. (200 g) mesclun salad (curly endive, oak leaf, etc.)
6 tbsp. (8 cl) hazelnut oil vinaigrette (pg. 295)

Pâté en croûte
7 oz. (200 g) pork jowl
1½ oz. (50 g) chicken livers
1 tbsp. pine nuts
2 tbsp. raisins
4 sage leaves
2 tbsp. (3 cl) rum
7 oz. (200 g) flaky puff pastry (pg. 296)
1 egg

Salt, pepper, and quatre epice (French 4 spice)

The quails

Preheat the oven to 350°F (180°C).

Clip off the quails' feet and tips of the wings. Season with salt and pepper and bard with strips of bacon. Truss with string.

Heat the butter and oil in a small casserole. Brown the quails and the garlic. Roast in oven for 8 to 9 minutes, basting frequently.

Remove from oven, debone, and set aside the fillets.

The gribiche sauce

Separate the yolks from the whites of the hard-boiled eggs. Chop the egg whites, gherkins, and capers. Mince the shallots. Mix the egg yolks, mustard and canola oil in a bowl. Add the tarragon, egg whites, gherkins, capers, and shallots. Remove the skin from the 2 breasts of 1 quail. Cut the meat into ¼ in. (½ cm) cubes and add to the egg mixture. Season well to bring out the flavors.

The warm pâté en croûte

Preheat the oven to 350°F (180°C). Grind the pork jowl in a meat grinder. Add the finely diced chicken livers, pine nuts, raisins, chopped sage, and rum. Season with salt, pepper, and *quatre epice*. Refrigerate.

Roll the flaky pastry dough onto a work surface. With a pastry cutter or coffee cup, cut 4 rounds 2 in. (5 cm) wide and 4 rounds 2¼ in. (6 cm) wide. Place a ball of pâté in the center of each small round. Brush around the pâté with the beaten egg. Place a large round on top of each small round, sealing well. Brush the surfaces with the beaten egg and crimp the edges. Refrigerate 15 minutes, then bake 20 to 25 minutes. Check for doneness. Remove from oven and keep warm.

The salad

Sort and wash the salad greens. Season with 4 tbsp. of vinaigrette to taste.

Presentation

Reduce the chicken jus to obtain a thickened sauce. Add a touch of vinaigrette, according to taste.

Place the *gribiche* garnish on one side of the plate and lay a quail fillet on top. Drizzle with slightly warmed vinaigrette. Place the salad on the other side, next to a warm sage pâté *en croûte*.

266

Warm Fillets of Red Mullet
in a "Venetian Carnival" Sauce

Appetizer
Serves 4

Ingredients
4 fillets of red mullet,
4 oz. (120 g) each, bones
removed

**Piquillo peppers with
salt-cod mousse**
4 piquillo peppers (canned)
or small red peppers
7 oz. (200 g) lightly salted cod
2 cups (50 cl) milk
1 sprig of thyme
¼ bay leaf
6 tbsp. (8 cl) olive oil
1 medium shallot, minced
1 onion, minced
1 clove of garlic, finely chopped
½ cup (12 cl) crème fraîche + ¾ cup
(18 cl) whipped cream

Marinade
¾ cup (18 cl) olive oil
1 carrot, diced
½ onion, diced
1 celery stalk, diced
1 garlic clove, crushed
2 thin slices fresh ginger, chopped
3 pinches ground star anise
Fresh thyme
1 Espelette pepper, finely diced (or
hot red pepper)
½ cup (12 cl) vinegar

Green lentil salad
⅔ cup (120 g) green lentils
½ tsp. dijon mustard
4 tbsp. (6 cl) oil
4 tsp. (2 cl) vinegar
1 tsp. chopped parsley

Decoration
Salmon eggs

Salt, pepper, and Espelette pepper

The salt-cod mousse
One day in advance, remove the bones from the cod. Cut into cubes and remove the salt by rinsing overnight under a gentle stream of cold water. The following day, drain the cod. Heat the milk with a little water, thyme, and bay leaf. Bring to a boil and poach the cod for 8 minutes. Remove the cod and drain. In the olive oil sauté the shallot and onion and add the cod to the pan. Flake the fish with a wooden spatula and add the chopped garlic. When the cod has absorbed the oil, add the crème fraîche and bring to a boil. Correct the seasoning and add a little Espelette pepper. Transfer to the bowl of a food processor. Blend to a purée and cool.

The marinade
Heat the olive oil in a sauté pan and add the diced carrot, celery, and onion. Cook for 5 minutes and add the garlic, ginger, star anise, thyme, and Espelette pepper. Stew gently for about 5 minutes. Deglaze with the vinegar and a little water. Cook for another 5 minutes or more, add salt, and transfer to a bowl. Cool.

The lentil salad
Cook the green lentils (page 142). Add remaining ingredients. Season.

The stuffed piquillo peppers
Whip ½ cup of cream and gently fold it into the cod mousse. Stuff the piquillo peppers with the cod mousse. Stand them on a tray and refrigerate.

Presentation
Place a little lentil salad on each plate. Whip the ¼ cup cream and spoon or pipe small rosettes onto the plate. Top the cream with salmon eggs or caviar. Stand a stuffed piquillo pepper, which looks like a carnival hat, at the top of the plate. Heat olive oil in a pan and quickly sear both sides of the fish fillets. Season with salt and pepper and place on top of the lentil salad. Stir the marinade and spoon over the fish. Serve immediately.

I like the contrast of warm mullet and cold marinade. I made this starter on the Orient Express during a journey to Venice for the carnival, so the dish evokes memories of flamboyant head wear and magnificent masks, Venice and its history and secrets.

Roasted Sea Bream with Red Cabbage Confit and Juniper Butter Cream Sauce

Ingredients
2 medium-sized sea bream, 9 to 10 oz. (280 g) each
4 cloves of garlic, finely chopped
1 sprig of rosemary
8 juniper berries
1 cup (25 cl) fish stock (pg. 291)
6 tbsp. (8 cl) olive oil

Red cabbage confit
⅓ large red cabbage
4 oz. (120 g) lightly salted slab bacon
2 tbsp. (30 g) butter
1 onion, chopped
4 tbsp. (6 cl) wine vinegar
1 green apple
Juice of 1 lemon

Juniper butter cream sauce
¾ cup (18 cl) white wine
4 tbsp. (6 cl) white wine vinegar
2 shallots, minced
1¼ cups (30 cl) crème fraîche (or heavy cream)
6 juniper berries, crushed
2 tbsp. (30 g) butter
1 capful of gin, or more

Salt and pepper

I like the flavor of red cabbage that has been braised with tart apples for a long time in the oven. I serve it with pork or game. In this recipe, I cook the cabbage a little differently, so that it is crunchier, and I add fresh apples as a garnish when serving.

The red cabbage
Remove the thick stalks and finely chop the red cabbage leaves. Brown the bacon and onion in the butter over medium heat. Add the cabbage leaves and sprinkle with vinegar. Season with salt and pepper.

Add a little water, cover, and slowly braise for about 30 minutes. The cabbage should remain slightly crunchy.

Cut the unpeeled apple into fine sticks. Toss in lemon juice and set aside. The apples will be added to the red cabbage before serving.

The juniper butter
Pour the white wine and vinegar into a sauté pan and add the minced shallots. Reduce over gentle heat until there are only 2 tbsp. of liquid in the pan. Add the crème fraîche, bring to a boil, then reduce again. Add the crushed juniper berries, remove from heat, and let infuse. Whisk the sauce with an immersion blender and pass through a fine china cap. Keep warm.

The braised sea bream
Clean the fish and remove the scales. Wipe with a clean cloth.
Lay the fish in a baking pan. Sprinkle the garlic, rosemary, and juniper berries around the fish. Drizzle the pan contents with the fish stock and olive oil. Season with salt and pepper. Bring to a boil and then braise in a 350°F (175°C) oven about 20 minutes. Check for doneness by inserting a sharp knife into the thickest part of the fish. The fish is done when the knife pierces the flesh easily.

Presentation
Arrange the drained sea bream on a serving platter. Boil the sauce and whisk in the butter with an immersion blender. Add the gin and check the seasoning.

Serve the sauce separately with the cabbage-apple garnish.

Cod Tournedos with Salted Pork Belly
and Sweet and Sour Tomato Butter

Fish
Serves 4

Ingredients
1 fillet of fresh cod,
about 2 lbs. 2 oz. (1 kg)
4 slices salted pork belly,
smoked bacon, or caul fat
4 tbsp. (6 cl) peanut oil
2 tbsp. (30 g) butter

Garnish
2 large handfuls of
fresh spinach leaves
1 lemon
3 tbsp. (40 g) butter
1 clove of garlic, halved

Sweet-and-sour tomato butter
4 oz. (120 g) tomato concasse
(pg. 293)
1 tsp. honey
1 tsp. sherry wine vinegar
1 tbsp. soy sauce
1 sprig of thyme
6 tbsp. (80 g) butter,
cut into small cubes

Coarse salt and fish spices (pg. 291)

The cod
Cut the cod into four pieces and coat with coarse salt. Set aside for only 10 minutes. Brush off the salt and then rinse quickly under running water to wash off remaining traces. Wipe with paper towels. Season with the fish spices. Wrap each piece with a slice of pork belly and tie with string. Set aside.

The spinach
Sort and wash the spinach leaves. Drain and spin dry. Remove the zest from the lemon and slice into thin strips. Place the zest in a saucepan and cover with cold water. Boil for 1 minute, remove, and drain. Rinse under cold water.

The sweet and sour tomato butter
Heat the tomato concasse and 4 tsp. (2 cl) of water. Add the honey, vinegar, soy sauce, and thyme and bring to a boil. Pass the sauce through a fine china cap. Return to the boil and reduce to obtain 2 tbsp. (3 cl) of concentrated sauce. Just before serving, whisk in the cubes of butter. This sauce does not keep well, so serve immediately.

The garnish
Heat the butter in a pan. Add the clove of garlic and spinach. Stir with a fork and salt lightly—the spinach will wilt and decrease in volume. At the end of the cooking, add the lemon zest. Keep warm on paper towels.

Presentation
Heat the peanut oil and butter in a pan. Brown the cod on both sides and check for doneness.

Place some spinach in the center of each plate and lay a cod fillet on top. Pour the sweet and sour tomato butter sauce around the plate.

Truffade, My Way

Peel the potatoes and slice into rounds ⅛ in. (3 mm) thick. In a large pan, heat the butter and brown the bacon and the potatoes. Season with salt and pepper. Add a pinch of garlic as the potatoes finish cooking.

When the potatoes are ready, add the cheese and let it melt into the potatoes. Line the sides and bottom of a mold or shallow casserole with the firmest potato rounds. Fill the mold with the softer rounds. Bake for 20 minutes to brown the surface, then unmold onto a serving platter.

Fresh Tome cheese is an essential part of traditional Auvergne cooking. It is used in the puréed potato aligot, *the* patranque *bread pancake, and the* truffade *featured here.*

Main dish or vegetable accompaniment
Serves 6

Ingredients
2 lbs. 2 oz. (1 kg) potatoes
6 tbsp. (80 g) butter
5 oz. (150 g) lightly salted slab bacon, cut into cubes
2 cloves of garlic, crushed
14 oz. (400 g) fresh Tome or Cantal cheese

Salt and pepper

Jambonette
with Green du Puy Lentils

Ingredients
Jambonette
1 jambonette (shoulder of pork, with pork fat, and wrapped in pork fat)
1 leek, halved
2 carrots, finely sliced
1 onion, studded with a clove
1 bouquet garni

Lentils
1¾ cups (300 g) green du Puy lentils
8 cups (2 l) chicken stock (pg. 290)
2 tbsp. (30 g) butter
1 onion, chopped
1½ oz. (50 g) tomato concasse (pg. 293)
1 tbsp. of chopped parsley
½ tsp. Charroux mustard (substitute dijon)
1 tbsp. butter
½ clove of garlic, chopped

Charroux mustard sauce
Vinegar
½ cup (12 cl) white wine
2 shallots, finely chopped
Black pepper
¾ cup (18 cl) pork jus (pg. 292)
8 tarragon leaves, minced
3 tbsp. (40 g) butter
1 tsp. Charroux mustard (substitute dijon)

Salt, pepper, and arrowroot

The jambonette

Dry the *jambonette* by leaving it at room temperature for at least 24 hours—this will bring out its rich color when cooked.

Heat 8 cups (2 l) of cold water. Add the leek, carrots, studded onion, and bouquet garni. Add the *jambonette* and simmer gently, allowing 30 minutes for every 2 lbs. 2 oz. (2kg). When the cooking is done, leave the *jambonette* in the cooking stock.

The lentils

Blanch the lentils in a pan of cold water, drain, and cool. Return them to the pan and moisten with the chicken stock. Bring to a boil and then simmer for about 20 minutes.

Check for doneness. The lentils are ready when they are still slightly al dente; they should not purée between the teeth. Drain the lentils, reserving the cooking juice. Reduce the liquid to obtain ¾ cup (18 cl) of gravy.

Heat the tbsp. of butter in a sauté pan. Sweat the onion, then add the tomato concasse, lentil jus and cooked lentils.

Stew until the lentils begin to thicken the sauce. Add the chopped parsley, mustard, a tbsp. butter, and a pinch of garlic. Keep warm.

The Charroux mustard sauce

Pour the vinegar and white wine into a separate sauté pan. Add the shallot and black pepper and reduce by three-quarters. Add the pork jus and ½ cup (12 cl) of the *jambonette* cooking stock. Return to a boil. Add the minced tarragon.

Whisk the butter and mustard into the sauce. Check the seasoning and thicken if necessary with a little arrowroot (or cornstarch) diluted in cold water.

Presentation

Remove the *jambonnette* from the stock, out into slices, and arrange the slices on a serving platter. Pour the sauce over the meat and serve the lentils separately.

The jambonette *is a large sausage packed in pork rind, so it does not have sausage casing. This dish is a specialty of the Haute Loire and the Ardèche. We can pinpoint its exact provenance to the village of Yssingeaux between Firminy and Saint-Agrève. In one of his famous books on local produce and cuisine, Forot, the famous local chef of the early twentieth century, writes that the finest* jambonette *he ever tasted was, indeed, in the village of Saint-Agrève.*

I serve it here with green lentils. My mother used to prepare it with creamed spinach tartlets. The flavor of the sauce is enhanced by the Charroux mustard, a product from a local medieval village in the Auvergne county of Allier. The idea of adding mustard to the lentils comes from friends of mine, the Durieux, who live in the village of Yssingeaux.

Roasted Half Pigeon
with Fresh White Beans, Cockscombs, and Peanuts

Meat 🌲
The white beans may be replaced
by other local bean varieties.
Serves 4

Ingredients
Fresh white beans
6½ oz. (180 g) cockscombs
3 cups (75 cl) chicken stock
(pg. 290)
4 tbsp. (6 cl) olive oil
1 large onion, minced
1 carrot, diced
3½ oz. (100 g) smoked bacon, diced
9 oz. (250 g) fresh white beans
1 bouquet garni
½ clove of garlic, crushed
2 tbsp. (30 g) butter

Pigeons and sauce
2 young pigeons, each 12 oz. (350 g),
with livers
4 tbsp. (6 cl) peanut oil
2 tbsp. (30 g) butter
2 medium shallots, thinly sliced
4 tbsp. (6 cl) port
4 tbsp. (6 cl) white wine
1¼ cups (30 cl) chicken jus
(pg. 290)

4 tbsp. (60 g) butter
1 chicken liver
3 oz. (80 g) roasted peanuts
6 tbsp. (8 cl) hazelnut oil
Handful of baby spinach

Brochettes
3 cébettes (or small green onions)
1 tbsp. butter
3½ oz. (100 g) bacon

Salt

The fresh white beans

Clean the cockscombs and cover with cold water in a saucepan. Boil, drain, and refresh in cold water. Return to the saucepan and cover with cold water. Add a little chicken stock and cook, covered, for 30 minutes. Sauté the onion, carrot, and bacon in olive oil, in a heavy casserole. Add the white beans and sweat for 2 to 3 minutes. Moisten with a bit chicken stock and the cockscombs cooking liquid. Add the cockscombs and bouquet garni. Salt very lightly so that the beans do not harden. Cover and cook for 30 to 35 minutes. At the end of cooking, the juice should coat the beans. Add the garlic and butter, correct the seasoning. Keep warm.

The pigeons and sauce

Debone the pigeon breasts, thighs, and wings, or ask your butcher to do it for you. Reserve the carcasses and livers. Fold each wing around a thigh to form a small pouch. Secure with a wooden toothpick.

Chop the carcasses with a large, heavy-bladed knife. Heat the peanut oil and butter in a heavy sauté pan. Brown the carcasses, then add and brown the shallot. Deglaze with the port and white wine. Reduce by half, then add enough chicken jus to just cover the pan contents. Boil and skim. Simmer gently for about 30 minutes. Remove from heat and allow the flavors to infuse for about 10 minutes. Pass through a fine china cap lined with muslin into a sauté pan. Reduce to obtain ¾ cup (18 cl) of sauce.

The brochette

Halve the onions and sauté in butter. Thread the brochette, alternately, with a piece of pigeon liver, a piece of bacon, and a sautéed onion half.

Presentation

In a small sauté pan, brown the pigeon halves on all sides in 2 tbsp. (30 g) butter. Season with salt and pepper. Cover and cook about 15 to 20 minutes, basting frequently. Let the meat relax.

In a separate pan, sauté the chicken liver in a tbsp. of butter. Add and brown the brochettes. Add and color the peanuts. Keep warm on a plate.

Reheat the pigeon sauce and pour into a small saucepan. Add the chicken liver and mix with an immersion blender, gradually adding the hazelnut oil.

Heat a tbsp. of butter in a pan and quickly sauté the spinach. Sprinkle with salt.

Place some white bean garnish in the center of each plate. Lay the roasted pigeon on top. Place the brochette to one side. Scatter toasted hazelnuts and spinach around the beans. Pour on the pigeon sauce.

I still remember the morning when a friend of mine, Gilles Liège, came into the kitchen with a box under his arm, full of white beans called "Princesse de Chambord." He had brought the beans from his native Poitou, and their fine skins and almond flavor won me over in an instant. They are now among the ingredients I use regularly.

Cherries in Mulled Wine with Yogurt Ice Cream and Sweet Pastry Fritters

Dessert 🌲
*If you do not have an
ice-cream maker, substitute
a good quality ice cream.*
Serves 8

Ingredients
*1 jar of cherries, in syrup (preferably
bing, not marashino cherries)*

Sweet pastry fritters (pg. 296)
*4 cups (1 l) peanut oil
Confectioners' sugar, for sprinkling*

Yogurt ice cream
*3 cups (75 cl) milk
⅔ cup (160 g) crème fraîche
6 egg yolks
1 cup (200 g) sugar
¼ cup (60 g) powdered milk
¾ cup (180 g) plain yogurt*

Mulled wine sauce
*4 cups (1 l) red wine
1 stick of cinnamon
1 orange, peeled and segmented
2 cloves
6 tbsp. (80 g) sugar
1 tbsp. potato flour*

The fritters
Heat the oil in a deep saucepan.

Fry 3 or 4 fritters at a time, then drain on paper towels. Sprinkle with confectioners' sugar.

The yogurt ice cream
Bring the milk and crème fraîche to a boil. Whip the eggs and sugar until light and creamy.

Whisk the milk into the eggs, adding the powdered milk. Cook over medium heat until the mixture coats the back of a spatula. Pass through a medium china cap into a bowl and refrigerate for 2 to 3 hours.

Add the yogurt, mixing well, and process in an ice-cream maker.

The mulled wine sauce
Pour the wine into a saucepan and bring to a boil.

Flambé, add the cinnamon, orange segments, cloves, and sugar.

Reduce by half and then add a little of the syrup from the jar of cherries.

Dissolve the potato flour in a little cold water in a bowl. Return the wine to a boil. Whisk in the potato flour to thicken slightly. Add the cherries. Keep warm on the edge of the stove.

Presentation

Place a slice of the orange from the wine sauce in the center of each plate. Top with a scoop of yogurt ice cream. Arrange the cherries and warm mulled wine around the ice cream. Serve with the sweet pastry fritters.

This recipe reminds me of our return from the slopes during February skiing vacations, when my mother would serve us mulled wine—with a little too much water and not enough wine for our taste! But perhaps she had her reasons. . . .

It was also the time for the sweet pastry fritters called bugnes. *Here, I present my grandmother's recipe. Now, my family has no more secrets from you!*

279

Candied Vanilla Ginger Green du Puy Lentils with White Chocolate Mousse

Dessert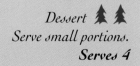
Serve small portions.
Serves 4

Ingredients
Green lentils
1 cup (150 g) green lentils
Zest of 1 lemon
2 cups (50 cl) mineral water
1¼ (250 g) sugar
2 pinches of ground star anise
1 vanilla bean pod
1–2 inch piece (20 g) ginger, grated

White chocolate mousse
1¼ cup (300 g) crème fraîche, chilled
9 oz. (250 g) white chocolate
2 large egg yolks
2 large whites

Accompaniment
½ cup (120 g) whipping cream
2 tbsp. (3 cl) kirsch

This is an idea I brought back from the TSUJI school in Japan, an exemplary cookery college that provides first-rate training. In a demonstration there, I wanted to use lentils to reproduce a typical Japanese dessert that features candied kidney beans. It was the first time that I had tried a candied lentil recipe—and I was surprised at how successful it was.

Wash the lentils and blanch in a pan of cold water. Drain and refresh.

Cook in a large volume of fresh water for at least 25 minutes. The lentils should be well cooked. Drain.

Blanch the zest and drain.

Boil the mineral water, sugar, star anise, vanilla, and ginger.

Gently candy the lentils in the syrup over low heat until they have totally absorbed the liquid. Refrigerate for about 2 hours.

The white chocolate mousse
Whisk the crème fraîche until firm. Break the white chocolate into small pieces and melt in a double boiler.

Beat the egg whites with a pinch of salt. At the same time, mix the egg yolks with a tbsp. of warm water.

Mix the chocolate and egg yolks in a bowl. Carefully fold in the whipped cream and the egg whites.

Refrigerate.

Presentation
Place some candied lentils in the center of each plate and crown with a scoop of white chocolate mousse. Then pour on some whipping cream flavored with kirsch.

Winter Luxury Squash Crêpes

1. The crêpes batter

Make the crêpe batter by combining the squash purée, eggs, flour, sugar, and a pinch of salt. Add the melted butter and milk. Mix well to obtain a smooth batter. Add the squash purée and let the batter rest for about 1 hour.

2. The crêpes

Pour a thin layer of batter into the crêpe pan. Cook the crêpes until lightly golden.

3. The pastry cream

Prepare the pastry cream (pg. 297).

When it is cold, add the finely diced orange zest, prunes, dried apricots, and hazelnuts.

4. The filling

Heat the clarified butter in a pan and sauté the diced squash. Sprinkle with a little sugar. Add the squash to the cold pastry cream and flavor with Grand Marnier.

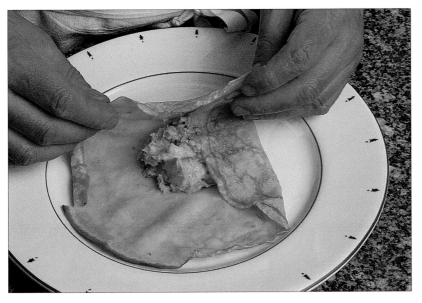

5.

Stuff each crêpe with the filling. Fold the 4 sides to create a small parcel.

6. Presentation

Reduce the orange and squash juices. Add the lemon zests and reduce by half.

Add the butter, mix well, and pour the sauce over the crêpes. Flambé with Grand Marnier, as you would a crêpe Suzette.

Complete recipe appears on page 216.

The Wine Cellar at Auberge des Cimes

At the Auberge, the choice of wine has to have the same personal touch as the cuisine or the atmosphere. Michèle Marcon appears very reticent when discussing the technical jargon that flows, monotonously, from the mouths of some experts. "I need to taste wine before being able to express my impressions about it," she says. In the mid-eighties, the Auberge needed a boost, but Michèle had not yet assembled the panorama of French wines that she had envisioned. Fortunately, at this point in the story, a bearded character appeared—George-Albert Aoust, who had a penchant for snooping around wine cellars. He was a well-known wine connoisseur who, over the years, had worked closely with the highly rated Château-Rayas and Beaucastel, producers in the Rhône region, and with a number of fine restaurants to whom he provided advice. By this time, he had already worked with Ginette Bras on the wine menu at Michel Bras's famous Laguiole restaurant in the Aubrac region. George-Albert's journey from Laguiole to Saint Bonnet was direct, despite the fact that the road between the villages is long and tortuous. In fact, Michèle and Ginette Bras recommended Aoust to the Marcons. At first, still reticent, Michèle imagined Georges-Albert to be a smooth-talking wine representative. She was, however, swiftly won over by his breadth of knowledge and, even more so, by his simple approach to wine. Devoid of pomposity, he would never drone on about the right time for malolactic fermentation or hide behind a smoke screen of enological complexities. In short, Michèle learned a great deal from Georges-Albert, who introduced her to wines from the Beaune region and confirmed her wine-tasting abilities. The vision had become a reality. In the meantime, Michèle had also begun to frequent some of the great chateaux of Bordeaux. She has kept close company with wines ever since.

Today, the wine menu at Saint-Bonnet-le-Froid is a fine balance of expertise and suggestion, chosen by Michèle and Georges-Albert together. Michèle's contributions focus on the areas north of Côtes-du-Rhône while Georges-Albert provides advice on the wines of Burgundy and the regions south of Côtes-du-Rhone and Languedoc, where he was born. A while ago, both of these southern areas experienced an upsurge in quality, and he has followed the developments closely.

The question is, are the wines a good enough reason to frequent the Auberge des Cimes? That is difficult to answer for certain. What is certain, however, is that wine producers now frequent the Auberge at Saint-Bonnet-le-Froid. And let us not forget the local wine experts, such as the Jaboulets, Gerard Chave, and others. Michèle has no complaints.

Georges-Albert Aoust
and Michèle Marcon

Meeting purveyors of fine products—whether they be wine, grain, cheese, or fruit producers—is part of the house philosophy. This is why the products served at the Auberge never seem to have just fallen off the back of a cart.

It remains to be seen exactly how the Auberge's clientele will react to such a carefully chosen wine cellar. The establishment's service is based on trust. In three out of four cases, the diner prefers to be advised. A vast wine list that reads like an instruction manual does not appeal to Michèle—and is simply beyond the scope of most people's knowledge. Instead, Michèle tries to quickly determine a comfortable budget for the table, a tricky task as the question is never asked. The most essential courtesy is not to place too heavy a weight on the final bill.

The Auberge's recommendations often have more to do with geography than with Michèle's personal preferences. Clients consume a lot of wine from the northern Côtes-du-Rhône: Condrieu, Côte Rôtie, and Hermitage (Crozes), or Saint Joseph. Each choice is well represented by several producers.

Another distinguishing feature of the wine list of the Auberge is the

outstanding collection of vintage wines, such as the Hermitage Chapelle de Jaboulet. Proof that the well-named Haute Loire, high on the mountainside at the source of the Loire, is not afraid to return to its source in the Rhône Valley. Family passions are so contagious that Régis Marcon's nephews and nieces (Johanès, Jean Régis, and Maguy) also have wine fever. They are now in charge of the Cave du Montagnard one of the Auberge's preferred suppliers.

Bread and Cheese

Breads served at the restaurant:
cereal flour bread, lentil flour bread,
chestnut bread, and rye bread

Cantal
One of the best known of the French cheeses traditionally produced in shepherds cottages in the hillsides. A large part of today's production happens at the dairy, however, and the cheese has lost much of its quality and character. It is eaten young (when mild) mature (when the flavor is more pronounced), and aged (when the flavor is strong).

Salers
Salers cheese is from the same region as Cantal and is produced exclusively between May and October. It is made only from Salers cows' milk. The quality specifications are strict. The cheese matures quickly, at an altitude of more than 2,789 feet (850 m) for at least three months. I prefer the hard variety uncooked. I tasted one recently that had aged for 18 months at Louis Verdier's farm in Raulhac and was surprised that the cheese had developed a nutty flavor. This cheese, which is my son Paul's favorite, is particularly delicious with wines from the Jura.

Saint-nectaire
In Besse, my friend Antoine Sachapt introduced me to another great cheese from the Auvergne. It may be farm-made (with an oval, green casein label on its rind) or dairy-made (with a rectangular label). It is matured in damp cellars on a bed of rye straw and turned every day. First, a down forms on the cheese then a rind, which subsequently takes on color, releasing an aroma of mushrooms. The cheese itself is soft with a pleasant fragrance. I prefer this cheese when ripe—it's ideal at four months old. I recommend a white wine with it. *Saint-nectaire* is my oldest son Jacques's favorite.

Fourme d'Ambert or de Montbrison
Making *fourme* cheese is a real craft. This cheese is one of the finest blue-veined cheeses that I know of. It matures in two to five months and has a gray or red rind. There are also cheeses that are similar to *fourme d'Ambert* such as *fourme de Rochefort, fourme d'Araules,* or *tome du Mezenc.* Enjoy any of these with a mellow Jurançon-style white wine.

Bleu d'Auvergne
Auvergne blue cheese may be made with pasteurized or raw milk. It is matured in a cellar on a bed of rye straw, like the *saint-nectaire, bleu de Laqueuille bleu, de Trizac,* and *bleu de Caynes.*

Lavort

This is a new ewe's milk cheese which matures in three months. It is produced by Patrick Beaumont on his aptly named farm, "God's Earth" (*Terre Dieu*). It is sometimes fermented in rolls and then smoked. The result is reminiscent of Eastern European cheeses.

Blanchardon

Our goat cheese is farm-produced by Christine, Yvette, Daniel, and Christian—a quality team that is also one of our favorite suppliers (page 55) This cheese should be eaten with a white wine.

Velay cheese

This cow's milk cheese is produced exclusively in the Velay region. The surface is covered with acarids called *artisous* which help it mature and give it an exceptional flavor.

Milk runs in streams down the Auvergne mountainsides, so it is no surprise to find five cheeses in the region that have been recognized for quality and awarded AOC certificates. Farm traditions and farm-made cheeses are still very much with us.

Cooking Tips

n the gas stove
Low heat: The smallest flame possible, which should just lick the bottom of the saucepan.
Electric stove setting: low.

Medium heat: Medium-sized flame which should heat the entire underside of the saucepan.
Electric stove setting: medium.

High heat: The flame heats the underside and edges of the pan. If the flame climbs too high up the sides, use a larger saucepan.
Electric stove setting: high.

Approximate cooking times are calculated according to the type of meat and its weight. Special cooking thermometers can be inserted into the center of the meat to check its temperature. If you do not own one, insert a thin knife into the meat. If its blade is still cold when you remove it, the meat is not cooked. If the blade is hot, the meat is rare. If it is burning hot, the meat is well done.

Generally speaking, beef is served rare to medium, lamb is served medium rare, veal medium, and pork, well done. Remember to let the meat relax after cooking.

Albumin coagulates at about 150°F (62°C), which means that above this temperature, meat begins to change color and texture.

Temperature equivalents for your oven type

Convection oven	Regular oven	Oven with number settings
140°F (60°C)	150°F (65°C)	T2
190°F (90°C)	200°F (95°C)	T3
250°F (120°C)	260°F (125°C)	T4
300°F (150°C)	310°F (155°C)	T5
350°F (180°C)	360°F (185°C)	T6
410°F (210°C)	425°F (220°C)	T7
440°F (230°C)	460°F (240°C)	T8
460°F (240°C)	500°F (260°C)	T9
500°F (260°C)	520°F (270°C)	T10

The Basic Recipes

Chicken stock

Makes 8 cups (2 l)

2¼ lbs. (1 kg) chicken parts
(carcass, wings, etc.)
1 onion, finely diced
1 carrot, finely diced
2 cloves of garlic, crushed
1 bouquet garni (celery leaves,
thyme, leek, parsley stems)
1 clove
2 thin slices of fresh ginger
(optional)

Chicken jus

Makes 2 cups (50 cl)

2 to 4 lbs. (1 to 2 kg) poultry neck
and chicken pieces (save meat
for another recipe)
6 tbsp. (8 cl) peanut oil
2 tbsp. (20 g) butter
1 large onion
2 carrots, finely diced
5 cloves of garlic, unpeeled and
crushed
1 bouquet garni (leek, thyme, ¼ bay
leaf, parsley sprigs)
2 black peppercorns
1 fresh tomato, quartered

Pork jus

Makes 4 cups (1 l)

6 tbsp. (8 cl) peanut oil
2 lbs. 2 oz. (1 kg) pork bone, with
meat
2 onions, finely diced
2 carrots, finely diced
3 cloves of garlic
4 tbsp. (6 cl) soy sauce
½ cup (12 cl) rosé wine
1 tomato, quartered
1 pig's foot, blanched and cut into
small pieces
1 sage leaf
4 peppercorns or Szechwan
peppercorns

Combine all ingredients into a good-sized deep pot. Cover with cold water and bring to a boil. Lower heat.

Skim the surface foam from time to time.

Simmer gently for 2 hours.

Remove from heat and let the flavors infuse for 10 minutes. With a ladle, pass the stock through a fine china cap. Refrigerate.

The following day, remove the fat from the surface.

Storage

In the freezer: Store in small sealed plastic containers to enable you to prepare a small quantity at a time. Reduce the stock so that it takes up less space.

In the refrigerator: Store in a sealed container. Use within 48 hours.

Use

This stock is often used in soups, to braise vegetables, or to moisten poultry dishes.

Cut each neck into thirds.

Heat the oil and butter in a heavy saucepan. Brown the neck pieces on all sides about 4 to 5 minutes. Add the onion, carrots, and garlic cloves. Cook until the ingredients caramelize.

Deglaze with ½ cup of water and reduce until the ingredients start to caramelize again.

Add 8 cups (2 l) of cold water. Add the bouquet garni, peppercorns, and tomato quarters with seeds. Bring to a boil, lower heat, and simmer for 1 hour. Skim the surface foam from time to time.

Remove from heat and let flavors infuse for 10 minutes. Pass through a fine china cap and refrigerate.

Storage

In the freezer: Store in small plastic containers, covered with a layer of fat.

In the refrigerator: Store in small covered plastic containers.

Heat the peanut oil in a sauté pan over high heat. Brown the pork pieces on all sides.

In a separate pan, sauté the onions, carrots, and garlic with the remaining oil and a pinch of salt. Deglaze with a little soy sauce and coat the vegetables with the cooking juices. Transfer to the sauté pan and stir with a wooden spatula. Deglaze with rosé wine, scraping the meat juices on the bottom of the pan. Reduce by half and add enough water to just cover the contents of the pan. Salt lightly. Add the tomato quarters, pig's foot, sage and, pepper. Simmer for 1½ hours. Remove from heat, pass through a fine china cap and refrigerate.

Storage

In the freezer: Store in small sealed plastic containers. Unlike veal jus, pork jus is only used with pork meat. Do not make too much.

In the refrigerator: Store in a container covered with the fat to keep it for several days.

Cut the fish bones, place in a bowl, and rinse under cold water about 30 minutes. Drain. Heat the butter in a heavy sauté pan. Sweat the shallots, onion, and mushrooms with a pinch of salt. Add the fish bones and sweat 3 minutes. Moisten with the white wine and reduce by half. Add the vermouth, bouquet garni, and tomato quarters. Add enough water, about 6 cups (1,5 l), to just cover the pan contents.

Bring to a boil and skim the surface foam. Lower the heat and simmer gently for about 30 minutes.

Remove from heat and carefully pass through a fine china cap. Refrigerate.

Storage

In the freezer: Store in small sealed plastic containers. Reduce the liquid if you have too much.

In the refrigerator: Store in a container covered with plastic wrap. Use within 24 hours.

Rinse the fish bones under cold water about 30 minutes and drain. Cut into small pieces and dry on a cloth.

Melt the butter in a heavy casserole over a medium heat. Brown the fish bones about 30 minutes. The bones will break apart and caramelize at the bottom of the pan. Add the shallots, mushrooms, and garlic. Brown another 10 minutes and deglaze with white wine. Scrape the bottom of the pan well, add the fennel seeds, reduce the liquid by half. Add enough water to just cover the bones. Cover the pan with plastic wrap, allowing the wrap to touch the liquid. Simmer gently about 30 minutes. Remove from heat and let rest for 10 minutes. Pass through a fine china cap, pressing the bones well. Refrigerate immediately, leaving the fat on the surface.

Storage

In the refrigerator: Leave the fat on the surface and cover with plastic wrap. Use within 24 hours. Because there is such a small quantity of sauce, you should use it quickly.

Mix the spices together well and store in a sealed container.

Use

This mixture may be added to all sautéed, oven roasted, or grilled fish.

Fish stock

Makes 4 cups (1 l)

2 lbs. 2 oz. (1 kg) fish bones (sole, monkfish, turbot, and lake pike, ideally)
3 tbsp. (40 g) butter
2 large shallots 5 oz. (150 g), finely chopped
1 medium onion, 3 oz. (80 g), finely chopped
5 oz. (150 g) white mushrooms or mushroom pieces
½ cup (12 cl) white wine
½ cup (12 cl) white vermouth
1 bouquet garni (leek, thyme, ¼ bay leaf, parsley stems)
1 tomato, quartered

Fish jus

Makes 2 cups (50 cl)

2 lbs. 2 oz. (1 kg) fish bones (sole, monkfish, turbot, and lake pike, ideally)
3 tbsp. (40 g) butter, preferably salted
3 large shallots, 6 oz. (180 g), finely sliced
4 oz. (120 g) mushroom pieces
2 cloves of garlic, crushed
⅔ cup (15 cl) dry white wine
½ tsp. fennel seeds

Fish spices

½ cup (100 g) fine sea salt
1 tbsp. galanga
1 tbsp. freshly ground pepper
1 tsp. cinnamon
1 tsp. fennel seed
1 tsp. nutmeg

Veal jus

Makes 4 cups (1 l)

2 lbs. 2 oz. (1 kg) veal trimmings
(pieces of flank, knuckle, etc.)
4 tbsp. (6 cl) peanut oil
2 tbsp. (20 g) butter
1 large onion, finely diced
2 medium-sized carrots, finely diced
2 cloves of garlic
4 tbsp. (6 cl) soy sauce
4 tbsp. (6 cl) white wine
1 calf's hoof, blanched and chopped
1 sprig of thyme
1 tomato, quartered
3 crushed peppercorns

Venison sauce

Makes 2 cups (½ l)

Jus
2 bottles of Syrah red wine
2 lbs. 2 oz. (1 kg) venison and hare
bones, with trimmings
6 tbsp. (8 cl) peanut oil
5 shallots, finely diced
2 carrots, finely diced
1 onion, finely diced
2 cloves of garlic
6 tbsp. (8 cl) cognac
1 tbsp. tomato paste
1 bouquet garni
10 juniper berries, crushed
1 pig's foot, blanched and chopped

To finish
1 tbsp. red currant jelly
1¼ cup (30 cl) wine vinegar
Peppercorns, crushed
½ cup (12 cl) hare or pig's blood
1 tbsp. mustard
2 tbsp. (30 g) butter

Cut the veal trimmings into pieces. Heat the oil and butter in a sauté pan over high heat. Brown the veal pieces on all sides, stirring with a wooden spatula.

In a separate pan, brown the onions, carrots, and garlic about 3 to 4 minutes over high heat. Add a pinch of salt. Deglaze with soy sauce. Cook until the cooking juices coat the vegetables. Transfer to the sauté pan and brown for another minute. Deglaze with the white wine, scraping the juices on the bottom of the pan. Reduce by half and then add enough water to just cover the contents of the pan. Add the calf's hoof, thyme, tomato quarters, and pepper. Salt lightly and simmer about 1½ hours. Skim the surface foam from time to time.

Remove from heat and let rest for 10 minutes. Pass through a fine china cap and refrigerate.

Storage

In the freezer: Store in small sealed plastic containers.

In the refrigerator: Store in a container covered with the fat, to keep for several days.

Boil the red wine in a heavy bottomed pot, flambé, and set aside. Cut the bones and trimmings into small pieces. Heat the oil in a heavy sauté pan and brown the bones on all sides.

Add and brown the onion, carrots, and garlic. Then flambé with the cognac and add the tomato paste. Brown again and moisten with the red wine. Add the bouquet garni and crushed juniper berries. Add enough water to just cover the pan contents. Add the meat from the pig's foot. Bring to a boil and skim the surface foam. Simmer gently for about 2 hours.

Remove from heat and let the flavors to infuse for 15 minutes. Pass through a fine china cap, pressing well.

Reduce this stock by half and remove the surface fat with a small ladle.

Heat the red currant jelly in a sauté pan. Caramelize slightly and deglaze with the vinegar. Reduce to obtain a syrupy consistency. Add the stock and reduce until sauce begins to thicken. Whisk in the crushed peppercorns and blood, then the mustard and butter. Pass through a fine china cap. Check the seasoning and thickness of the sauce. Refrigerate if you do not use it immediately.

Storage

In the refrigerator: Store in a container with a lid or covered with plastic wrap.

eat the olive oil in a deep heavy bottomed pot.
Add the leek, carrots, mushrooms, fennel, celery, parsley, ginger, and garlic. Brown for 3 to 4 minutes with a pinch of salt. Add enough water to just cover the contents. Add the lemongrass, thyme, bay leaf, tarragon, and tomato quarters. Simmer gently for 45 minutes.

Storage
In the refrigerator: Store in a covered container for 2 to 3 days.

eel and halve the tomatoes. Remove the seeds and finely chop the pulp.
Brown the onions in olive oil in a sauté pan. Add the tomatoes, crushed garlic, thyme, and tomato paste. Add salt and a little sugar if necessary.
Reduce the heat and cover with parchment paper until the tomatoes have dried. Refrigerate.

o make the orange powder, remove the zest from several oranges and boil in cold water for 30 seconds. Drain and dry.
Spread the zest on a sheet of parchment paper and dry in the oven at 180°F (80°C) for 2 to 3 hours. Grind the dried zest in a coffee grinder or pulverize them with a rolling pin. Mix this powder with the other dry ingredients.

Use
This spice mix is served with lamb in a straw crust, game, etc.

lace the mushrooms in a spice grinder.
Process until they are finely powdered.
Sift the powder through a fine strainer and store in a cool place.
Mushroom powder should be made with top-quality mushrooms that have been trimmed and dried in the open air or dried indoors on grates or straw.

Vegetable stock

Makes 4 cups (1 l)

4 tbsp. (6 cl) olive oil
1 leek, thinly sliced
2 medium-sized carrots, finely diced
5 oz. (150 g) white mushrooms
1 fennel bulb, finely diced
2 stalks of celery, finely sliced
Handful of parsley
2 thin slices of ginger
2 cloves of garlic
1 stalk of lemongrass
Fresh thyme
¼ bay leaf
5 or 6 leaves of tarragon
1 tomato, quartered

Tomato concassé

8 ripe tomatoes
2 onions, finely minced
Olive oil
½ clove of garlic, chopped
1 sprig of thyme
1 tbsp. tomato paste

"Wolf spices"

2 tbsp. orange powder
2 tbsp. juniper berries, ground
1 tsp. garlic powder
1 tsp. ginger powder
1 tsp. black pepper

Mushroom powder

(This may be made with just the dried porcini.)

Top-quality dried porcini
Dried parasol mushrooms, stems removed
Dried fairy ring mushrooms

Mushroom duxelle

Makes 2 cups (½ l)

1 tsp. (3g) dried porcini (optional)

2 lbs. 2 oz. (1 kg) fresh white mushrooms
1 tbsp. (10 g) butter
½ cup (50 g) olive oil
2 shallots, minced
1 medium onion, minced
Juice of ½ lemon
1 tbsp. heavy cream

Mushroom stock

Makes 1 cup (25 cl)

3½ lbs. (1.5 kg) white mushrooms
4 tbsp. (6 cl) olive oil
2 tbsp. (30 g) butter
3 shallots, finely sliced
¼ fennel bulb, finely diced
1 tbsp. mushroom powder

Seafood stock

2 lbs. 2 oz. (1 kg) seafood shells
6 tbsp. (8 cl) olive oil
1 onion, minced
4 shallots, finely sliced
2 carrots, finely diced
½ fennel bulb, finely diced
6 cloves of garlic, chopped
4 tsp. (2 cl) cognac
1 tbsp. tomato paste
2 tbsp. (3 cl) white wine
2 tsp. (1 cl) port
3 tomatoes, quartered
2 star anise
2 thin slices of fresh ginger
½ teaspoon paprika
Pinch of cayenne pepper

Soak the dried porcini in a little warm water. Drain and coarsely chop.

Peel or clean the fresh mushrooms with a brush. Cut them into quarters or sixths, depending on their size.

Heat the butter and olive oil in a sauté pan. Cook the shallots and onion with a pinch of salt for 2 to 3 minutes, stirring with a spatula. Do not brown. Add the porcini and white mushrooms, with a pinch of salt. Stir frequently. The mushrooms will release their juices. Cover with butter and add a few drops of lemon juice. When the mushrooms have released all their juices, add the cream. Reduce again to allow the mushrooms to absorb the cream.

Process in a food processor until the mushrooms are finely chopped, or until a purée, depending on your needs.

Quarter the white mushrooms. Sauté the mushroom quarters in the oil and butter over high heat, stirring with a wooden spatula. Salt lightly. The mushrooms will release their juices. Cook until the mushrooms start to brown, then add the shallots and fennel. Cook for 2 to 3 minutes, then add enough water to cover the pan contents. Add a little salt and the mushroom powder. Bring to a boil and skim the surface foam. Simmer gently, covered, for 30 minutes. Refrigerate.

Storage
In the refrigerator: Store in sealed plastic containers for 2 to 3 days.

In the freezer: Reduce the mushroom stock by half and freeze in small containers.

Heat the olive oil in a large heavy sauté pan. Add the crushed shells and brown slightly to dry.

Add the onion, shallots, carrots, fennel, and garlic. Heat for 3 to 4 minutes. Flambé with the cognac, then add the tomato paste. Heat again, moistening with the white wine. Scrape the bottom of the pan and reduce the liquid by half. Add the port, fresh tomatoes, star anise, ginger, paprika, and cayenne pepper. Add enough water to just cover the contents of the pan.

Simmer gently for 45 minutes, skimming the surface frequently. To retain as much of the aroma as possible, cover the surface of the stock with plastic wrap. Remove from heat and let rest for 10 minutes. Pass through a fine china cap and cool.

Storage
In the refrigerator: Store, covered, for 24 hours.

In the freezer: Gently reduce the stock so that it does not take up too much space.

294

In a narrow stainless-steel pot, mix the two vinegars, salt and cumin with an immersion blender. Add the two oils and the slightly warmed truffle juice. Keep cool.

In a stainless-steel pot, pour the boiling water onto the chopped herbs, salt, and pepper. Purée with an immersion blender gradually adding the oil and vinegar.

Strain the fresh orange juice and reduce by half.
Add the salt, pepper, and orange zest. Gradually mix in the lemon juice and grape seed oil.

Whisk the vinegar, salt, and pepper in a bowl, gradually add the two oils.
Finish by vigorously whisking in the boiling water.

Whisk the vinegar, mustard, salt, and pepper in a bowl, gradually add the oil.
Finish by vigorously whisking in the boiling water.

Mushroom vinaigrette

4 tbsp. (6 cl) cider vinegar
4 tbsp. (6 cl) balsamic vinegar
1 tsp. (6 g) salt
Pinch of cumin
¾ cup (18 cl) mushroom oil
½ cup (12 cl) canola oil
4 tbsp. (6 cl) truffle juice, slightly warm

Pistachio herb vinaigrette

4 tbsp. (6 cl) boiling water
Chopped parsley, tanagon, chervil, and chives
1 tsp. (6 g) salt
Pinch of pepper
1¼ cups (30 cl) pistachio oil
½ cup (12 cl) cider vinegar

Citrus vinaigrette

½ cup (10 cl) orange juice
1 tsp. (6 g) salt
Pinch of pepper
1 tsp. orange zest
½ cup (12 cl) lemon juice
1¼ cups (30 cl) grape seed oil

Hazelnut oil vinaigrette

½ cup (12 cl) sherry wine vinegar
4 tbsp. (6 g) salt
Pinch of pepper
¾ cup (18 cl) hazelnut oil
½ cup (12 cl) grape seed oil
4 tbsp. (6 cl) boiling water

Mustard vinaigrette

½ cup (12 cl) sherry wine vinegar
1 tbsp. mustard
1 tsp. (6 g) salt
Pinch of pepper
1¼ cup (30 cl) grape seed oil
4 tbsp. (6 cl) boiling water

Sweet pastry fritters: *bugnes*

5 eggs
15 tbsp. (200 g) softened butter
1 tsp. yeast
1 cup milk, slightly warm
1 tbsp. vanilla sugar
3⅓ cups (500 g) cake flour
A few drops of orange flower water
Orange and lemon zest

Flaky puff pastry

3⅓ cups (500 g) bread flour
2 tsp. (10 g) salt
12 oz (350 g) + 1½ oz (50 g) butter
1 cup (25 cl g) water

Tart dough

1⅔ cups (250 g) bread flour
9 tbsp. (125 g) butter
1 tsp. (5 g) salt
1 egg
½ cup (12 cl) water
Sugar (optional)

Short pastry dough

1⅔ cups (250 g) bread flour
9 tbsp. (125 g) butter
1 tsp. (5 g) salt
2 tbsp. (20 g) sugar
1 egg
½ cup (12 cl) water

Mix the eggs and softened butter in a bowl. Mix the yeast into the milk. Add the milk mixture and the sugar to the bowl. Gradually sprinkle in the flour. Flavor with the orange water and zest. Cover with a damp cloth and refrigerate.

Let rise for several hours before kneading and cutting the dough.

Prepare one day in advance. Sift the flour. Add the salt and rub the 1½ oz. (50 g) of butter into the flour until it resembles fine bread crumbs. Gradually add the water. Knead the dough and form into a ball. Do not work the dough too vigorously or it will become elastic and difficult to work with later. Cover with plastic wrap and let it relax for at least 1 hour. Work the 12 oz. (350 g) of butter until it is malleable by sandwiching it between 2 sheets of parchment paper and tapping with a rolling pin. Form the butter into a square.

Roll the pastry dough into an 8 in. (20 cm.) square, ¾ in. (2 mm) thick. Place the butter square on top, at a 45° angle to the pastry square. Fold the corners of the pastry toward the center of the butter square, overlapping and sealing the ends. Even out the square by tapping with a rolling pin. Roll the pastry evenly to form a strip about 16 in. (40 cm) long and 7 in. (18 cm) wide. Fold the pastry dough back on itself, making 3 equal-sized folds.

Turn the pastry a quarter-turn to change the direction in which you are working it. Roll and fold the dough again.

Cover the dough with plastic wrap to keep it from drying out, and let relax for 45 minutes. Roll and fold the dough again two more times. Let relax for 45 minutes and repeat the process once again. Let the dough rest for 1 hour before use.

Note
Making this pastry requires some experience. You may also buy good pure butter flaky pastry at a bakery. Charentes butter works well in this recipe because it contains less water.

These pastry doughs are made the same way, but their ingredients (short pastry contains sugar) and the way they are used differ: tart dough is used for savory recipes (porcini quiche, for example) and short pastry is used for desserts that require a sweet pastry crust (such as blueberry pie). Use bread flour if possible.

Sift the flour. Rub in the butter until the mixture resembles fine crumbs. Form a well in the middle of the flour, add the salt (or salt and sugar) and dissolve with a little water. Combine the remaining water and egg, then mix in gently. Knead the pastry gently with the palm of your hand until smooth and even.

You may make this dough in your food processor but be careful not to overmix or the dough will become too hard.

Let the dough rest for at least 30 minutes before use.

These two pastries are slightly different.

There is proportionately more sugar in the sugar pastry dough, which produces a drier more dense pastry.

There is more butter in the shortbread dough, which produces a delicate pastry with a light texture.

Sift the flour. Work the sugar into the butter with your hands or with a food processor to produce a smooth creamy mixture. Fold in the egg (and vanilla), mix well. Add the flour, powdered almonds, and salt. Mix until the dough forms a ball. Knead the dough until it is smooth and even. Roll into a ball and wrap in plastic wrap to prevent the dough from drying out.

Uses

Sugar pastry dough is used for pies without liquid fillings. It is blind-baked or precooked first (as for the Baked Strawberry Tart) at 300° to 325°F (150 to 160°C)

Shortbread dough is used for petits fours (Rose Shortbread with Wild Strawberries) small cookies, and as a base for tartlets, custard pies, and fine small tarts (Chestnut Pie).

Pour the milk into a heavy saucepan. Split and scrape the vanilla bean pod and add the pod to the milk. Bring to a boil.

Meanwhile, separate the eggs. Whisk the yolks and sugar in a bowl until light and creamy. Whisk in the cornstarch and pour the mixture into the boiling milk.

Return the milk to the saucepan and return to boil, whisking constantly. Continue to stir for 30 seconds after the custard boils. Remove from heat. Stir in the butter and pour into a bowl. Sprinkle with confectioners' sugar or cover with plastic wrap to prevent a skin from forming. Refrigerate and use within 24 hours.

Pour the milk into a heavy saucepan. Split and scrape the vanilla bean pod and add to the milk. Bring to a boil.

Meanwhile, separate the eggs. Whisk the yolks and sugar in a bowl until light and creamy. Pour the mixture into the boiling milk. Return to the saucepan and heat, stirring with a large spatula. When the custard begins to coat the back of the spatula and begins to boil, remove from heat. Pass it through a fine china cap into another container. Refrigerate and use within 24 hours.

Sugar pastry dough

1⅔ cups (250 g) all purpose flour
¾ cup (100 g) confectioners' sugar
9 tbsp. (125 g) butter
1 egg
4 tbsp. (30 g) powdered almonds
Pinch of salt

Shortbread dough

1⅔ cups (250 g) all purpose flour
¾ cup (100 g) confectioners' sugar
10⅔ tbsp. (150 g) butter
1 egg
5 tbsp. (50 g) powdered almonds
Pinch of salt
Vanilla

Pastry cream

2 cups (50 cl) whole milk
1 vanilla bean pod
6 egg yolks
½ cup (100 g) sugar
½ cup (50 g) cornstarch
4 tbsp. (50 g) butter
Confectioners' sugar

Custard sauce

2 cups (50 cl) whole milk
1 vanilla bean pod
8 egg yolks
7 tbsp. (80 g) sugar

For their invaluable contributions I am especially grateful to:

The regional administration of Auvergne and the Haute-Loire departmental administration
My sponsors (Revol, Weiss, and Celnat)
The photographers (Jean-Jacques Arcis, Philippe Barret, Yves Chupin, Joël Damase, Pierre Guibert, Bernhard
    Winkelmann, Philippe Schaff, Patrick André, and Jean-Paul Chapelon, my brother-in-law)
The Auvergne chefs' association, my colleagues in the hotel profession, and the restaurateurs of the Haute-Loire
    and elsewhere
All my suppliers and producers
The Prom'hôte group
I also thank everyone else who had any direct or indirect input in creating this work.